Civil Procedure in South Korea

Civil Procedure in South Korea

Nam-Geun Yoon

This book was originally published as a monograph in the International Encyclopaedia of Laws/Civil Procedure.

Founding Editor: Roger Blanpain
General Editor: Frank Hendrickx
Volume Editor: Wannes Vandenbussche

Wolters Kluwer

Published by:
Kluwer Law International B.V.
PO Box 316
2400 AH Alphen aan den Rijn
The Netherlands
E-mail: international-sales@wolterskluwer.com
Website: lrus.wolterskluwer.com

Sold and distributed by:
Wolters Kluwer Legal & Regulatory U.S.
7201 McKinney Circle
Frederick, MD 21704
United States of America
Email: customer.service@wolterskluwer.com

ISBN 978-94-035-2673-7

e-Book: ISBN 978-94-035-2674-4
web-PDF: ISBN 978-94-035-2675-1

The Author

Nam-Geun Yoon (1956) is a professor of law at Korea University School of Law (KU Law School) in Seoul, where he teaches civil procedure, enforcement of judgment and bankruptcy law. Prior to joining KU Law School in 2007, he served on the bench from 1987 to 2007 as a judge, high court judge and then as a presiding judge in various courts including the Seoul Central District Court, the Seoul High Court and the Seoul Eastern District Court. While in the judiciary, he researched American bankruptcy law at Yale Law School as a visiting scholar (1995-1996).

He was the chairperson of the Korea Bankruptcy Law Association from 2017 to 2019; the chairperson of the Advisory Committee for the Seoul Bankruptcy Court from 2018 to 2020. He has served as an arbitrator of the Korean Commercial Arbitration Board (KCAB) since 2008 and a board member of KCAB since 2016. He was the chairperson of the Subcontract Dispute Resolution Council which is annexed to the Korea Fair Trade Commission from 2011 to 2018. He was an editorial writer for Law Times (Seoul) from 2008 to 2018 and is currently a member of its editorial board. He served as a commissioner of the National Human Rights Commission from 2011 to 2017.

He received an LL.B. from Seoul National University in 1984 and passed the Jurisprudence Examination in the same year. He completed two-year Judicial Research and Training Institute course in 1987.

The Author

Table of Contents

List of Abbreviations

(Acts)

AA	Arbitration Act
AAJA	Act on Appointment, Etc. of Judge Advocates
AALA	Attorney-at-law Act
ACPCT	Act on Citizen Participation in Criminal Trials
AEMPL	ACT on the Establishment and Management of Professional Law Schools
AGER	Act on the Guarantee of Employees' Retirement Benefits
AIJMA	Act on International Judicial Mutual Assistance in Civil Matters
ALA	Administrative Litigation Act
ALSP	Act on Litigation to which the State is a Party
APAR	Act on Press Arbitration and Remedies, Etc. for Damage Caused by Press Reports
APNJ	Act on the Prescribed Number of Judges of Various Levels of Courts
ARTC	Act on the Regulation of Terms and Conditions
AUEDC	Act on the Use, Etc. of Electronic Documents in Civil Litigations, Etc.
ASA	Aviation Safety Act
ASACL	Act on the Stamps Attached for Civil Litigation, Etc.
ASPTS	Act on Special Cases Concerning Procedure for Trial by the Supreme Court
CA	Civil Act
CCA	Constitutional Court Act
CEA	Civil Execution Act
CMMA	Construction Machinery Management Act
COA	Court Organization Act
ComA	Commercial Act
Cons	Constitution

List of Abbreviations

CPA	Civil Procedure Act
CrA	Criminal Act
CrPA	Criminal Procedure Act
DJA	Discipline of Judges Act
DRBA	Debtor Rehabilitation and Bankruptcy Act
EOA	Enforcement Officer Act
FA	Fisheries Act
FAC	Framework Act on Consumers
FANT	Framework Act on National Taxes
FLA	Family Litigation Act
FMAMA	Factory and Mining Assets Mortgage Act
GAACA	Guarantee of Automobile Accident Compensation Act
HLPA	Housing Lease Protection Act
JCCDA	Judicial Conciliation of Civil Disputes Act
LAA	Legal Aid Act
LoAA	Local Autonomy Act
LSA	Labor Standards Act
LTA	Local Tax Act
MCA	Military Court Act
MIA	Mining Industry Act
MVMA	Motor Vehicle Management Act
NAA	National Assembly Act
NBEA	National Bar Examination Act
NcCPA	Non-contentious Case Procedure Act
PA	Patent Act
PCSA	Protection of Communications Secretes Act
POEA	Public Official Election Act
PRSA	Provisional Registration Security Act
RREA	Registration of Real Estate Act
SA	Ship Act
SCA	State Compensation Act
SCAA	Securities-related Class Action Act
SPOA	State Public Officials Act
TSCA	Trial of Small Claims Act
TrA	Trust Act

(Treaties)

Hague Service Convention	Convention on the Service Abroad of Judicial and Extrajudicial Documents in Civil or Commercial Matters

SOFA	Agreement under Article IV of the Mutual Defence Treaty between the Republic of Korea and the United States of America, Regarding Facilities and Areas and the Status of United States Armed Forces in the Republic of Korea
VCC	Vienna Convention on Consular Relations 1963
VCD	The United Nations Vienna Convention on Diplomatic Relations 1961

(Presidential Decrees, Regulations and subordinate laws)

AEMPL-ED	Enforcement Decree of ACT on the Establishment and Management of Professional Law Schools (Presidential Decree)
GACM	Guidelines on Administration of Civil and Family Mediation (Supreme Court Guideline No. 1735)
GDTC	Guidelines for Distribution of Tasks and Cases among Judges (Supreme Court Guideline No. 1732)
GMLA	Guidelines on Management of Legal Aid (Supreme Court Guideline No. 1679)
RAF	Regulation on Inclusion of Attorney's Fee into Litigation Cost (Supreme Court Regulation)
RCE	Regulation on Civil Execution (Supreme Court Regulation)
RCP	Regulation on Civil Procedure (Supreme Court Regulation)
REO	Regulation on Enforcement Officers (Supreme Court Regulation)
RJPM	Regulation on Judicial Personnel Management (Supreme Court Regulation)
RMC	Regulation on Mediation Commissioners
RKBA	Rules of the Korean Bar Association
RPE	Regulation on Professional Examiners (Supreme Court Regulation)
RPIA	Rules on Public Interest Activities (internal rules of KBA)
RSACL	Regulation on the Stamp Attached for Civil Litigation, Etc. (Supreme Court Regulation)
RSMJCFC	Regulation on Subject-Matter Jurisdiction in Civil and Family Cases (Supreme Court Regulation)

List of Abbreviations

Foreword

Wolter Kluwers International Encyclopaedia of Laws online brings together contributions from countries around the world in one of the biggest comparative law exercises currently available. The series dealing with Civil Procedure covers many countries.

In this outstanding monograph, Professor Nam-Geun Yoon of Korea University School of Law, describes Civil Procedure in South Korea. He brings to this task both his academic experience and his experience serving on the bench in Korea for more than twenty years as a judge and a presiding judge in various courts.

At a time of global interaction, it is more important than ever to have an understanding of the procedures applicable in countries where disputes may arise. There are of course many foreign law firms and lawyers doing business in Korea, but despite its position as a leading global economy, there has been no book written in English which gives an extensive description of Korean civil procedure. This monograph is written from a practical perspective and is intended to fill that gap.

Professor Nam-Geun Yoon has produced a work of outstanding thoroughness and clarity. He describes the background to civil procedure in Korea, without which no real understanding is possible. The description of the organization of the courts and legal profession gives a roadmap to the reader. Increasingly important issues such as pro bono are covered too. There follows a comprehensive description of the substance of civil procedure from the beginning of the claim to enforcement, with the system of explanatory headings and sub-headings making navigation straightforward. The monograph concludes with sections on arbitration and mediation.

Professor Nam-Geun Yoon's monograph on Civil Procedure in South Korea is a model of how such an account should be written and presented. It will be an invaluable source of reference lawyers, judges, arbitrators, academics and others who wish a clear and authoritative description of how civil procedure in Korea actually works.

Sir William Blair
London, England
May 2020

Preface

Recently, Korea has emerged as an important player in the international community with respect to economy and geopolitics, and the number of foreign or multinational enterprises trading with Korean counterparts, or those having invested in the Korean market, are on the rise. Korea has been opening its legal market step-by-step since 2012 in accordance with the U.S.-Korea Free Trade Agreement. There are dozens of foreign law firms providing legal services in Korea. The Regulation on Establishment and Operation of Judicial Panels for International Cases, which is a Supreme Court Regulation, took effect in 2018. Under the Regulation, the Patent Court and the Seoul Central District Court operate a three-judge panel respectively wherein the proceedings English is the official language. Such judicial panels can be expanded to other courts if demand for them increases.

In this context, it is natural for foreign practitioners and academics to have a lot of interest in Korean dispute resolution procedures. However, Korea has a unique language and legal system, which makes access to Korean civil procedure difficult for foreigners. Until now, there has been no law book written in English, which introduces the Korean civil procedure extensively. This work is an effort at filling this gap.

Korea was under Japanese colonial rule for thirty-five years from 1910, during which Japanese law was applied in Korea with some exceptions. Japanese legal system is rooted in German law. On the other hand, the United States Army Military Government governed Korea for three years from 1945 when the World War II ended. Moreover, in contemporary times the relations between the U.S. and Korea have been close. This is the reason why so many legal principles of the United States have been adopted in Korean law, although in essence, Korea is a civil law country. In sum, German, Japanese and American features of law have, all in varying degrees, informed the Korean legal culture, thus enriching the legal system of Korea.

I have served in Korea on the bench as a judge including as a presiding judge in various courts for over twenty years since 1987, after which I became a professor of law in 2007 at Korea University School of Law teaching civil procedure and bankruptcy law. During my career as an academic, I have been actively engaged in arbitration practice as an arbitrator of the Korean Commercial Arbitration Board. This work is based both on my judicial experience and academic one as a professor.

This book endeavors to make Korean civil procedure understood by foreign legal experts from a practical perspective. I tried to show how statutory provisions and legal principles are applied to real cases in the proceedings. I made it a point, if possible when explaining legal theories, to show different results when different theories are applied to a case. I placed more emphasis on court precedents over academic treatises so as to make the subject more accessible to foreigners. Most of the examples taken in this book originate from court cases.

At first, I thought writing this book was not so challenging since the subject of civil procedure was part of my everyday life as a judge, an arbitrator and a professor of law. However, it did not take long to realize that too many legal terms of art used readily among Korean legal professionals did not have a corresponding parlance in English. Of course, such difficulties were expected to some degree because Korea and common law countries have little in common in their legal history and culture.

This book will also be used as a textbook in classes for foreign law students at Korea University School of Law. The American Law Center of Korea University provided me with financial support under its program to develop legal textbooks written in English. I would like to express my gratitude to the Center.

I would also like to acknowledge with appreciation the cooperation of my colleagues, lawyers, teaching assistant and former students, who contributed to the writing of this book, in particular lawyer Jinkyu "David" Lee who practices law in Seattle, U.S. for translating Korean legal terminologies into English and my colleagues Kee-chang Kim and Asif H. Qureshi for their precious advice. Lawyer Mel Kang in Seattle and assistant professor Jung-won Jun in the college of law at Kookmin University proofread the text along with lawyers Ji-young Jung and Hyun-woo Kim. Fang Dan who is my former teaching assistant worked on footnotes. My son Ho-yeol Yoon, a teaching fellow at Seoul National University School of Law helped me with researches and other miscellaneous works.

Professor Nam-Geun Yoon
April 28, 2020

General Introduction

§1. General Background

I. Political System

A. Liberal Democracy

1. Korea was under Japanese colonial rule from 1910 until the end of World War II in 1945. Thereafter Korea was governed by the United States Army Military Government for three years. In 1948, the Republic of Korea (ROK) was founded according to its own Constitution promulgated in the same year. The First Constitution adopted a presidential system based on a liberal democracy and strict separation of the presidential, legislative and judicial branches of government. However, the first President, Rhee Syngman, and the then ruling Liberal Party created an autocratic regime through fraudulent elections and illegitimate revisions of the Constitution.

2. President Rhee's regime collapsed in 1960 under the pressure of the April 19 Student Uprising. This uprising was caused by widespread and systematic election fraud. While the National Assembly initiated democratization measures, in 1962, General Park Chung-hee led a military coup and seized power. Park was officially sworn in as President and ruled as a dictator with support of the military until he was assassinated in 1979. Just after the demise of Park's regime, another military general Chun Doo-hwan mobilized the military, usurped power and extended the military dictatorship.

3. In 1987, the June Democracy Movement against President Chun's regime successfully ended military rule. The Constitution was revised through a national referendum and eliminated the undemocratic elements in the prior Constitution. Since the 1987 Constitution, to the date of this writing, seven presidents have been directly elected by the citizens. The separation of powers and principles of liberal democracy are enshrined in the Constitution. It decrees that the basic free and democratic order be ensured; that a policy of peaceful unification be pursued (Art. 4 Cons); and if the purposes or activities of a political party contradict and threaten the fundamental democratic order, that party can be dissolved in accordance with the decision of the Constitutional Court (Art. 8(4) Cons). It also provides that the freedom and creative initiatives of enterprises and individuals in economic affairs be respected (Art. 119(1) Cons).

B. Democratic Republic

4. Korea is a democratic republic with a presidential form of government. Power is equally divided among three branches of government: the legislature, the executive branch and the judiciary. Each of these branches enjoys autonomy and independence. The President is elected by universal, equal, direct and secret ballot by the people (Art. 67(1) Cons). The term of office for the President is five years with a limit of one term (Art. 70 Cons). The President has the power to sign and ratify treaties; accredit, receive or dispatch diplomatic envoys; and declare war and conclude peace (Art. 73 Cons). As the head of the executive branch, the President appoints the Prime Minister, Ministers and senior public officials (Arts 86(1),87(1); §32 SPOA). The heads of each executive ministry are appointed by the President from among members of the State Council (Art. 94 Cons). The President also appoints the Chief Justice of the Supreme Court, the Supreme Court Justices, the President of the Constitutional Court and the Constitutional Court Justices. Consent of the National Assembly is needed when the President appoints the Chief Justice of the Supreme Court, the President of the Constitutional Court, the Prime Minister, and Supreme Court Justices (Arts 104(1),(2);111(4);86(1) Cons).

5. The National Assembly is unicameral. It is composed of members elected by universal, equal, direct and secret ballot by the citizens (Art. 41(1) Cons). The term of office for each member is four years (Art. 42 Cons). There are 300 National Assembly members, of which 253 members are elected in the same number of local constituencies and 47 members are allocated to the parties based on the percentage of nationwide votes that each party received (§§21(1),189 POEA).

6. The National Assembly introduces, deliberates and votes on legislative bills (Arts 51,53 Cons). Legislative bills may be introduced by any member of the National Assembly supported by at least nine other members or by the executive branch (Art. 52 Cons; §79(1) NAA). The National Assembly deliberates and decides the national budget submitted by the executive, including the budget for the National Assembly and the judicial branch (Art. 54(1),(2) Cons). The National Assembly has the authority to audit state affairs or investigate matters related thereto (Art. 61(1) Cons). The National Assembly may pass a motion for impeachment against the President, the Prime Minister, members of the State Council, Justices of the Supreme Court, Justices of the Constitutional Court, judges, and other public officials (Art. 65(1) Cons). The Constitutional Court adjudicates impeachment cases (Art. 111(1) Cons).

7. The court system is composed of the Supreme Court which is the court of last resort and lower level courts including five High Courts, eighteen District Courts, six Family Courts, one Administrative Court, one Bankruptcy Court, and one Patent Court (Art. 101(2), §3(1) COA). The National Court Administration which is annexed to the Supreme Court takes exclusive charge of judicial administrative tasks. The Ministry of Justice is part of the executive branch and manages the legal affairs thereof and does not take part in court administration.

C. *Municipal Autonomy*

8. Korea is a unitary state, not a federal system. However, Korea has a system of municipal autonomy in which municipalities are in charge of local administrative functions. Types of municipal governments, election procedures for elected positions and other matters pertaining to municipal organization and operation are regulated by statutes enacted by the National Assembly (Arts 117,118 Cons). A municipality is a legal person and can have and enjoy property rights (§3(1) LoAA).

9. Cities are divided into metropolitan cities and basic cities. The Seoul Special Metropolitan City, six Metropolitan Cities including the Busan Metropolitan City, eight Provinces including the Gyeonggi Province, the Jeju Special Self-governing Province, and the Sejong Metropolitan Autonomous City are classified as the metropolitan. Cities and districts governed by provincial governments are considered basic cities. So too are districts within metropolitan cities including districts within the Seoul Special Metropolitan City (§2 LoAA). The head of a municipality and members of municipal councils are directly elected by the residents of the municipality (§§31,94 LoAA). Municipalities have legislative councils that can adopt ordinances that are within the scope of the relevant statutes (§§22,26(1) LoAA).

II. Legal System

A. *Civil Law System*

10. Korea has a civil law system. Written laws in Korea include the Constitution, Acts, Presidential Decrees, Regulations of constitutional bodies including the Supreme Court, Ordinances of the Prime Minister, Ordinances of Ministries, Municipal Ordinances and international laws.

11. The Korean Constitution was promulgated on July 17, 1948 and has been revised nine times. The last revision was in 1987. The Korean Constitution is the highest law of the nation. A proposal to revise the Constitution can be introduced either by the National Assembly with a resolution of an absolute majority or by the President (Art. 128(1) Cons). If the proposal is passed by the National Assembly with an absolute two-thirds majority (Art. 130(1) Cons), it is referred to a national referendum. When approved by a simple majority of all ballots cast in the referendum where more than one half of eligible voters participate, the resolution takes effect as a revised Constitution (Art. 130(2) Cons).

12. Legislative bills may be introduced by members of the National Assembly or by the executive (Art. 52 Cons). Each bill passed by the National Assembly becomes a law when the President promulgates it (Art. 53(1) Cons). The President can also send a bill back to the National Assembly for reconsideration. If the legislature repasses the bill with a simple two-thirds majority, it automatically becomes a law (Art.53(4) Cons). A name (e.g., Civil Act, Income Tax Act, etc.) is given to each Act. Under the name of an Act, the promulgation date and serial number according to the chronological order of enactment are indicated.

13. The Korean legal code is composed of the Six Codes and other Acts. "Six Codes" refers to the six main legal codes including the Constitution, the Civil Act, the Commercial Act, the Criminal Act, the Civil Procedure Act and the Criminal Procedure Act that make up the main body of law in Korea.

B. Adjudication on the Constitutionality of Laws

1. The Constitutional Court

14. When the adjudication of a case turns on the constitutionality of an Act, the court in which the case is pending refers the case to the Constitutional Court upon petition by a party or by its own authority (§41(1) CCA). The prerequisites for a constitutional decision are: a specific case pending in a court, the Act at issue is applicable to the case, and a final judgment in the case could be different depending on constitutionality of the Act.[1] There is no appeal of a court's decision to refer a pending case to the Constitutional Court (§41(4) CCA). While the case is pending in the Constitutional Court, the proceedings in the original court are suspended until the Constitutional Court delivers a decision (§42(1) CCA).

2. Courts

15. When a Presidential Decree, a Regulation or Ordinance that is applicable to a pending case, runs afoul of the Constitution or an Act, the court must reject the application of subordinate laws passed pursuant to that particular constitutional provision or Act. The Constitutional Court does not have jurisdiction in such a case. This is distinguished from a case where the constitutionality of an Act is in question. Rather, the Supreme Court has the final authority regarding constitutionality and legality of these subordinate laws (Art. 107(2) Cons). This means that lower courts are also authorized to put aside the subordinate laws, and the Supreme Court is the ultimate authority on this matter.

C. Adversarial System

16. Civil litigation begins by the plaintiff's filing of a complaint in the appropriate court. In a trial, the plaintiff and the defendant assert claims and defenses and stand as equal parties before the court. The court presides over the proceedings as a neutral adjudicator and renders a judgment on whether the plaintiff's claim is

1. Supreme Court Decision 2002ChoGi113 decided on September 27, 2002.

upheld or not, based on the evidence presented by the parties. The court has authority to have the parties clarify the facts and law but may not urge submission of a new allegations or evidence.

17. Criminal litigation starts when an individual is charged with a crime by a prosecutor. In criminal trials, the roles of prosecutors and defendants are similar to those of plaintiffs and defendants in a civil case. A judge plays the same neutral role as in civil litigation.

18. In the past, the prosecutor initiated criminal proceedings by submitting to the court records of investigations conducted by the police and prosecutors. The court heard witnesses and examined evidence based on these investigations and decided if there was enough evidence to find the defendant guilty. The criminal investigation lay at the core of criminal procedure and the prosecution took a leading role in courtroom proceedings. However, the Criminal Procedure Act was revised several times from 1995 to 2007, gradually adopting adversarial procedures. As a result, the focus of criminal proceedings moved from investigations to a trial. This trend is called the principle of trial-centered adjudication.

D. Jury Trial

19. In Korea, a jury trial is allowed only in criminal cases. The Act on Citizen Participation in Criminal Trials was enacted on June 1, 2007 and took effect on January 1, 2008. Criminal cases assigned to a judicial panel can be adjudicated by a jury trial. However, the jury is advisory and its verdict is nonbinding on the court (§48(4) ACPCT). If the court reaches a verdict contrary to the jury verdict, the panel's presiding judge must explain its reasoning to the defendant. In civil litigations, there are no jury trials. As a result, the judge is exclusively responsible for findings of fact and conclusions of law.

E. Norms for Adjudication

20. The court adjudicates cases by applying laws to the facts found in the trial. In the hierarchy of laws, lower level laws are made within the scope delegated by higher level laws. The Constitution is the ultimate legal authority and Acts are one step below the Constitution.

21. Presidential Decrees or Enforcement Decrees are one step below Acts. The President may issue Presidential Decrees in accordance with the scope of delegation specifically defined by an Act (Art. 75 Cons). In addition, the Prime Minister and Ministers may issue Ordinances on matters specified in higher level laws (Art. 95 Cons). These Ordinances are subordinate to Presidential Decrees and effective insofar as they do not run counter to higher level laws. These Presidential Decrees and Ordinances are collectively referred to as Orders.

22. Constitutional entities, including the National Assembly, the Supreme Court, the Constitutional Court and the National Election Commission, may make rules called Regulations. The hierarchical order of these Regulations is equal to that of Presidential Decrees. The Supreme Court has issued about seventy regulations pertaining to judicial proceedings, internal discipline and regulations on administrative matters of the court (Art. 108 Cons), including the Regulation on Civil Procedure, the Regulation on Criminal Procedure, the Regulation on Family Procedure, and the Regulation on Registration of Real Estate. The Supreme Court Regulations become effective by a resolution of the Council of Supreme Court Justices.

23. International treaties duly concluded and promulgated under the Constitution, and the generally recognized principles of international law have the same effect as domestic statutes (Art. 6 Cons). This means treaties concluded and joined by the ROK immediately take direct effect on Korean citizens without separate legislation. The President is empowered by the Constitution to conclude and ratify treaties with the consent of the National Assembly (Art. 60 Cons).

24. As in other civil law countries, the doctrine of *stare decisis* is not applied in Korea. Precedents of the court do not have binding force. Judges are not bound by decisions rendered by the same court or higher courts. However, Supreme Court decisions strongly influence lower courts. Since lower court judges do not want their decisions reversed by higher courts, Supreme Court decisions have become *de facto* case law.

25. There are statutory provisions which reflect the fact that Supreme Court decisions function as a source of law. In the Supreme Court, there are panels composed of three or more Justices. A panel can adjudicate a case when the Justices are unanimous. However, when the validity of a previous Supreme Court opinion is an issue, the panel refers the case to an *en banc* proceeding consisting of not less than two-thirds of all Justices (§7(1) COA). In addition, in a small claims case, a party is allowed to appeal the judgment, decision or order of an intermediate appellate court to the Supreme Court, but only on the grounds that the appellate court's opinion on the constitutionality or legality of the laws was erroneous or contrary to Supreme Court precedents (§3 TSCA). These provisions reflect the fact that Supreme Court decisions have a similar effect to written laws.

§2. DELIMITATION OF THE SUBJECT-MATTER

I. Definition of the Term "Civil Procedure"

26. Civil procedure involves litigation. "Litigation" is a dispute resolution proceeding presided over by the court as a fair and neutral umpire, where concerned parties are given equal opportunities to present claims and defenses and the court rules on the dispute.[2]

27. "Civil procedure" is the dispute resolution process for civil cases. A "civil case" is a dispute arising out of claims and obligations based on personal status or property, which are governed by private laws such as civil and commercial law. A civil case is premised on a dispute. A "dispute" in this context means an actual dispute with respect to legal rights and obligations.[3] For instance, a dispute between individuals on the truthfulness of a factual allegation or the interpretation of a law in a hypothetical situation are outside of subject area of civil procedure.

28. Disputes between the State or municipalities and individuals are subjects of civil procedure provided such disputes are regulated by private law. In contrast, disputes regarding a legal relationship in which the State or a municipality exercises administrative power are subjects of administrative litigation, not civil.[4]

II. Distinction with Other Types of Procedures

A. *Criminal Procedure*

29. Criminal procedure is the process in which the State exercises its penal power against a person who violates criminal laws. Criminal procedure begins with the filing of charges by a public prosecutor. Prosecution by a private individual is not allowed (§246 CrPA). Because the adversarial system is used to determine facts in the adjudication process as in civil litigation, the prosecution and defense present evidence regarding the charges as equal parties except that the prosecution bears the burden of proving the defendant's guilt. A judge, as a neutral referee, determines the truth and passes judgment based only on evidence presented and admitted in the trial. However, in a criminal case, the principle of substantive truth is applied. Thus, there are no arraignments or plea bargaining.

30. In criminal proceedings, fact finding is based only on the evidence (§307(1) CrPA). When the confession of a criminal defendant is the only evidence against him/her, it is not admissible as evidence of guilt (§310 CrPA). In contrast, in civil litigation, when a defendant fails to submit an answer within thirty days from the

---

2. Neung-hwan Kim et al., *Civil Procedure Commentaries (I)* 33 (Judicial Administration Association 2003).
3. *Ibid.*
4. *Ibid.*

date he/she received a copy of a complaint, the court may render a judgment in favor of the plaintiff on the assumption that the defendant admitted the truth of the facts constituting the legal elements of the claim (§257(1) CPA). Courts do the same when a defendant submits an answer admitting the truth of all the facts alleged by the plaintiff without presenting an affirmative defense (§257(2) CPA). The facts admitted by the parties before the court have binding effects, and a court should find the facts regardless of evidence (§288 CPA).

31. In criminal procedure, any evidence obtained in violation of due process is not admissible (§308-2 CrPA). Also, hearsay evidence is admissible only when certain requirements are met (§316 CrPA). On the other hand, in the Civil Procedure Act, there is no provision limiting the admissibility of hearsay evidence or any evidence obtained in violation of the law. According to Supreme Court case law, an audiotape containing a surreptitiously recorded conversation by one party is admissible.[5] However, mail obtained through illegal inspection, or the content of communication acquired or recorded by a third party through illegal means are not admissible in a trial or disciplinary proceedings including the civil litigation (§4 PCSA). In addition, the Supreme Court held that a medical examiner's report was inadmissible because the examiner had not taken an oath before preforming examination of the object designated by the court, as prescribed in the Civil Procedure Act.[6]

32. In a criminal case, only when the prosecution has proved that the defendant committed the crime beyond a reasonable doubt, can the court find the defendant guilty (§307(2) CrPA). However, in civil cases, the Civil Procedure Act does not define the standard of evidence required to prove facts. Scholarly opinions on this issue are divided. A few jurists suggest a preponderance of the evidence standard. Under this standard, the burden is met when the evidence shows that the alleged fact is more likely to be true than not.[7] However, a majority of scholars and case law require a higher level of plausibility. According to this standard, when the evidence is sufficient to convince a reasonable person that the alleged facts are true in light of their experiences in their daily lives, or when the trial judge is more than 80% sure that the facts are true, the burden is satisfied.[8]

33. Because the degree of proof and admissibility of evidence are different in criminal and civil cases, it is possible for a court to find inconsistent facts based on the same evidence depending on whether the pending case is criminal or civil. However, considering the higher threshold of proof in criminal cases, factual findings of guilt by judges warrant a much higher degree of proof. In this context, the Supreme Court ruled that a trial court in a civil case could find facts inconsistent with the guilty verdict in a related criminal case, only when new and persuasive evidence

5. Supreme Court Decision 99Da1789 decided on May 25, 1999.
6. Supreme Court Decision 82DaKa317 decided on August 24, 1982.
7. Dong-yoon Chung et al., *Civil Procedure Law* 545-546 (Bobmunsa 6th ed. 2017).
8. Si-yoon Lee, *New Civil Procedure Law* 525-526 (Parkyoungsa 9th ed. 2015); Supreme Court Decision 2011Da1828 decided on April 13, 2012; Supreme Court Decision 2009Da56603,56610 decided on December 10, 2009.

was presented in the civil case.[9] The theoretical ground for this case is weak because it restricts a judge's discretion to evaluate the evidence. However, public trust in the courts would be seriously damaged if a civil court found facts suggesting that an innocent defendant was wrongly convicted in a criminal court. In this regard, maintaining public confidence in the courts was probably the basis of this decision.

B. Administrative Litigation

34. Typical types of administrative litigation are appeals suits and party suits. Appeals suits include revocation suits, suits seeking confirmation of nullity, and suits seeking confirmation of illegality of an omission.

35. Revocation suits are brought to revoke or alter an illegal disposition by an administrative agency. Most of administrative litigations belong to this category. A suit seeking confirmation of nullity is a suit instituted to confirm the invalidity or nonexistence of a disposition by an administrative agency. A suit seeking confirmation of an illegal omission is a suit to confirm an omission by an administrative agency when the administrative agency has a legal obligation to act on a petition within reasonable period of time, but fails to provide any response.[10] The defendant of an appeals suit is not the State or municipalities, but the specific administrative agency that imposed the disposition or has obligation to do so.

36. A party suit is a lawsuit concerning claims related to public laws or those caused by an administrative disposition. The party to this type of administrative litigation is the State or a municipality even when the disposition of an administrative agency is a basis of such litigation.[11] There are different theories regarding the standard for distinguishing party suits and civil suits in which the State or a municipality is a party. A majority of scholars suggest that a lawsuit based on a legal relationship regulated by public law is a party suit, whereas a civil case is one based on relationships governed by private law.[12] A small number of scholars believe that the dividing line should be based on the nature of the claim itself. Thus, in a party suit the claim is based directly on a public right. The claim in a civil lawsuit comes from a private right.[13]

37. Decisions of the Supreme Court seem to be in line with this latter opinion. In a lawsuit filed by a civil servant seeking confirmation of his/her status as such or seeking unpaid salary, the Court held that this was under the jurisdiction of the

9. Supreme Court Decision 92Da31453 decided on January 15, 1993.
10. Seoul Administrative Court Practice Research Association, *Theory and Practice of Administrative Litigation* 7-8 (Judicial Development Foundation, 2014).
11. Seoul Administrative Court Practice Research Association, *supra* n. 10, at 9.
12. Myung-ho Ha, *Relationship between an administrative lawsuit for civil remedies and a civil action* 380 Human Right and Justice 52, 56 (2008).
13. Seoul Administrative Court Practice Research Association, *supra* n. 10, at 26.

Administrative Court.[14] On the other hand, a lawsuit seeking confirmation of ownership or return of unjust enrichment should be brought in a District Court. This is true even when the claim is based on a relationship governed by public law.[15]

38. Because the adjudicative process in administrative litigation and civil litigation are very similar, the procedural aspects of administrative and civil litigation do not significantly differ.[16] For this reason, the Civil Procedure Act and its subordinate laws including the Regulation on Civil Procedure apply to administrative litigation.[17]

39. However, since the legitimacy of administrative proceedings and protecting individuals' rights are fundamental goals in administrative litigations, judges play an active role in fact finding, limiting the principles of civil procedure including party-disposition and the adversarial principle. For example, if there is a third party whose rights and interests are likely to be infringed upon by the outcome of a suit, the court may, on its own motion, have the person intervene in the suit (§16 ALA). If the court deems it necessary to have another administrative agency intervene in a suit, the court may decide to do so (§17 ALA). The court may examine evidence on its own authority and render a judgment based on facts not asserted by a party (§26 ALA). Also, even when claims filed by the plaintiff are deemed legitimate, if they are remarkably inappropriate in terms of the public interest, the court may dismiss them (§28 ALA).

C. Family Litigation

40. The Family Court has exclusive jurisdiction over familial relationships recognized in the law. This includes both contentious and noncontentious cases (§2(1) FLA). A contentious case is premised upon the existence of a dispute between opposing sides. In noncontentious cases, there are no disputing parties. Rather, the court is asked to determine the status or rights of an individual litigant. Contentious family cases are divided into two groups: those based on family relationships and those based on property relationships. Family relationship-based cases are further divided into those involving marriage and those involving parent-child relationships.

41. Contentious family cases based on property relationships include suits that seek damages arising out of family and parent-child relationships. Thus, damages may be claimed in cases involving the cancellation of an engagement or ending a de facto marriage relationship, as well as the nullification or revocation of a marriage, divorce, or adoption.

---

14. Supreme Court Decision 2012Da102629 decided on March 28, 2013.
15. Supreme Court Decision 2011Da95564 decided on March 21, 2013.
16. Seoul Administrative Court Practice Research Association, *supra* note 10, at 16.
17. *Ibid.*

42. Noncontentious family cases include a petition for adult guardianship; declaration of death in absentia; creation of a surname and its origin; cohabitation, support, cooperation or providing living expenses for a spouse; child support and visitation rights; etc.

43. The Family Litigation Act applies to contentious and noncontentious family cases. The Civil Procedure Act supplements where matters are not covered by the Family Litigation Act (§12 FLA). However, contentious family cases are fundamentally different from civil cases. Civil cases deal with individuals' economic and proprietary claims which parties can freely manage in their own self-interest. In contested family law cases, the court also considers the public interest. These differences are reflected in the respective litigation procedures. In a family relationship-based case, considering the public interest, the adversarial principle is sometimes ignored or restricted and a family court conducts fact-finding by its own authority regardless of allegations by the parties (§17 FLA).

44. In a contested divorce case, reversal of adoption and property-related disputes, mediation is required before the parties can proceed to litigation (§50(1) FLA). This is the same for a noncontentious case where there is an interested third party. If a party files a suit or petition without first applying for mediation, the family court will nevertheless refer the case to mediation (§50(2) FLA).

D. Noncontentious Proceedings

45. Civil cases can be divided into two categories, litigation and noncontentious cases. Presence of a dispute is the essential nature of litigation. For this reason, the procedural structure of civil litigation is built on an assumption that parties have competing claims and defenses that they will assert in front of a judge. On the other hand, in noncontentious cases, despite lack of a dispute, the court, acting in the public interest, adjudicates an individual's legal status, rights and obligations upon a petition from an interested party or a prosecutor acting as the guardian of the public interest.

46. In theory, one can clearly distinguish litigation cases from noncontentious cases. However, in practice, there is a large gray area between them, making it difficult to categorize such cases. The Non-contentious Case Procedure Act defines matters which are to be regulated thereby. This Act enumerates noncontentious civil cases, noncontentious commercial cases and administrative fines. Noncontentious family cases are governed by the Family Litigation Act.

47. Under the Non-contentious Case Procedure Act, there are two types of cases, civil and commercial. Civil cases include ones related to a legal person, trust, permission for creditor's exercise of debtor's rights on behalf of the debtor (§404(2) CA), deposit in court (§488 CA) and registration of spousal agreement (§829(4) CA). Commercial cases encompass ones related to oversight of a corporation, voluntary liquidation and issuance of corporate bonds.

48. The Non-contentious Case Procedure Act does not govern all noncontentious cases. Some of them are regulated by separate statutes such as the Civil Execution Act, the Family Litigation Act, the Registration of Real Estate Act and the Debtor Rehabilitation and Bankruptcy Act. Such statutes including the Non-contentious Case Procedure Act, have provisions stipulating that the Civil Procedure Act applies to the noncontentious proceedings, except as otherwise provided for.

49. The features of noncontentious proceedings are as follows. When dealing with noncontentious cases, courts may *sua sponte* find facts and examine evidence as needed (§11 NcCPA). Hearings are not open to the public. However, the court may allow specific persons to observe the court proceedings when it deems it appropriate (§13 NcCPA). The court gives notice of hearing dates to the public prosecutor and the public prosecutor, acting in the public interest, may submit opinions and participate in the hearings (§15 NcCPA).

50. Unlike civil litigation cases where the court renders a judgment in open court, in noncontentious cases, the judge delivers a decision in a manner the judge finds appropriate (§17(1) NcCPA). If a court later finds its own decision unlawful or unjust, it may annul or alter it on its own motion (§19(1) NcCPA). In a civil case, a judgment has a binding effect on the court that rendered it. Thus, the court may not modify the judgment once it is rendered.

§3. Sources of Civil Procedure Law

I. History

51. During the *Joseon* (also called as *Chosun*) Dynasty (1392˜1897), legislative power was exclusively vested in the king. The first code of law was published in 1397 by order of King Taejo and was based on law codes of the *Goryeo* Dynasty (918˜1392). Revised codes were published several times until the final years of *Joseon* Dynasty. Such codes reflected Confucianism from the Chinese *Ming* Dynasty. The Codes of the *Joseon* Dynasty consisted of six codes: the *Yijeon* (), the *Hojeon* (), the *Yejeon* (), the *Byeongjeon* (), the *Hyeongjeon* (), and the *Gongjeon* (). The *Yijeon* Code applied to administrative organization and human resources; the *Hojeon* Code governed tax and financial matters; the *Yejeon* Code applied to personal status and rituals; the *Byeongjeon* Code applied to the armed forces and national defense; the *Hyeongjeon* Code governed criminal punishments and execution; and the *Gongjeon* Code regulated transportation and maintenance of facilities. In the *Joseon* Dynasty, there was no clear distinction between laws governing civil matters and criminal cases. In addition, administrative power was not separated from adjudicative power. Thus, local administrators appointed and dispatched by the central government took charge of judicial tasks as well.

52. In 1894, in the waning days of the *Joseon* Dynasty and amid a power struggle between the Chinese *Qing* Dynasty and the Japanese Empire, the *Donghak*

Peasant Revolution erupted in Korea. The Chinese *Qing* Dynasty and Japan dispatched their armed forces to Korea to put down the uprising. This triggered the Sino-Japanese War. Japan won this war and further increased its influence on *Joseon*. In June 1894, Japan established a group of government officials who supported the modernization of the nation. This was a legislative body () which exercised political power beyond the government. This council enacted and promulgated 208 reform rules that were aimed at transforming *Joseon* from an autocratic monarchy to a modern western style nation.[18]

53. In April 1895, the Court Organization Act was promulgated and the adjudication system of *Joseon* was entirely reformed. In the same month, the Civil and Criminal Litigation Rule () was enacted. This Rule was the first modern litigation procedure law in Korea. It governed both civil and criminal litigation.[19] In July of the same year, the Enforcement and Disposition Rule () was enacted to regulate enforcement of civil judgments.

54. After the Japanese Empire won the Russo-Japanese war in February 1904, it took measures to colonize the Empire of *Dai Han*.[20] In January 1907, twenty-nine Japanese judges and prosecutors were dispatched to Korea to advise Korean judges and supervise litigation management.[21] On July 12, 1909, the prime minister of the Empire of *Dai Han* and a Japanese representative concluded an agreement named "Protocol of delegation of Korean adjudication and prison management to the Japanese Government". According to this protocol, Korea entrusted litigation tasks and criminal punishment to the Japanese government. By doing so, the Korean court system was abolished and replaced with Japanese courts. Japanese and Korean personnel were appointed as judges of the Japanese Empire.[22] At that time, litigation procedure was governed by the Civil and Criminal Litigation Rule () enacted in July 1908. This rule had provisions regarding amount in controversy, jurisdiction, litigation representation, litigation costs, settlement, withdrawal of a lawsuit, seizure, enforcement of judgment, preservative measures.[23]

55. In August 1910, Japan coerced Korea into signing the Treaty for Japanese Annexation of Korea, by which the Empire of *Dai Han* was deprived of sovereignty and placed under the rule of the Japanese Empire. Japan changed Korea's official name to *Joseon* and instituted a Japanese Governor-General of *Joseon* to rule the country. The *Joseon* Rules of Civil Cases was promulgated in 1912 and applied the Japanese Civil Procedure Act to civil litigation in Korea with some exceptions. The Japanese Civil Procedure Act was modeled after German law.

---

18. *History of Courts* 16 (National Court Administration 1995).
19. *Supra* n. 18, at 37.
20. King Gojong, the King of *Joseon*, abolished the *Joseon* Dynasty on October 12, 1879 and founded Empire of *Dai Han* (also called the Great Korean Empire) and became the first emperor. He made efforts to modernize Korea in the mold of western advanced countries. However, it turned out to be beyond his capacity to repel the invasion of the Japanese Empire.
21. *Supra* n. 18, at 45.
22. *Supra* n. 18, at 46.
23. *Supra* n. 18, at 60.

56. Korean independence from Japan occurred in August 1945 with the defeat of Japan in World War II. Immediately after that, the US Army Military Government ruled the country. It quickly abolished unjust draconian laws and regulations of the former colony. However, in November 1945, through Rule 21, the US Army Military Government declared that the Japanese statutes and regulations that were not abolished by that date would remain in effect until further measures were taken. Following this decree, the Japanese Civil Procedure Act remained effective during the US Army Military Government in Korea.[24]

57. Korea promulgated its Constitution in July 1948. In August of the same year, the Republic of Korea was founded as an independent nation. However, it took a long time for the new-born nation to have its own civil procedure statute. Immediately after Korea's independence, the Code Drafting Committee composed of jurists was formed to make Korea's own unique laws.

58. The committee submitted its first draft of the Civil Procedure Act to the National Assembly in January 1953. After repeated delays in different terms of the National Assembly, the bill finally passed in December 1959 and was promulgated on April 4, 1960. The Code Drafting Committee wrote the Civil Procedure Act on the basis of Japanese law, while at the same time reflecting Korea's unique family culture and with references to Chinese law.[25]

II. Rules on Civil Litigation Procedure

59. The most important source of law for civil procedure is the Civil Procedure Act that was enacted on April 4, 1960, and most recently revised on October 31, 2017 with act number 14966. This Act initially included provisions on proceedings for civil lawsuits as well as enforcement of judgment and provisional remedies such as prejudgment seizure and injunction regarding the object of the litigation.

60. Later, the enforcement provisions and provisional remedies were removed and incorporated into the Civil Execution Act which was enacted in January 2002. As a result, the current Civil Procedure Act mainly governs adjudication procedure.

61. Disputes concerning the enforcement of a judgment are adjudicated by the court of enforcement. However, some cases are treated as civil litigation. For example, an action raising an objection to the claim being enforced and an action brought in support of an opposition lodged to a distribution plan are tried by civil courts and the Civil Procedure Act applies to these cases.

62. The Civil Procedure Act consists of seven parts with 502 sections. The Supreme Court may also prescribe rules, not inconsistent with the Constitution and

24. *Supra* n. 18, at 172.
25. Young-seob Lee, *Reading Summary of Publishing Civil Procedure Act,* 4-3 Beob Jeong 4, 4 (1949. 3.).

statutes, pertaining to litigation proceedings, internal discipline and regulations on administrative matters of the court (Art. 108 Cons). Accordingly, the Regulation on Civil Procedure prescribed by the Supreme Court regulates all aspects of civil procedure just as the Civil Procedure Act does. The Regulation consists of 144 rules based on those of the Civil Procedure Act.

63. The Court Organization Act governs the organization and jurisdiction of different courts, judges and judicial councils. It also applies to maintaining order in the courtroom and the decision-making process of a judicial panel.

§4. General Features of Civil Procedure

I. Characteristics of the Procedure

A. Role of the Judge in Court

64. In civil litigation, a judge plays two roles simultaneously: finding facts and applying the law. Only a legal practitioner who meets certain qualifications can become a judge. Unlike the European lay judge system, a Korean judicial panel only includes professional judges.

65. In an adversarial system, parties to litigation play a leading role in alleging facts, presenting evidence and making arguments as to the points each side has the burden to prove. On the other hand, the court has the responsibility to reach a fair and just solution through the proper exercise of its procedural authority to lead the proceedings smoothly, to treat both parties equally and to conduct a speedy and truthful trial.[26]

66. The following are areas where judicial authority is exercised to direct the course of the proceedings.

(a) Initiative in the proceedings: designation or alteration of a hearing date (§165 CPA); determination, extension and reduction of a period (§172 CPA); and resumption of the interrupted proceedings (§244 CPA), etc.
(b) Authority on case management: limitation, separation or consolidation of proceedings (§141 CPA), resumption of the hearing after close thereof (§142 CPA), discretionary transfer of a case to another proper venue (§35 CPA), referring cases to trial preparation proceedings (§§258,279 CPA), setting the time limit to submit a brief or evidence (§147 CPA), issuance of order to submit a summarized brief (§278 CPA), requesting parties to clarify points of arguments (§136 CPA), etc.

26. Si-yoon Lee, *supra* n. 8, at 355.

(c) Control of hearings: opening, continuing and closing of a hearing (§§169,207 CPA); permission or prohibition of making a statement in the courtroom (§135 CPA); exercising courtroom policing authority (§58 COA), etc.

B. *Principle of Orality*

67. The principle of orality is conceptually opposite to the principle of written forms. The former directs courts to adjudicate cases based only on what was stated verbally in a hearing. Even when a brief containing important legal elements is submitted to the court, the brief cannot be grounds for a ruling unless the content of the brief is stated point-by-point orally in the courtroom. In line with this, examination of evidence is centered on hearing testimony of witnesses. Documentary evidence can contribute to the judgment only when a witness testifies or a party states in court its content in detail.

68. The principle of written forms takes the opposite approach. Here, judges read and review briefs and documentary evidence before the trial date. In the courtroom, judges usually ascertain the main points of arguments contained in such briefs to the extent it is necessary. Also, when authenticity is verified, the court takes into account documentary evidence in adjudicating the case, even if the specific content was not presented orally.

69. Although the Civil Procedure Act stipulates that the parties present a case orally in court (§134 CPA), in practice, the principle of written forms prevailed. As a result, a judge usually relied on reading and reviewing litigation records including documentary evidence. For example, if a party said before the court, "I am making a statement as written in my brief submitted on such and such date," the court accepted the statement as if the party orally stated the facts and points of law as stated in the brief. Such a practice contributed to processing a large number of cases simultaneously in a short period of time.

70. In 2007, the Supreme Court revised the Regulation on Civil Procedure to adopt the principle of orality, departing from the long tradition of relying on written documents.[27] The Supreme Court recognized that a procedure based on oral statements would better serve truth finding and improve public confidence in the court. This change was in line with the 2007 reform of the criminal procedures and the adoption of jury trials in criminal cases.

71. Since the Regulation on Civil Procedure established the principle of orality, lawyers have significantly changed the way they present their cases and judges

27. Regulation on Civil Procedure, rule 28 (1) Oral hearings shall be conducted in a way that parties to the litigation state important factual or legal matters or the court confirms with the parties that such matters are correct. (2) Courts shall provide the parties with opportunity to state his or her opinion on important factual or legal issues.

spend a longer time in the courtroom. However, practitioners are so accustomed to written documents that it is too early to say whether orality is being completely implemented.

C. Principle of Directness

72. Under the principle of directness, only the judge who heard oral arguments and examined evidence in person in the courtroom can render a judgment on the case. Under the principle of orality, this principle of directness is strongly required because a judge is supposed to render a judgment after hearing oral testimony in person. In contrast, under the principle of written forms, where judges reach their decision through reading and reviewing litigation records, the principle of directness applies to a lesser degree.

73. To strictly comply with the principle of directness, a judge has to hear the case from the opening to the closing. If a member of a judicial panel is replaced during trial, the panel must open a new trial.

74. However, in Korea, judges are not appointed to a specific court or panel but are supposed to move from one court or panel to another every two or three years. In such a circumstance, if the judiciary strictly followed the principle of directness, many pending cases would undergo stops and restarts resulting in a massive backlog of cases.

75. For this reason, the Civil Procedure Act provides that the final decision on a case should be made by the judge or judges, who have taken part in the hearing or hearings which form the foundation of the litigation (§204(1) CPA). When a single judge or the majority of judges in a judicial panel are replaced, upon a motion of a party, the court should have witnesses who have already testified, reappear and give testimony before the new judge or newly formed panel. According to this court practice, when the judge or judges who participated in the final hearing make the decision on the case, the requirement of directness is met.

D. Principle of Concentration

76. The principle of concentration requires that once the main hearing commences, all claims, grounds thereof, evidence and arguments should be presented directly to the judge or panel deciding the case, in one block of time until the case closes. The concentrated main hearing is conducted in one day or consecutive days to the final stage of the proceedings. This practice depends on well-organized pre-trial proceedings.

77. By contrast, in piecemeal hearings, the judge designates a trial date for multiple cases and hears each case for a short period of time. The short hearings are repeated at intervals of three or four weeks. When the presentation of evidence is concluded, the judge closes the record and passes judgment.

78. The piecemeal approach works well with the principle of written forms because judges are supposed to decide a case relying on reading and reviewing litigation records and documentary evidence. They need not close a case with only one concentrated hearing. However, if hearings are held multiple times over a long period under the principle of orality, a judge's memory could be challenged and potentially seriously hamper or distort his/her understanding of the case. Therefore, the principle of orality is successfully implemented when it is combined with concentrated proceedings.

79. When revising the Civil Procedure Act in 1990, Korea adopted the principle of concentration and included provisions for trial preparation. Under these provisions, the trial should converge in one main hearing, and parties should prepare for it in writing (§272(1) CPA). The judge in charge of the preparatory proceedings helps parties clarify the points of their allegations and sort out evidence, so that the trial becomes efficient and concentrated (§279(1) CPA). After the 1990 changes to the Civil Procedure Act, the number of hearings for one case was significantly decreased. However, practitioners are so used to the tradition of piecemeal trials that there is still some way to go to fully implement this new trial procedure.

E. Principle of Party Disposition

1. Definition and Meaning

80. Under this principle, parties control the course of litigation. They initiate the action, determine the object and scope of a case and any voluntary termination of the action. Party autonomy, a fundamental guideline in private law, is reflected in the Civil Procedure Act. The Civil Procedure Act stipulates that a court should not render any judgment on matters which have not been claimed by the parties (§203 CPA).

2. Contents

a. Commencement of the Proceedings

81. Civil litigation begins when the plaintiff files a complaint with a court. A lawsuit is not pending until the plaintiff files a complaint even if there is a long-standing dispute.

b. Object and Scope of Adjudication

(1) Specification of subject-matter

82. The object and scope of a court's adjudication of a case are bound by the subject-matter in the plaintiff's complaint. Courts can rule only on the subject-matter determined by the plaintiff's pleadings. This principle protects the defendant's ability to defend against a claim. According to Supreme Court decisions, a claim for damages due to a breach of contract and a tort claim are separate subject-matters even though both are based on the same accident. Thus, the court may not render a judgment on a claim arising from a breach of contract, when the plaintiff only sought tort damages.[28]

(2) Quantitative limit of an identical subject-matter

83. The court may not render a judgment granting relief exceeding the amount prayed for by the plaintiff. For example, if the plaintiff seeks tort damages in the amount of KRW 100 million, but the court finds that the damage sustained by the plaintiff amounted to KRW 150 million, the court must nevertheless render a judgment awarding only KRW 100 million.

84. The responsibility of the plaintiffs to accurately state their damages is further refined in personal injury cases. According to case law, damages in personal injury cases are divided into three categories: actual damages, passive damages and compensation for pain and suffering (hedonic damages). Each category is a separate subject-matter and the court may not award the plaintiff more than the amount prayed for on each of these separate subject-matters.[29]

85. In a monetary claim, the plaintiff must specify the principal amount, the interest rate and the relevant period for calculating interest as damages. The court then rules on the claim within the limits of each of these factors specified and asserted by the plaintiff.[30]

86. Of course, the plaintiff will be granted judgment for the amount of the claim proven when the court finds that part of the debt in dispute lacks evidence. Also, when the plaintiff seeks unconditional performance of an obligation, and the defendant presents an affirmative defense of simultaneous performance with evidence to support it, the court may render a judgment ordering the defendant to perform his/her obligation in exchange for counter-performance by the plaintiff.

28. Supreme Court Decision 2010Da28604 decided on May 17, 2012.
29. Supreme Court Decision 2002Da34581 decided on September 10, 2002.
30. Supreme Court Decision 2012Da55198 decided on October 11, 2012.

3. Termination of the Proceedings

87. The plaintiff, according to his/her own decision, may end litigation proceedings through withdrawal of the lawsuit, withdrawal of an appeal, waiver of a claim, a settlement or mediation. However, in a derivative suit or a securities-related class action, the court's permission is needed for a withdrawal of the lawsuit, waiver of a claim or a settlement (§403(6) ComA, §35(1) SCAA).

F. Adversarial Principle

1. Definition and Meaning

88. Under the adversarial principle, parties have the right and responsibility to present their own factual allegations and to produce evidence. The court relies only on facts alleged by the parties when ruling on a case. Undisputed facts automatically bind the court and disputed facts must be established by evidence produced by the parties. The adversarial system is the opposite of an inquisitorial system. An adversarial system is applied to hearings on the merits of the case. An inquisitorial system is used in determining the procedural requirements of a lawsuit.

89. The Civil Procedure Act does not explicitly require an adversarial system, although it has been generally accepted as the fundamental mode in civil litigation. However, there exist several complementary opinions regarding the theoretical grounds for this system.[31] One theory holds that adversarial proceedings come from the basic nature of civil procedure. It is a mechanism to resolve disputes arising from economic and proprietary relationships governed by the principle of party autonomy. Another opinion suggests that litigation procedures based on the parties' self-interest better serve truth finding. A third opinion posits that ruling within the scope of what was stated by a party serves to protect the other party from unexpected claims and evidence and guarantees the right to due process.

2. Contents

a. Responsibility to State Facts

90. Facts to be found at trial are categorized as material facts, basic facts and evidentiary facts. Material facts directly satisfy the requirements of the substantive laws that define specific rights or legal relationships. Material facts work to identify, modify or extinguish legal rights. Basic facts or subsidiary facts are facts from which the court may draw a factual inference about a material fact. For example, if A is in possession of B's seal and its official certificate (basic facts), it can be inferred that B gave A the authority to act as his/her agent (a material fact). Evidentiary facts support or impeach the admissibility or probative value of evidence.

31. Si-yoon Lee, *supra* n. 8, at 320-321.

For example, if a witness is a relative of one party or was previously convicted of perjury, which is an evidentiary fact, that might impeach the credibility of the witness.

91. The adversarial principle applies only to material facts. Moreover, courts can determine that material facts exist only if a party orally asserted the facts. If a party admits material facts that the other party has the burden to prove, those admissions are binding on the court. By contrast, with respect to basic facts and evidentiary facts, courts may find these facts without a stated assertion by a party. In addition, such facts must be supported with evidence even when they are admitted by the party who does not bear the burden of proof.

92. Material facts are categorized further into different groups of facts; a group of facts raising legal rights, a group impeding the rise of legal rights, a third group extinguishing legal rights, and a fourth impeding the exercise of legal rights.

93. Facts that give rise to a legal right are a set of facts that constitute the legal elements of a claim. For example, entering into a contract for sale creates a buyer's right to seek transfer of ownership of the property he/she bought, and a seller's right to seek payment of the purchase price. A tort gives rise to a victim's right to seek monetary compensation for his/her loss or injury by the person committing the tort, or tortfeasor. Thus, in a claim seeking the payment of a purchase price, the material facts are that the seller and buyer entered into a contract in which the buyer, the seller, the property, the contract price and the contract date are all properly described. In a claim for unintentional tort damages, the material facts are that the plaintiff was owed a duty of care by the defendant, the defendant failed to take due care, the plaintiff suffered an injury or property loss, and that the damages suffered by the plaintiff were caused by the defendant's negligence.

94. An example of facts that impede a legal right would be a purchase and sale agreement that is a sham transaction or when a party to an agreement is incapable of entering into the agreement. In these examples, impeding facts might be that each party did not actually intend to buy or sell the item or one party knew of the other party's lack of intent. Another example would be that one party to the agreement was unconscious or lacked the mental capacity to enter into the agreement.

95. Another category of facts is those which cause the extinction of existing rights. For example, parties to a contract have legal contractual rights. But these rights are lost when the contract is lawfully terminated. The facts or circumstances that justify termination of a contract and the act of doing so fall into this category. Completion of performance, waiver, satisfaction of requirements for termination, setoff and expiration of the statute of limitations all belong to this category of facts.

96. Facts impeding the exercise of legal rights do not affect the existence of legal rights but block the exercise of such rights. Examples of this type include the due date of performance, conditions precedent, an affirmative defense based on simultaneous performance, or an affirmative defense based on a right of retention. For example, if Person A entered into a contract but the date of performance by Person B has not yet arrived, Person A may not exercise his/her rights under the contract even though such rights exist. In this example, existence of the due date for performance of the obligation is a fact impeding exercise of legal rights.

97. Facts giving rise to, impeding the rise of, extinguishing, or impeding the exercise of legal rights are all relatively determined with regard to claims in a case. When a plaintiff files a lawsuit based on his/her rights under a purchase and sale agreement, the fact that the contract was terminated is a fact that extinguishes legal rights. However, if the plaintiff claims restitution of a paid purchase price or delivered property based on the termination of the contract, the facts relevant to the contract's termination are facts giving rise to legal rights.

b. Burden of Pleading and Principle of Statement for Mutual Interest

98. Material facts are derived from legal provisions that provide grounds for the creation, modification or extinction of legal rights. Private substantive laws such as the Civil Act and the Commercial Act define certain legal requirements and effects. For example, a person who has kept possession of real estate for twenty years peacefully and openly with an intention to own it, acquires ownership by registering the property (§245 CA). Here, "holding peaceful and open possession of another person's real estate for twenty years" is a legal requirement. This legal requirement gives rise to a claim to transfer title of the property. This is a legal effect corresponding to a legal requirement. A fact, or a set of facts, satisfying this legal requirement are material facts. Therefore, facts giving rise to a legal right are derived from the requirement prescribed by the laws regulating the creation of a legal right. This principle applies in the same manner to other types of material facts.

99. Each party has the responsibility to assert the legal elements of his/her claim. When exercising a legal right, the plaintiff has the burden to state facts which give rise to that right. The defendant then has the responsibility to state facts in an affirmative defense, which impedes or extinguishes that right or impedes the exercise of it.

100. When a party with the burden to plead material facts does so and the opposing party admits these facts, the court takes these facts as proven. There is no need for the party pleading the facts to present evidence to prove them. But if the opposing party disputes these facts, then the other party with the burden to plead must go forward and satisfy its burden of proof by presenting evidence. Therefore, in principle, the burden of pleading and burden of proof coincide.

101. If a party states material facts which the opposing party has the burden to assert, the court decides the case based on those facts. As to material facts stated before the court, which side makes such a statement does not matter. This is the principle of statement for mutual benefit. For example, in a case seeking repayment of a loan, the fact that the defendant paid off the debt extinguishes the plaintiff's claim. While the defendant bears the burden of pleading this material fact, if the plaintiff makes statements to the effect that the debt has been paid, the court should decide the case based on those statements.

c. Distinction Between Litigation Material and Evidentiary Material

102. What the parties say at trial regarding material facts is referred to as litigation material. What is inferred or asserted as a result of the examination of evidence is called evidentiary material. Korean civil procedure law strictly distinguishes one from the other. Thus, even if evidence is enough to establish material facts, the court may not find these facts as a basis of a judgment unless a party states them. For example, in a claim for repayment of a loan, if the defendant does not assert repayment of the debt, the court decides the case ignoring the repayment even when an item of evidence supporting the repayment was presented in court. This is because repayment is a material fact. Similarly, the court may not find the lapse of the statute of limitations when the defendant did not raise this affirmative defense even if the lapse is clearly shown on the face of the plaintiff's complaint. The burden of pleading and litigation materials are two sides of the same coin.

d. Implicit Statement of Material Facts

103. In principle, parties' assertion of material facts should be made explicitly before the court. However, the court may find material facts if it concludes that a party stated these facts implicitly in view of his/her whole argument and explanation of the evidence made in court. This is true even if the party failed to state them explicitly. This is called an indirect statement or argument.

104. In some cases, the court can also rely on facts established by evidence even when the facts are inconsistent with the factual allegations in court. This can occur when the discrepancy is due to a party's mistake, memory lapse or misstatements. Further provided such discrepancy is deemed insignificant and the opposing party's ability to assert or defend its case is not impaired.

105. However, courts have interpreted indirect statements very narrowly. The Supreme Court held that a statement of actual authority of an agent does not include a statement about apparent authority.[32] Similarly, an assertion of voidness of a contract due to coerced expression of intent does not include a statement about avoidance of declaration of intent by reason of unlawful duress.[33]

e. Offer of Proof

106. In principle, courts may only examine evidence presented by the parties. However, if a court fails to obtain the required degree of conviction from the evidence presented by parties, or otherwise deems it necessary, the court may conduct a *sua sponte* examination of the evidence (§292 CPA). However, in practice, it is

32. Supreme Court Decision (*en banc*) 83DaKa1489 decided on December 13, 1983.
33. Supreme Court Decision 95Da40038 decided on December 23, 1996.

very rare when courts examine evidence not submitted by the parties. It is because such *sua sponte* examination might give an impression of partiality.

f. Authority to Ask for an Explanation

(1) Definition and meaning

107. The presiding judge may, in order to clarify points, ask the parties questions, and prompt them to explain factual or legal matters (§136(1) CPA). The court should give the parties an opportunity to state their opinions on core issues, which may have been overlooked (§136(4) CPA). This authority is referred to as the authority to clarify. If the court follows the adversarial principle very strictly, it must not intervene in pleadings or arguments of the parties. However, such strict compliance with the adversarial principle would result in legal issues being ambiguous and trials going adrift. Also, the parties might be faced with unexpected results due to trivial mistakes or ignorance.

(2) Scope of the authority

108. Under the adversarial principle, the responsibility to assert and to prove a case lies with the parties. Thus, court's authority to clarify is only allowed to the extent that it does not infringe on this principle. Accordingly, the authority to clarify must be exercised in ways that provide the parties an opportunity to correct and supplement their motions or statements only when they are ambiguous, incomplete or inconsistent.

109. While in principle, active exercise of this authority does not permit a court to recommend that a party take such actions as submitting a new motion, claim or defense, such a measure may be exceptionally permitted when the recommended acts are legally and logically predictable when considering their reasonable connection with previously submitted litigation materials. In these particular circumstances, an opposing party's right to an effective defense is not likely to be harmed by such a recommendation.

110. For example, if a plaintiff (landlord) requests a defendant (tenant) to vacate the land and demolish a building thereon, and the defendant exercises his/her tenant's right to sell the building to the landlord (§643 CA), then the contract of purchase and sale between them is automatically established and the plaintiff's claim would be dismissed. In this situation, the Supreme Court held that the trial court must clarify whether the plaintiff intends to pursue the claim to vacate and demolish – a claim that would in all likelihood be dismissed, or whether he/she intends to amend the claim or join an alternative claim for delivery of the building based on the statutory contract for sale. If, taking the hint from the judge, the plaintiff modifies the complaint, the court could then render a judgment and resolve the dispute.[34]

34. Supreme Court Decision (*en banc*) 94Da34265 decided on July 11, 1995.

(3) Method of exercising the authority

111. Since the authority to clarify comes from the court's responsibility to preside over the proceedings, it is exercised by a presiding judge in a judicial panel or the judge in the single-judge court. Other members of a judicial panel may exercise this authority after consulting with the presiding judge of the panel.

g. Exclusion of the Adversarial Principle

112. The court may inquire into matters *sua sponte* because the court's ruling affects the public interests or relates to the public policy. The court, not the parties, has the responsibility to collect litigation materials on such matters as international jurisdiction, foreign laws, customary laws and exclusive jurisdiction. On matters to be inquired *sua sponte*, the burden of pleading does not apply and admission of alleged facts does not have any binding effect.

113. Some matters are examined *sua sponte* but the court need not actively collect materials thereon because the effects of the ruling is limited to the parties. With respect to such matters, the court finds facts based on the evidentiary materials presented by the parties even though they are not pleaded by a party.[35] Examples include matters concerning a proper venue, the amount in controversy, the plaintiff's legitimate interest to sue, etc.

II. Fundamental Guarantees

A. Right to Be Adjudicated

114. All citizens have the constitutional right to a trial in conformity with the law, by judges qualified under the Constitution and statutes (Art. 27(1) Cons).

115. The appellate system is one of the tools to serve the right to a fair trial because higher courts review whether the appealed case was adjudicated correctly in the lower courts and fix any errors. The Korean court system has three main levels and the Supreme Court is the court of last resort. However, the right to a fair trial does not include the right to appeal up to the Supreme Court in all cases.[36]

116. A party to a civil case may appeal when the party is dissatisfied with the final judgment of the trial court. A party who loses in part can appeal on that part of the claim. In appealing to an intermediate appellate court, the aggrieved party need not assert factual or legal grounds for appeal. The court of intermediate appeal adjudicates the claim as a trial court within the scope of the judgment challenged by the appealing party. However, results of the examination of evidence in the first

35. Supreme Court Decision 81Da124 decided on June 23, 1981.
36. Constitutional Court Decision 90HunBa1 decided on January 20, 1995.

instance court still have valid effects in the court of appeals. Thus, the intermediate appellate court can find facts based on the testimony of a witness who testified in the lower court and, if necessary, examine evidence newly produced at the appellate hearing.

117. The Supreme Court only decides the legal issues. Parties may appeal to the Supreme Court only on the ground that the intermediate court of appeals erred in interpreting or applying the law. The party appealing to the Supreme Court must submit a statement of reasons for the final appeal (§427 CPA).

B. Open Court Principle

118. The court conducts trials and delivers its judgment in a courtroom open to the public, unless an open trial might endanger national security, public peace and order, or good public morals (Art. 109 Cons, §57 COA). Accordingly, even when the court decides to have closed hearings, it delivers its judgment in open court.

119. Only the proceedings for cases tried and finalized by a judgment are open to the public. For the cases specified by statutes to be resolved by a decision, the court may adjudicate the case based only on written documents or in-person hearings. The proceeding for such a case is usually conducted in camera, not open to the public.

120. The open court principle has two parts: litigation conducted in open court and litigation records open to the public. Thus, citizens who are not the parties to the litigation are allowed to visit the courtroom and watch the progress of the litigation without any restriction. They can also inspect the files of the case pending in the court or when it is finalized.

121. In practice, this principle is strictly followed in attending trials, whereas public access to court records is limited. Those who are not a party may inspect the litigation records only after the case has been resolved with a final and binding judgment. Nonparties can inspect the records for the purpose of academic research or public interest research, as prescribed by the Supreme Court Regulation (§162(2) CPA). Thus, litigation records of a case still pending are closed to the public.

122. Under a democracy, citizens may visit the courtroom to watch first-hand every stage of the trial and examine whether the proceedings are administered fairly and justly. Also, a transparent litigation process plays a critical role to protect the parties from judges' possible prejudice or arbitrariness and enhance public confidence in the court system. It provides learning experiences by showing how laws made by their representatives apply to real cases. This principle contributes to securing independence of the judiciary because it is more difficult for people with power to exert influence on a judge's decision-making when all aspects of litigation are subject to public scrutiny.

C. Independence of Judges

123. Fair and impartial adjudication of a case hinges upon the independence of individual judges and the institution of the courts. Independence of individual judges is protected by the Constitution and statutes regulating the appointment and transfer of judges, their term of office and mandatory retirement age, the guaranty of political neutrality, and protection of their official status. A judge may not be removed from office except by impeachment, criminal conviction accompanied by imprisonment or heavier punishments, or judicial disciplinary measures (Art. 106(1) Cons).

124. The independence of the courts guarantees autonomous and independent adjudication free from outside influences. Judges exercise their judicial function independently according to their conscience and in conformity with the Constitution and related laws (Art. 103 Cons). "Conscience" in this context is interpreted as an evaluation and determination by a career judge based on legal reasoning, rather than personal subjective judgment.[37]

---

37. Young-soo Jang, *State Organization Theory* 365 (Hongmunsa 2005).

Part I. Judicial Organization

Chapter 1. The Courts and Their Members

§1. Courts

I. Structure of the Court System

A. General Adjudicative Body

1. The Supreme Court

125. The Supreme Court is the highest appellate court. There are fourteen Justices including the Chief Justice (§4(2) COA). Judicial panels may be established in the Supreme Court (Art. 102(1) Cons) and these panels decide cases by consensus of all the sitting Justices on the same panel. The cases on which the Justices fail to reach a unanimous decision are referred to a hearing by the Supreme Court *en banc*, which is composed of at least two-thirds of the sitting Justices. Also, when a panel determines that an administrative decree or Regulation to be applied to a pending case is in violation of the Constitution or an Act; or when a panel deems it necessary to alter a previous opinion of the Supreme Court; or when it otherwise believes that adjudication of the case by a panel is not proper, the panel refers the case to an *en banc* proceeding (§7(1) COA).

126. As the court of last resort, ruling only on legal issues, the Supreme Court generally has appellate jurisdiction over cases tried or decided in the intermediate appellate courts. An exception to this rule is cases brought by a party disputing the validity or results of a presidential election or general election for the National Assembly. In such a case, the Supreme Court has original jurisdiction and acts as the trial court (§§222,223 POEA).

2. Courts of Appeals and Courts of First Instance

127. The High Court, as a second-tier court, has jurisdiction over appeals from judicial panels of District Courts (including their Branch Courts), Family Courts (including their Branch Courts) and appeals from the Bankruptcy Court and the Administrative Court (§28 COA).

128. District Courts are trial courts for civil cases and criminal cases (§32(1) COA). Family Courts have exclusive jurisdiction over family matters regarding marriage relationships, adoptions, parental rights, support, guardianship, inheritance, and testamentary matters (§40(1) COA, §2 FLA). There is also a Family Branch Court of a District Court where there is no Family Court in the judicial district (§31-2 COA).

129. The Administrative Court has jurisdiction over appeals suits (a suit instituted against a disposition or an omission by an administrative agency); party suits (a suit over legal relations under public law filed by one of the parties to the legal relationship); public suits (a suit instituted by a person without any direct interest in order to seek the correction of violations by the State or organs of public entities); and agency suits (a suit instituted when disputes arise over the existence or exercise of power between agencies of the State or organs of public entities, except for a suit instituted against matters under the jurisdiction of the Constitutional Court) (§40-4 COA, §3 ALA).

130. The Bankruptcy Court administers and adjudicates cases concerning business rehabilitation, bankruptcy, and individual rehabilitation (§3(1) DRBA).

131. When there is no Administrative Court or the Bankruptcy Court in a judicial district, judicial panels of the District Court substitute for each of these courts [§2 COA Addenda (Act No.4765, Jul. 27, 1994); §2 COA Addenda (Act No.14470, Dec. 27, 2016)].

132. The Patent Court adjudicates cases regarding patent rights, utility model rights, design rights, and trademark rights (§28-4 COA).

133. Within a District Court, there are Branch Courts and a Family Branch Court if there is no Family Court in the region (§31 COA). Family Courts also have Branch Family Courts (§39 COA). A City Court or a Town Court is under a District Court, a Family Court, or one of their Branch Courts; and has jurisdiction over small claims cases, settlements prior to filing a lawsuit (§§385,386 CPA), summary proceedings for a payment order (§§462,474 CPA), mediation, and minor criminal cases punishable by a fine not exceeding KRW 200,000, misdemeanor imprisonment, or a petty fine (§§3(2), 34(1) COA).

3. Appellate System

134. The Supreme Court, sitting at the top of appellate system, has jurisdiction over final appeals against judgments rendered by High Courts and appellate panels of first instance courts. The Supreme Court also hears the final appeal from the High Military Court which is an intermediate appellate court for military crimes.

135. Though the Patent Court is a court of first instance, its status is similar to that of a High Court in that the Supreme Court hears cases brought directly from the Patent Court (§14 COA). This means that there is no intermediate appellate court concerning cases under the jurisdiction of the Patent Court.

136. A District Court, a Family Court, the Administrative Court, and the Bankruptcy Court are courts of first instance. Among these courts, District Courts, Family Courts, and the Bankruptcy Court have appellate panels, which have jurisdiction over cases tried by single judges of their court or their respective subordinate courts including Branch Courts, City Courts and Town Courts.

4. Composition of Judicial Panels

137. In the Supreme Court, the entire bench and three judicial panels hear cases. Among the fourteen Justices, twelve Justices, excluding the Chief Justice and the Minister of the National Court Administration, compose three panels, each of which has four Justices. When the entire bench exercises the adjudicating authority of the Supreme Court, the Chief Justice presides over the proceeding (§7(1) COA).

138. In the High Courts and the Patent Court, judicial panels adjudicate all cases. A judicial panel is composed of one High Court Presiding Judge and two judges. High Court presiding judges enjoy higher status than other judges and are appointed by the Chief Justice of the Supreme Court. However, this system is in transition. The position of High Court Presiding Judge is being done away with and High Court judicial panels will have three High Court judges of equal status.

139. When cases are distributed to judicial panels by the President of a court (usually using a computer program), a member judge of the panel is designated the "case management judge" and this judge takes a leading role in deciding the case.

140. Since the presiding judges have to take care of the proceedings for all the cases assigned to their judicial panel, they are designated as the case management judge in a relatively small number of cases. At the close of a trial, the case management judge briefs the other two judges on the case and its factual and legal issues, and thereafter the panel deliberates until reaching a conclusion. The case management judge then writes the form and contents of their judgment reflecting the opinions of the panel members.

141. There are judicial panels and single judges in District Courts (including their Branch Courts), Family Courts (including their Branch Courts), the Administrative Court, and the Bankruptcy Court. Judicial panels in these courts dispose of cases in the same manner as those in the High Courts. In first instance courts, a judicial panel and a single judge have different subject-matter jurisdiction based on the amount in controversy. A judicial panel adjudicates relatively serious cases, while a single judge takes relatively less serious cases.

5. Personnel Supporting Judicial Tasks

a. Supreme Court Law Clerk

142. In the Supreme Court, law clerks conduct legal research and analysis, and brief various legal issues under the direction of the Justices. Most, but not all, clerks are judges. All Justices have three law clerks available exclusively to them. There is also a common research team composed of law clerks who are not assigned to a specific Justice and conduct research as a team member.

b. Judicial Researcher

143. Judicial researchers are appointed to courts of various levels except the Supreme Court. They conduct legal research, prepare bench memos and assist judges in other matters regarding hearings and trials. Judicial researchers are appointed by the Chief Justice of the Supreme Court from among those admitted to the bar. They are employed for a definite period of up to three years. Every year, third year law school students and military advocates whose term of service is near expiration compete for the position of judicial researchers. Around eighty are selected for the following year.

c. Judicial Assistant Official

144. The judicial assistant officials are assigned to the Supreme Court as well as other courts (§54(1) COA). Tasks of the judicial assistant officials include determining the amount of litigation costs and enforcement costs, proceedings for a payment order, judicial public notice, proceedings to order issuance of a court certificate of enforceability (enforcement clause), entry into the defaulters list, proceedings for an inquiry into a debtor's property and the judicial sale of immovable property (§54(2) COA).

145. Judicial assistant officials are recruited from among the court clerks who have served not less than five years in positions corresponding to grade 5 or higher, or not less than ten years in positions corresponding to grade 7 or 6 (§54(4) COA).[38]

146. A judicial assistant official has the status similar to that of a judge in that he/she adjudicates matters prescribed by the Court Organization Act. Originally, matters now assigned to judicial assistant officials were assigned to judges even though they are routine matters. However, a judicial assistant official is not a judge and if a party raises an objection to a decision by a judicial assistant official, a judge in the same court adjudicates the case from the beginning. Judicial assistant officials also do not enjoy the legal status as a judge.

38. South Korea has a grade structure for the civil service. All the career civil service positions are classified into 9 grades with the 1st grade being the highest.

d. Court Clerk

147. "Court clerk" collectively refers to court officials who are assigned to various levels of the court and conduct subsidiary tasks. Their ranks are divided into administrative officer, junior administrative officer, junior official, and assistant junior official. Their duties include making various trial transcriptions (records of the hearing), examining the procedural requirements of complaints and answers, dealing with service of process, issuing various certificates including certification that a judgment is no longer appealable, issuing court certificates of enforceability, and keeping litigation records.

e. Professional Examiner

148. In litigation proceedings where special expertise is helpful to adjudicate a case, the court may appoint professional examiners *sua sponte* or on motion of a party (§164-2(1) CPA). Professional examiners may submit a written explanation or opinion on questions raised by the court or parties. They can also present such explanation or opinion in person at a hearing (§164-2(2) CPA).

149. The Minister of the National Court Administration keeps a list of candidates who are eligible to work as a professional examiner, and based on the list, may appoint full time professional examiners whose term of employment is two years (§2-2 RPE).

f. Investigation Officer

150. Investigation officers are assigned to the Supreme Court and other courts. They collect and investigate materials necessary for court proceedings at the request of judges, and perform other necessary duties (§§54-3(1),(2) COA). For example, prior to a sentencing hearing, a criminal court may issue an order to investigate sentencing factors such as the defendant's previous character, motivation for the offence, personal circumstances of the victim, etc.

151. The Chief Justice of the Supreme Court may request other government agencies to dispatch public officials under their control to the court to serve as investigation officers (§54-3(3) COA). Investigation officers are usually used in Family Courts for family relationship cases, juvenile cases and family protection cases.

B. Special Adjudicative Bodies

1. The Constitutional Court

152. In principle, courts adjudicate all legal disputes. The Constitutional Court is an exception and it rules only on constitutional disputes. The Constitutional Court is a part of the Korean Judicial system, however, despite its title, it is separate and independent from the rest of the judiciary. Thus, a party may not appeal a judgment to the Constitutional Court, nor may a party to a constitutional case appeal a decision of the Constitutional Court to the Supreme Court. The Constitution also treats the Constitutional Court in a separate chapter from the other courts.

153. The Constitutional Court is composed of nine Justices who are appointed by the President (Art. 111(2) Cons). The President appoints three justices directly. Of the other six, three are appointed from candidates nominated by the National Assembly and three from candidates nominated by the Chief Justice of the Supreme Court (Art. 111(3) Cons).

154. The President of the Constitutional Court is appointed by the President from among the Justices with the consent of the National Assembly (Art. 111(4) Cons). The term of office for Justices is six years and they may be reappointed (Art. 112(1) Cons). However, to date, no Justices have been reappointed.

155. The Constitutional Court rules on the following matters: (a) on the constitutionality of a statute at the request of a court, (b) on charges of impeachment in accordance with the resolution of the National Assembly, (c) on the request of the Government for dissolution of a political party, (d) on conflicts of powers between administrative agencies of the Government or municipalities, and (e) on constitutional petitions as prescribed by statutes (Art. 111(1) Cons; §2 CCA). The adjudication proceedings of the Constitutional Court are initiated by submitting a written request (§26 CCA).

156. Those who are subject to impeachment include the President, the Prime Minister, members of the State Council, Ministers of each Ministry, Justices of the Supreme Court, judges, Justices of the Constitutional Court, Commissioners of the National Election Commission, and the Chairperson of the Board of Audit and Inspection and Commissioners thereof.[39]

157. In impeachment proceedings, the Chairperson of the Legislation and Judiciary Committee of the National Assembly is the prosecution commissioner (§49(1) CCA). The prosecution commissioner initiates the procedure by submitting an impeachment resolution to the Constitutional Court. The prosecution commissioner may examine the respondent (impeached official) in an impeachment hearing (§49(2) CCA).

158. If the platform or activities of a political party seriously run counter to the democratic basic order, upon a deliberation of the State Council, the Government

39. In Korea, two presidents have been impeached: Roh Moo-hyun and Park Geun-hye. The resolution to impeach Roh Moo-hyun on the ground that he violated his duty to remain neutral in the election for the National Assembly was adopted in the National Assembly on March 12, 2004. However, he was acquitted on May 14 in the same year in the Constitutional Court (Constitutional Court decision 2004HunNa1 decided on May 14, 2004). On the other hand, Park Geun-hye was impeached for corruption and abuse of power on December 9, 2016. She was convicted and removed from office on March 10, 2017 (Constitutional Court decision 2016HunNa1 decided on March 10, 2017).

may request the Constitutional Court dissolve that party (§55 CCA).[40] In this proceeding, the Minister of Justice serves as the claimant representing the Government; and the respondent is the political party.

159. When there is a dispute between administrative agencies of the Government or municipalities over their authority over certain matters, a party to the dispute may bring the case to the Constitutional Court to confirm the scope of their authority (§61(1) CCA). In these particular proceedings, the opposing Government agencies or municipalities are the parties (§62 CCA).

160. Anyone suffering a breach of fundamental rights guaranteed by the Constitution may lodge a constitutional complaint. However, complaints against judicial decisions of a court are not admissible. In addition, all legal remedies available in courts must be exhausted before a constitutional complaint can be lodged (§68(1) CCA).

161. Among the matters placed under the jurisdiction of the Constitutional Court, the proceedings for impeachment, dissolution of a political party and jurisdictional disputes are conducted in oral hearings (§30(1) CCA). However, in proceedings related to a ruling on the constitutionality of a statute or a constitutional complaint, an oral hearing is not required (§30(2) CCA).

162. The Civil Procedure Act generally applies to the proceedings in the Constitutional Court. In addition, the Criminal Procedure Act applies to impeachment proceedings, and the Administrative Litigation Act generally applies to proceedings for jurisdictional disputes between government agencies and constitutional complaints (§40 CCA).

2. Military Court

163. The military court is a special court to conduct military trials (Art. 110(1) Cons). The military court has jurisdiction over military personnel, civilian employees of the military, and military prisoners who are charged with crimes specified in the Military Criminal Act. Ordinary citizens may be subject to the jurisdiction of the military court for certain military crimes involving important military secrets, sentinels, sentry posts and military facilities (§§2,1 MCA).

164. There are two kinds of military courts: general military Courts of First Instance and the High Military Court which is the appellate court (§5 MCA). The Supreme Court has the final review of military cases (Art. 110(2) Cons; §9 MCA).

165. A general military court consists of one or three military judicial officers. The High Military Court consists of three or five military judicial officers (§22

40. For the first time in Korean history, the Unified Progressive Party was dissolved following the Constitutional Court decision 2013HunDa1 decided on December 19, 2014.

MCA). Military judicial officers include military judges and adjudicators. Military judges are appointed from among the military judge advocates. Adjudicators are military officers who are appointed by the Minister of National Defense or the commanding officer of the military unit where the military court is located.

II. Administration of the Court

A. *The Supreme Court*

1. The Chief Justice of the Supreme Court

166. The Chief Justice of the Supreme Court has responsibility for the administrative affairs of the judicial branch as a whole and supervises court officials (§9(1) COA). The Chief Justice may delegate part of this authority to the Minister of the National Court Administration, the heads of various courts, the Director of the Judicial Research and Training Institute, the Director of the Court Officials Training Institute or the Director of the Court Library in accordance with related statutes or Supreme Court Regulations (§9(2) COA).

167. When the National Assembly considers legislation related to court organization, personnel affairs, operations of the courts, litigation procedures, registry, registration of family relationships, and other court affairs, the Chief Justice may present his/her opinion, in writing, to the National Assembly (§9(3) COA). The Chief Justice also appoints court officials (§53 COA).

2. The Supreme Court Justices' Council

168. The Supreme Court Justices' Council is composed of all the Justices of the Supreme Court including the Chief Justice. It deliberates and decides matters concerning consent to the appointment and reappointment of judges, the collection and publication of judicial precedents, the request for the budget, expenditure of reserve funds, etc. (§17 COA).

169. The Supreme Court Justices' Council makes decisions by a two-thirds quorum of all Justices and an affirmative vote of a majority of Justices present (§16(2) COA). The Chief Justice of the Supreme Court chairs the Council (§16 COA).

3. The National Court Administration

170. The National Court Administration is the Supreme Court-affiliated organization which generally governs court administration nationwide. It performs functions and duties in relation to personnel affairs, budgets, accounting, facilities, statistics, litigation affairs, registration of immovable properties, registration of legal persons, registration of family relationships, deposits in court, enforcement officers, certified judicial scriveners, research of legislation and study of judicial systems (§19(2) COA).

171. The Ministry of Justice has the authority and responsibility to handle matters related to public prosecutors and legal affairs of the Government excluding the judicial branch.

172. The Minister of the National Court Administration is appointed by the Chief Justice of the Supreme Court from among the Justices, and the Vice Minister of the National Court Administration is a judge and appointed by the Chief Justice (§68 COA). In administrative litigation regarding a disposition by the Chief Justice, the defendant is the Minister of the National Court Administration (§70 COA).

173. The Vice Minister assists the Minister and performs the duties of the Minister when the Minister cannot perform his/her job and may be the acting Minister in case of a vacancy (§67(3) COA). The Minister and the Vice Minister of the National Court Administration may attend the National Assembly or the State Council and speak about judicial administration (§69 COA).

174. In the National Court Administration, there are three offices and four bureaus, under each of which sections are established. Division of duties among these subunits is prescribed by Supreme Court Regulations (§71 COA). Judges are assigned to some positions of the National Court Administration to manage judicial administrative affairs working together with nonjudge officials.

4. Affiliates of the Supreme Court

175. In addition to the National Court Administration, the Judicial Research and Training Institute, the Judicial Policy Research Institute, the Court Officials Training Institute, the Court Library, and the Sentencing Committee are part of the judicial branch.

176. The Judicial Research and Training Institute was set up in 1971 to educate judges and judicial trainees (§20 COA). With changes to law school system and the elimination of the judicial examination, the last class of judicial trainees graduated in 2018. Under the prior system, the Institute's two-year training course was required to practice law. Currently, the Judicial Research and Training Institute trains judges and the Institute also sends judges to law schools nationwide to teach law classes (§20 COA).

177. The Judicial Policy Research Institute is an organization that conducts research to improve the judicial system and trial procedures (§20-2 COA). The Court Officials Training Institute takes charge of training and educating court officials and enforcement officers (§21 COA). The Court Library is charged with researching, collecting or compiling judicial decisions, statutes, legal materials, historical records, data and other information (§22 COA).

178. The mission of the Sentencing Committee is to reduce sentencing disparities by establishing and amending sentencing standards. The Committee also conducts studies and deliberations on sentencing policies (§81-2(2) COA). The sentencing standards are nonbinding but provides important guidelines for judges when determining the kind of punishment, the period of imprisonment, the amount of fines, and the possibility of suspending a prison sentence, within the scope of the minimum or maximum sentence prescribed in criminal law.

B. Courts

1. President of a Court

179. The President of a court is appointed by the Chief Justice of the Supreme Court (§44 COA). The President of a court is in charge of judicial administrative affairs and supervises court officials in their respective courts.

2. Judges' Council

180. The Judges' Council consists of the judges of a particular court. It is an advisory body that offers the group's opinion on judicial matters (§9-2(1) COA). The President of the court serves as the Chairperson of the Council. It advises on internal rules and management of the court. It also offers suggestions to the Supreme Court concerning revision of the Supreme Court Regulations, standards for distributing cases and other work to judges and the assignment of judges to a wide array of committees of the court.

3. Secretariat

181. The Secretariat of each court is in charge of general administrative affairs, personnel management, maintenance of facilities, statistics, accounting, receipt of litigation documents, and management of litigation records of the court. The Secretariat is not a judge and leads nonjudge court officials in the court.

§2. MEMBERS OF THE JUDICIARY

I. Qualifications

A. The Chief Justice and Justices of the Supreme Court

182. The judicial officers of the Korean judiciary are the Chief Justice, Justices of the Supreme Court, and lower court judges (§5(1) COA). The Supreme Court consists of the Chief Justice and Justices (§§4(1),13(1) COA). Power to appoint the Chief Justice and Justices of the Supreme Court is vested in the President. Appointments are made with the consent of the National Assembly (Art.104(1) Cons). In addition, in appointing Justices, the recommendation of the Chief Justice is needed (Art.104(2) Cons).

183. The Chief Justice and Justices of the Supreme Court are required to be at least 45 years of age and to have practiced law or taught law as a member of the faculty at a college or university for at least twenty years (§42(1) COA).

184. The Chief Justice position is at the same level as the Speaker of the National Assembly, the President of Constitutional Court, the Prime Minister, and the Chairperson of the National Election Commission. In terms of ranking for protocol, the Chief Justice is the third position following the President and the Speaker of the National Assembly.

185. Candidates for Supreme Court Justices are recommended according to the following process. When a Justice's term is about to expire, the Recommendation Committee is formed ad hoc several months in advance. The Committee has ten members including the retiring Justice, the Minister of the National Court Administration, the Minister of Justice, the President of the Korean Bar Association, the President of the Korea Law Professors Association, the President of the Korean Association of Law Schools, one judge, and three laypersons (§41-2(3) COA). A chairperson is appointed from among the committee members by the Chief Justice (§41-2(4) COA).

186. Any person or organization may recommend candidates to be a Supreme Court Justice. Organizations of legal practitioners such as the Korean Bar Association have been active in recommending candidates. The Committee recommends at least three times the number of retiring Justices (§41-2(6) COA). Based on these recommendations, the Chief Justice recommends the most suitable candidate to the President by way of an in-person meeting. Although it is not officially confirmed, it is known that the Chief Justice and the President communicate concerning the selection of the candidate to be recommended in advance.

B. Judges

187. Lower court judges are assigned to courts of different levels and jurisdictions nationwide (§5(2) COA). Judges are appointed by the Chief Justice with the consent of the Supreme Court Justices' Council (Art.104(3) Cons, §41(3) COA). To become a judge, the candidate must have practiced law or taught jurisprudence as a member of the faculty at a college or university for at least ten years (§42(2) COA). As of January 1, 2019, the sanctioned number of judges stands at 3,214 (§1 APNJ).

188. The Personnel Committee of the Supreme Court, which is formed ad hoc, reviews matters of basic personnel planning; appointment of judges; judges' consecutive appointments; and retirement of judges (§25-2(2) COA). The Personnel Committee is composed of eleven members including a chairperson. There are three judges, two prosecutors recommended by the Minister of Justice (participating only in the deliberation on new appointments of judges), two attorneys recommended by the President of the Korean Bar Association, two professors of law recommended respectively by the President of the Korean Law Professors Association and the President of the Korean Association of Law Schools, and two citizens who are not lawyers (§§25-2(3),(4) COA).

189. Judges are not appointed to a specific court but serve nationally at-large. The Chief Justice may transfer judges from one court to another considering each court's workload and programs of personnel management. Most judges want to work at the courts in the Seoul area. As a result, judges are periodically assigned to different courts nationwide. In general, judges move to a different court every two or three years.

II. Incompatibilities

A. Incompatibilities of Judicial Officers

190. The following persons are excluded from appointment as a judicial officer: (a) those who are disqualified as a public official under other statutes; (b) those who have been sentenced to imprisonment or a greater punishment; and (c) those for whom five years have not passed since they were removed from office by impeachment (§43 COA).

191. A person for whom bankruptcy proceedings commenced and a court decision granting reinstatement is not issued is disqualified as a public official (§33 SPOA). It is notable that the statutory provisions regulating qualifications of public officials are applied to private school teachers according to Section 57 of the Private School Act. The Constitutional Court held that this provision is constitutional. The Court opined that this provision is aimed at enhancing teachers' devotedness to education and the public trust in them, taking into account the fact that societies have high expectations of them and it would be difficult for them to dedicate themselves to teaching students while they are in the bankruptcy proceedings.[41]

B. Prohibition of Dual Office Holding

192. In order to secure independence, fairness, and integrity, and to encourage judicial officers to concentrate only on adjudication, statutes prohibit judicial officers from having additional offices or jobs. Impermissible activities include: (a) to be a member of the National Assembly or a municipal council; (b) to be a public official in any administrative agency; (c) to participate in political campaigns; (d) to be engaged in paid activities without the permission of the Chief Justice of the Supreme Court; (e) to do business; and (f) to hold a title, regardless of its reward, as an advisor, officer, or employee of a corporation, organization, etc., other than government agencies, without the permission of the Chief Justice of the Supreme Court (§49 COA).

C. Prohibition from Adjudicating Specific Cases

1. Judicial Disqualification

a. Causes of Disqualification

193. The following are causes for disqualification in civil litigation (§41 CPA). These grounds for disqualification also apply to criminal litigation, with the addition that a judge is disqualified if he/she was a victim or a prosecutor or a judicial police officer in the case (§17 CPA).

(a) When a judge, his/her spouse, or his/her former spouse becomes a party to a case, or is related to a party as a co-creditor, co-debtor or a third party liable for redemption.

"Spouse" here means a legal spouse, not a spouse in de facto marriage.[42] In case of the latter, a challenge to the judge would still be possible. A party includes a plaintiff, defendant, intervener, and a third party to whom preclusive effects reach.[43] The relationship as a co-creditor, co-debtor or a third party liable for redemption means there is a common legal interest regarding rights and obligations with a party, which might impair the judge's impartial adjudication. Such a relationship exists when the judge is one of the multiple interest holders in the litigation concerning claims and obligations of multiple parties or when the judge is the third party in a subrogation relationship.

---

41. Constitutional Court decision 2005HunGa21 decided on November 27, 2008.
42. Si-yoon Lee, *supra* n. 8, at 81.
43. *Ibid.*

In litigation concerning proprietary rights of a corporation, a judge who is a shareholder of the company might not be disqualified but is likely to be challenged. However, in litigation challenging the validity of a resolution at a shareholders' meeting, the judge who is a shareholder would certainly be disqualified.

(b) When a judge is, or has been, a relative of a party to the case

The "relative" here means blood relatives within the eighth degree of relationship, in-laws within the fourth degree of relationship, and a spouse (§777 CA).

(c) When a judge has given testimony or conducted an expert examination

When a judge previously testified or was an expert examiner in a case and later became a judge in the same case, the judge is disqualified.

(d) When a judge was, or becomes, an agent of a party to a case.

An "agent" here refers to a person defined as such in the Civil Act, a statutory agent, and a counsel. It is interpreted to include a representative of a legal person, and a representative or an administrator of an association or foundation without legal personality. This is true because provisions regarding a statutory agent apply to representatives of such entities.

(e) When a judge heard a case at the trial level and is later assigned to the appeals court.

When an appellate case is assigned to a judge who previously participated in a trial held in a lower court, the judge is disqualified. If a judge of the appellate court is allowed to adjudicate the very case he/she tried when on the lower court bench, the basic function of appellate system would be seriously compromised.

The prior trial noted above means the last oral hearing or deliberation for a final judgment of the lower court or an intermediate judgment to be reviewed by the appellate court together with the final one. Proceedings prior to the last oral argument and making procedural decisions such as the admissibility of evidence, or the designation of hearing date, do not count as a "trial" in this context.[44]

Similarly, in a retrial proceeding, the hearings against which a retrial is directed, do not constitute a prior trial. So, a judge may adjudicate a retrial even when he/she participated in the last hearing of the same case previously terminated by the final judgment.[45]

When the Supreme Court reverses the judgment and remands the case to the lower court or transfers it to another court, the judge who participated in the judgment in the original court may not adjudicate the remanded or transferred case (§436(3) CPA). This prohibition is to secure the binding effects of the decision of the final appellate court, by excluding the judge from the case, who is highly likely to have a dissenting opinion. In this sense, it has nothing to do with the causes of disqualification in this Section.[46]

---

44. Supreme Court Decision 96Da56115 decided on June 13, 1997.
45. Supreme Court Decision 2000JaeDa87 decided on August 18, 2000.
46. Sang-won Kim et al., *Commentary on Civil Procedure Act (I)* 596 (Association of Judicial Administration 2003).

b. Decision on Disqualification

194. Causes of disqualification are matters to be investigated *sua sponte* by the judge himself/herself or by the panel on which the judge is a member. When grounds for disqualification certainly exist, a judge is supposed to recuse himself/herself voluntarily. Even when in doubt, the judge is likely to do so. Otherwise the court usually decides issues of disqualification on motion of a party (§42 CPA).

195. When there is a cause to disqualify a judge, the judge lacks the authority to adjudicate the case without regard to any motion. As a result, a court decision on disqualification is just a declaration of an inherent fact

2. Challenge to a Judge

a. Causes of Challenge

196. As for causes of disqualification, the Civil Procedure Act enumerates typical situations where it is difficult to expect a judge to perform his/her duty impartially. When this type of situation arises, the judge is automatically removed from the case.

197. However, there are occasions where no grounds for disqualification are found but special circumstances exist, which justify doubt about the impartiality or integrity of the judge. In such cases, the court examines the related facts on motion of a party and decides whether the judge should be removed.

198. In practice, judges usually recuse themselves when there exists a fact that might foster doubt about their fairness. Thus, in most of cases, a motion to challenge the judge is denied. Oftentimes, a motion to challenge a judge is brought to delay the proceeding or to vent a party's dissatisfaction with the court's handling of a case.

b. Motion to Challenge

199. A motion to challenge a judge on a judicial panel must be submitted to that panel. A motion to challenge a single judge must be submitted to the judge (§44(1) CPA). The reasons for the challenge and the methods for proving them must be set out in writing and presented to the court within three days from the date of filing the motion (§44(2) CPA).

200. If a motion to challenge is filed, the litigation proceedings are suspended until a decision on the motion becomes final (§48 CPA). A judge against whom a motion to challenge has been lodged should submit a written opinion (§45(2) CPA).

c. Decision on the Motion to Challenge

201. When it is obvious that a motion to challenge is in violation of the forms and procedural requirements, or is filed to delay a pending case, the court rejects it

(§45(1) CPA). When such a motion meets procedural requirements, a judicial panel of the court decides on the motion without participation of the challenged judge (§46(2) CPA).

3. Self-Recusal

202. A judge may voluntarily recuse himself/herself in a case when there are causes for disqualification or justifiable grounds for a challenge, or when, considering all the circumstances, it is deemed desirable for him/her not to adjudicate the case. In doing so, permission of the court is required because another judge must be assigned to the case (§49 CPA).

III. Judicial Term and Discipline

A. Expiration of Term and Reappointment

203. As noted earlier, the term of office for the Chief Justice of the Supreme Court is six years with a one term limit. Justices serve for six years without any term limit. Lower court judges serve for ten years and are almost automatically reappointed at the end of their term (Art. 105 Cons).

204. The retirement age for the Chief Justice and the Justices of the Supreme Court is 70 and for lower court judges it is 65 (§45(4) COA). When the retirement age for a judge falls between February and July, the judge retires on July 31 in the same year. When the date is in between August and January of the next year, the judge retires on January 31 (§45(5) COA).

205. Judges who served a full term may apply to the Chief Justice for reappointment. After consulting with the Personnel Committee and the consent of the Supreme Court Justices' Council, the Chief Justice may reappoint them for another term (§45-2(1) COA).

206. The Chief Justice of the Supreme Court may not reappoint retiring judges if it is deemed difficult for them to perform their normal duties due to physical or mental impediments; if their service records substantially fall behind; or if it is deemed substantially impracticable to expect them to maintain the dignity of a judge (§45-2(2) COA).

207. There is almost no occasion where a judge fails to be reappointed. This is because judges usually seek reappointment only when their records of performance and reputation as a judge are sufficient for reappointment. Most judges meet this requirement.

B. Involuntary Resignation due to Mental or Physical Impediment

208. When any judicial officer is unable to perform his/her duties due to a grave mental or physical impediment, he/she must resign at the order of the appointing authority. Justices of the Supreme Court are subject to an order from the President following the recommendation by the Chief Justice. Lower court judges can be ordered to resign by the Chief Justice (§47 COA).

209. The Judicial Officer Personnel Committee of the Supreme Court deliberates on involuntary resignations at the request of the Chief Justice (r.21 RJPM). The Committee may request specialized institutions to provide examinations and their opinion; require related institutions or organizations to verify facts or to produce related materials; and summon specialists for their opinions (r.22(1) RJPM). When the Committee determines that there exist causes for an involuntary resignation, the Chief Justice of the Supreme Court, after deliberation of the Justices' Council, may order a judge to resign (r.23 RJPM).

C. Removal from Office

210. A judge is removed from office if convicted in an impeachment proceeding by the Constitutional Court, or a final and binding judgment with a sentence of imprisonment or heavier punishment (Art. 106(1) Cons).

211. The National Assembly initiates the proceeding for impeachment of a judge. A draft resolution for impeachment is submitted by one-third or more of the sitting members of the National Assembly and passed with an absolute majority (Art. 65(2) Cons). The impeachment trial is under jurisdiction of the Constitutional Court. For the Constitutional Court to convict, the concurrence of six Justices or more is required (Art. 113(1) Cons).

IV. Discipline

A. The Judicial Disciplinary Committee

212. The Judicial Disciplinary Committee is part of the Supreme Court and decides judicial disciplinary cases (§4(1) DJA). The Committee consists of a chairperson and six members (§4(2) DJA).

213. The Chairperson is a Justice of the Supreme Court, appointed by the Chief Justice. Other members of the Committee include three judges, one lawyer, one professor of law and one layperson. They are appointed or commissioned by the Chief Justice (§5(1) DJA). The term of office for the chairperson and members is three years (§5(3) DJA).

B. Reasons and Types of Discipline

214. The grounds for discipline of judges include a serious breach or dereliction of official duties, misconduct in office and conduct prejudicial to the dignity of a judicial officer (§2 DJA).

215. There are three types of judicial disciplinary measures: suspension, salary reduction and reprimand (§3(1) DJA). A disciplinary suspension removes the judge from performing his/her official duty for a period of time between one month and one year without pay (§3(2) DJA). In a salary reduction, the amount of pay is reduced by up to one-third for a period of one month to a year (§3(3) DJA). A reprimand is imposed by issuing a warning to the judge against inappropriate conduct (§3(4) DJA).

C. Procedure

216. The Judicial Disciplinary Committee considers disciplinary measures at the request of the Chief Justice or a Justice of the Supreme Court, the Minister of National Court Administration, the President of a court or other judicial officers who have supervisory authority over the judicial administrative matters in the court of the relevant judge (§7(1) DJA). When the request for disciplinary action is made, the chairperson issues a notice of a meeting of the Committee, designating the date of the deliberations (§12 DJA).

217. The attendance of a majority of the Committee Members and the Chairperson is required for a disciplinary proceeding (§13(1) DJA). The requestor and respondent may state opinions and arguments in writing or orally and present evidence (§14 DJA). The Committee may *sua sponte* or on motion of a party, request an expert examination; summon witnesses to testify; ask public institutions for a fact inquiry or production of documents (§16 DJA).

218. The Committee makes a decision on a disciplinary case, by a simple majority vote (§23(1) DJA). The Chief Justice implements the decision by issuing an order of disciplinary action (§26(1) DJA).

219. The respondent may bring a lawsuit in the Supreme Court seeking revocation of the disciplinary action. This action must be filed within 14 days from the date the respondent learned that the disciplinary measure was taken (§27(1) DJA). There is no appeal on a Supreme Court decision in this type of case (§27(2) DJA).

Chapter 2. The Legal Profession

§1. The Practice of Law

I. Admission to Bar

A. *Qualifications for Attorneys*

220. There were two ways to become an attorney: pass the National Bar Examination; or pass the Examination for Appointment of Military Advocates and complete Judicial Research and Training Institute course.

221. Beginning in 2009, a three-year post graduate law school program was phased in. Therebefore, a law degree was an undergraduate degree. As the first class under the new system graduated in 2012, the National Bar Examination was introduced that same year. The old Jurisprudence Examination was phased out in 2017.

222. Before 2017, an applicant for the Jurisprudence Examination was required to have received more than thirty-five credits for law courses from a college or university. The Jurisprudence Examination consisted of three parts. The first part was a multiple-choice test, the second was an essay test and the last was an oral interview. Before 2009, around 1,000 applicants passed this examination every year.

223. Under the new law school system, an applicant for the National Bar Examination must have a post graduate juris doctorate degree from an accredited three-year law school (§5(1) NBEA). An undergraduate degree or equivalent academic courses are necessary for admission to law schools (§22 AEMPL).

224. The Minister of Education prescribes the total number of enrollees at law schools, after consulting with the Minister of National Court Administration and the Minister of Justice (§7(2) AEMPL). There are twenty-five post graduate law schools with a total enrollment of 2,000 students nationwide. The number of students at each law school is determined by the Minister of Education according to the terms in a Presidential Decree. Currently, between 50 and 150 students are admitted to the various law schools (r.6(1) AEMPL-ED). Only the Seoul National University Law School is allowed to admit the maximum number of students.

225. The National Bar Examination tests subjects including public law (constitutional law and administrative law), private law (civil law, commercial law and civil procedure), criminal law including criminal procedure, and one subject of legal specialization (international law, labor law, international transaction law, economic law, intellectual property law, environmental law and tax law) chosen by the examinee (§9(1) NBEA). Unsuccessful applicants can retake the examination five times in five years including the year of law school graduation (§7(1) NBEA). The Minister of Justice determines the number of successful candidates (§10(1) NBEA). So far, the number has been between 1,500 to 1,600 per year.

226. Another route to take to become a lawyer without passing the National Bar Examination is to serve as a military advocate. Military advocates are attorneys or those who have completed the Judicial Research and Training Institute curriculum after passing the examination for appointment of military advocates (§3 AAJA). When a military advocate who belongs to the latter group is discharged after serving ten years as a judicial officer, he/she will maintain their status as an attorney. However, if he/she is discharged without serving the ten-year term, he/she is disqualified (§7 AAJA).

B. Registration and Practice of Law

227. Not every lawyer may practice law. Lawyers must be admitted to and registered with the Korean Bar Association. To register, an attorney submits an application to a local bar association with which he/she intends to be affiliated (§§7(1),(2) AALA). The local bar association examines the application, appends its written opinion on whether the applicant is well qualified and then sends it to the Korean Bar Association (§7(3) AALA).

228. An attorney's application for registration can be denied for a criminal prison sentence, bankruptcy, impeachment, a mental disorder or clearly inappropriate conduct. When an attorney-applicant has any of the above listed grounds for disqualification the Korean Bar Association may deny his/her application, pursuant to a resolution by the Registration Review Committee (§8(1) AALA).

229. A newly licensed attorney may not practice law independently, unless he/she has served a practice training period in a government agency or a law office or has completed a practice training course provided by the Korean Bar Association for at least six months (§21-2(1) AALA).

C. Registration Review Committee

230. The Registration Review Committee of the Korean Bar Association examines and decides matters related to the attorney registration, and the denial or revocation thereof (§9(1) AALA). The Committee is comprised of nine members, including one judge, one prosecutor, four attorneys, one professor of law, and two citizens who are not attorneys (§10(1) AALA). When the Committee passes a resolution, the Korean Bar Association should register the applicant or deny or revoke the relevant registration (§12(2) AALA).

II. Rights and Duties

A. Attorney's Individual Law Office

231. Any attorney may open a law office, located in the district of the local bar association with which he/she is affiliated (§21(2) AALA). Although an attorney is prohibited from having two or more offices, he/she may set up additional offices in an adjacent place if there are unavoidable reasons, such as insufficient office space (§21(3) AALA).

B. Legal Professional Corporation and Legal Professional Partnership

1. Legal Professional Corporation

232. There are two business models for providing legal services: legal professional corporations and legal partnerships. There are also two types of corporations that provide legal services: a professional corporation that does not limit the liability of its members and a limited liability law firm where the liability is limited. Both types of professional corporations provide services to clients in their own name, but they must designate an attorney to be in charge of a specific case (§§50(2), 58-16 AALA). The representative of a legal professional corporation undertakes general transactions on behalf of the corporation, but each attorney in charge of a case represents the corporation in providing specific legal services to a particular client (§§50(6),58-16 AALA).

233. In order to establish a legal professional corporation, an attorney who is to become a partner must submit the articles of incorporation to the Minister of Justice by way of the local bar association and the Korean Bar Association (§§41,58-3 AALA). When authorization is granted to incorporate a legal professional corporation, registration should be made within two weeks (§§43(1),58-5 AALA).

234. A legal professional corporation may have associate attorneys who are not partners (§§47,58-6(2) AALA). Every partner or associate attorney of a legal professional corporation is prohibited from having another law office (§§48(3),58-16 AALA). However, a legal professional corporation may open branch offices outside of the district of the local bar association with which it is affiliated (§§48(1),58-16 AALA).

235. The biggest differences between the two types of legal professional corporations are in the requirements for establishing them and the liability of their partners.

236. A law firm without limited liability is comprised of not less than three attorneys (§45(1) AALA). At least one of the partners must be at least 45 years of age with experience as a judge, prosecutor, attorney or faculty of law at a college or university, for at least twenty years (§45(1) AALA, §42(1) COA).

237. On the other hand, the minimum requirements for a limited liability law corporation is that there must seven attorneys, two of whom have professional experience as a judge, prosecutor, attorney, or faculty of law at a college or university, for at least ten years (§58-6(1) AALA); it must have three directors who are partners (§58-6(4) AALA); and total capitalization of KRW 500 million (§58-7(1) AALA).

238. With respect to liability of partners of an unlimited liability law firm, the provisions pertaining to unlimited liability partnership companies in the Commercial Act apply (§58 AALA). Accordingly, if a law firm has not designated a managing partner in the articles of incorporation, each of the partners will be deemed to represent the firm (§207 ComA). When an attorney representing the law firm causes someone a loss or harm in the course of his/her duties, both the firm and its partners are jointly and severally liable for any damages (§210 ComA). In addition, if assets of a law firm are insufficient to fully repay its debts, each of the partners is jointly and severally liable (§212(1) ComA). Thus, a partner of a law firm has unlimited liability for the obligations of the firm.

239. On the other hand, the liability of the partners of a limited liability law firm is limited to the amount of their respective investment (§58-10 AALA). When any attorney in charge of a case causes a loss to a client, both he/she and the firm are jointly and severally liable for the damage, but other partners do not have to reimburse the client for the loss (§58-11(1) AALA).

240. A limited liability law firm must maintain a reserve account to be used for damage claims resulting from torts or other violations of duty. Such a firm should also set aside a certain amount of money to be added to the fund every business year. In the alternative, a limited liability law firm may purchase malpractice insurance or participate in the mutual aid fund operated by the Korean Bar Association (§58-12(1) AALA). Except as otherwise provided for in the Attorney-At-Law Act, the provisions of the Commercial Act pertaining to limited liability companies apply to a limited liability law firm (§58-17 AALA).

2. Legal Professional Partnership

241. A legal professional partnership is not a legal person. The provisions of the Civil Act pertaining to a partnership apply to a legal professional partnership. However, a legal professional partnership has the capacity to be a party to a lawsuit (§58-26 AALA). Thus, it is treated as an association without legal personality in civil litigation proceedings.

242. The minimum requirements of a legal professional partnership are: there must be seven attorneys, two of whom have experience as a judge, prosecutor, attorney, or faculty of law at a college or university, for at least ten years (§58-22(1) AALA). A legal professional partnership may hire associate attorneys who are not partners (§58-22(2) AALA).

243. To establish a legal professional partnership, an attorney who is to become a partner must prepare a partnership contract and partnership rules, and he/she must obtain authorization from the Minister of Justice. This process should be done by way of the local bar association in the district where the principal office of the partnership is located and the Korean Bar Association (§58-19(1) AALA).

244. The partners are liable for the debts of the partnership according to their loss sharing ratio, effective at the time when the debts are incurred (§§58-24,58-25(3) AALA). However, when an attorney, in the course of his/her employment deliberately or negligently causes loss and harm to a client, he/she is liable for the damage without any limitation (§58-25(1) AALA).

C. Advertising

245. Legal advertising is restricted and regulated by the Attorney-at-Law Act. Attorneys including legal professional corporations and legal professional partnerships may advertise their educational backgrounds, career records, main practice areas and cases which they have dealt with. The means of advertisement include newspapers, magazines, broadcasts, computer-based communications, etc. (§23(1) AALA).

246. However, attorneys are prohibited from running an advertisement containing false or misleading information that could induce potential clients to have unreasonable expectations of the outcome of legal services; or any advertisement that carries statements slandering any other attorneys or comparing their own services to those of another (§23(2) AALA). Also, attorneys should not publicize their private relationship or connection with judges, court clerks or law enforcement officials, insinuating that they could exert influence on the results of trials or investigations (§30 AALA).

247. The Advertisement Examination Committee is charged with scrutinizing attorney advertising. This committee is established in the Korean Bar Association and each local bar association (§23(3) AALA).

D. Duties of Attorneys

1. Duties Concerning Taking Cases

248. Once an attorney shows an intention to take a case, the attorney may not represent the opposing party in the same case. Nor is an attorney allowed to take the cases from other parties in a case even though the cases are not related to his/her client's case.

249. An attorney cannot take a case which he/she dealt with officially in the past as a public official, a mediator or an arbitrator (§31(1) AALA). Also, an attorney who formerly served as a judge, a prosecutor, or a public official, should not accept a case that was in the court, the prosecutors' office or the government agency within one year prior to his/her departure (§31(3) AALA).

250. A nonattorney may not establish or operate a law office by employing or entering into a partnership with an attorney (§34(4) AALA). An attorney or his/her office staff may not offer money, valuables, entertainment or other benefits to anyone in return for introducing, referring or soliciting clients (§34(2) AALA). In addition, they may not solicit clients at any court, investigative agency, correctional institution or hospital, or send others to do so (§35 AALA).

251. A court clerk or law enforcement employee may not introduce persons with whom they are dealing to a specific attorney or office staff (§36 AALA).

252. All attorneys should prepare and keep records on cases they accept (§28(1) AALA). Also, every January, each attorney must report to their local bar association the number of cases he/she processed in the previous year and the amount of fees he/she received during the same period (§28-2 AALA).

253. An attorney including a law firm and legal professional partnership must submit a power of attorney and designation of counsel to the relevant court or the investigative agency before he/she can defend or represent a client in that court or a law enforcement agency (§29-2 AALA).

2. Prohibition of Dual Employment

254. An attorney may not be employed as a full-time public official and practice law at the same time. Nor can an attorney operate a private for-profit business or serve as a director, officer or employee while operating a private law practice (§38 AALA).

3. Pro Bono Services

255. Pro bono legal services include providing services for no fee or significantly reduced fees to individuals who cannot afford to hire an attorney, to nongovernmental organizations (NGOs), religious institutions, educational institutions and public interest organizations. In addition, serving as an executive member or committee member of the Korean Bar Association or local bar associations and acting as a public defender are all considered pro bono services (§27 AALA, §2 RPIA).

256. An attorney who has his/her own office should engage in pro bono activities for at least thirty hours a year. However, under compelling circumstances, this minimum may be reduced to twenty hours per year pursuant to a determination of the local bar association (§3 RPIA). The duty for an attorney to engage in such activities is exempted for attorneys with less than two-year experience or those 60 years old or older (§3(3) RPIA).

4. Mandatory Continuing Legal Education

257. All attorneys must receive training and education offered by the Korean Bar Association to improve lawyering skills and expertise, and to enhance awareness of legal ethics for at least 8 hours a year, including 1 hour of legal ethics training (§17-2 AALA Decree).

258. The Korean Bar Association may conduct such training and education itself or delegate the tasks to local bar associations. It can also commission appropriate institutions or organizations to undertake such programs (§85(2) AALA). In addition, the Korean Bar Association may recognize law related conferences and seminars hosted by other institutions or organizations as a substitute for its own training and education courses, and determine the hours of the attendance to be counted toward the mandatory education hours (§85(3) AALA).

5. Duty to Tell the Truth

259. In the course of his/her duties, an attorney is prohibited from concealing the truth or making false statements (§24(2) AALA). Prohibited conduct includes making false statements of material facts and law; falsifying, altering, destroying or fabricating evidence; and assisting others to do any of these acts.

260. To parse out this otherwise straight forward rule, take the case of a defendant who confessed to a crime he did not commit. The defendant did this to help the actual offender evade prosecution. The defense attorney knowingly overlooked his client's innocence and false confession, and he participated in a scheme to pay his client for the false confession. In this case, the Supreme Court ruled that the attorney was guilty as an accessory to the crime of escape (§151(1) CrA).[47]

261. However, this does not mean that an attorney has a duty to affirmatively cooperate with law enforcement authorities or any others in finding facts prejudicial to his/her client's interest. A criminal defense attorney must defend a guilty client even if his/her defense results in an acquittal because the prosecution failed to meet its burden of proof.[48]

---

47. Supreme Court Decision 2012Do6027 decided on August 30, 2012.
48. Jae-sang Lee & Gyun-seok Cho, *Criminal Procedure* 145 (Parkyoungsa 11th ed. 2017).

6. Duty of Confidentiality

262. An attorney may not disclose any confidential information that he/she has learned in the course of his/her duties (§26 AALA). To date, there are no statutory exceptions to this duty.

263. It is taken for granted that law enforcement officers may search an attorney's office with a search and seizure warrant when the attorney is a criminal suspect. However, it is debatable whether the police can search an attorney's office to find material regarding an attorney's client.

264. For example, in August 2016, officials of the Seoul Central District Prosecutors' Office pursuant to a warrant tried to search the office of Yulchon LLC, one of the largest law firms in Korea. They were investigating Shin Gyuk-ho, the then-President of the Lotte Group, who was suspected of tax crimes. The law firm immediately and voluntarily handed over the documents described in the warrant – thus giving up the opportunity to challenge the warrant in court.[49] The failure to challenge this warrant has been criticized by legal practitioners and academics on the ground that such a warrant was likely to infringe on the attorney-client privilege and the defendant's constitutional right to counsel.[50]

III. Discipline

A. Causes and Types of Discipline

265. Types of disciplinary actions against attorneys fall into the following five categories: permanent disbarment; disbarment; suspension for not longer than three years; a disciplinary fine not exceeding KRW 30 million ; and a reprimand (§90 AALA).

266. When an attorney is permanently disbarred, his/her registration with the Korean Bar Association is cancelled without the possibility of re-registration. This means that the attorney cannot ever practice law again, even though his/her status as a lawyer remains valid. An attorney who is disbarred, but not permanently is banned from practicing law indefinitely. However, this kind of penalty leaves open to the possibility of re-registration. A suspended attorney is prohibited from practicing law for a specific period of time prescribed by the disciplinary action. A disciplinary fine is not a criminal punishment, but a kind of administrative monetary penalty, which is enforced by a prosecutor and paid into the national treasury. A reprimand is a formal and public disciplinary action. It is an official warning to an attorney to exercise self-restraint and caution. However, it is not a bar to practice law.

49. *The Law Times* (Aug. 11, 2016).
50. *Ibid.*

267. The grounds for disciplinary actions include violations of: the Attorney-at-Law Act; rules of the Korean Bar Association or those of a local bar association; and a reasonable and decent standard of conduct. Also, a misconduct that brings discredit to the profession is included (§91(2) AALA).

268. Permanent disbarment is imposed when an attorney commits a crime in the course of his/her duties and is sentenced to imprisonment or a heavier punishment more than once. This penalty is also handed down to an attorney who has more than two prior suspensions or received heavier discipline pursuant to the Attorney-at-Law Act more than twice. An attorney can also be disbarred permanently if he/she is deemed highly unqualified to perform the duties of an attorney now and in the future (§91(1) AALA).

B. Disciplinary Procedure

1. Commencement of Disciplinary Proceedings

269. Disciplinary procedures against an attorney are initiated at the request of the President of the Korean Bar Association to the Bar Association's Attorney Disciplinary Committee (§97 AALA).

270. The chief prosecutor of a district prosecutors' office or the president of a local bar association can request the President of the Korean Bar Association to initiate disciplinary proceedings when they learn of an unethical or illegal conduct (§97-2 AALA). A client or his/her agent, spouse or relative may also file a petition with the president of the local bar association to take action so that the President of the Korean Bar Association begins disciplinary proceedings (§97-3(1) AALA). The President of the Korean Bar Association can ask the Investigative Committee to investigate whether disciplinary proceedings are necessary (§97-4(2) AALA).

2. The Korean Bar Association Attorney Disciplinary Committee

271. The Korean Bar Association's Attorney Disciplinary Committee is comprised of two judges recommended by the Minister of Court Administration; two prosecutors recommended by the Minister of Justice; three attorneys elected at a general meeting of the Korean Bar Association; one professor of law and one citizen who is not an attorney, recommended by the President of the Korean Bar Association (§93(1) AALA). The Committee makes decisions with an absolute majority of its members (§98-4(1) AALA).

272. The attorney-respondent may participate in disciplinary proceedings presenting oral or written statements of facts and favorable evidence (§98-2(2) AALA).

3. Objection to a Disciplinary Decision

273. The attorney-respondent may raise objection to a disciplinary decision by the Attorney Disciplinary Committee in the Korean Bar Association, with the Attorney Disciplinary Committee in the Ministry of Justice (§96 AALA).

274. The Committee in the Justice Ministry is composed of nine members, including the Minister of Justice (committee chair), two judges recommended by the Minister of Court Administration, two prosecutors appointed by the Minister of Justice, one attorney recommended by the President of the Korean Bar Association, and three citizens who are not attorneys. The Committee in the Justice Ministry makes decisions with an absolute majority of its members (§100(3) AALA).

§2. Other Institutions and Organizations

I. The Korean Bar Association

275. The Korean Bar Association is an organization with a legal personality, which was jointly established by all local bar associations nationwide for the purpose of improving legal services and supervising local bar associations (§78 AALA). Besides local bar associations, members of the Korean Bar Association include legal professional corporations, legal professional partnerships, registered attorneys and foreign legal consultants (§7 RKBA).

276. The Korean Bar Association is in charge of matters regarding attorney registration, protection of attorneys' rights and interests, training and education programs for attorneys, supervision of local bar associations, and legal aid. It is under the supervision of the Minister of Justice (§86 AALA).

277. The operating revenue of the Korean Bar Association comes from contributions by local bar associations, membership fees, special membership fees, and registration fees (§83 AALA, §9(2) RKBA).

II. Local Bar Associations

278. A local bar association is established in each judicial district. An exception is the Seoul Bar Association, which covers all five judicial districts in Seoul. Members of a local bar association include legal professional corporations, partnerships and registered attorneys operating in the district.

279. The tasks of a local bar association are similar to those of the Korean Bar Association. A local bar association is under the oversight of the Korean Bar Association and the Minister of Justice (§77(1) AALA).

III. The Legal Ethics and Professional Conduct Council

280. The Legal Ethics and Professional Conduct Council was established to draft conduct guidelines, enhance professional responsibility and build a healthy legal climate (§88 AALA). The Ethics Council is comprised of nine members. The Minister of the National Court Administration, the Minister of Justice, and the President of Korean Bar Association nominates three members respectively, among judges, public prosecutors, attorneys with at least ten years of experience; faculties of law; and ordinary citizens (§89-2(1) AALA).

281. The Council deliberates on statutes, systems and policies concerning legal ethics; conducts an evaluation of current compliance by attorneys with ethical norms and recommends appropriate responses to ethical problems. It can also request commencement of disciplinary proceedings by the Korean Bar Association or criminal investigations (§89(1) AALA). The operating costs and expenditures are subsidized by the Government (§89-3(4) AALA).

282. If necessary, the Ethics Council may demand any person, agency or organization to submit materials, attend meetings to present statements or explanations or allow an on-site examination (§89(2) AALA).

Chapter 3. Enforcement Officers

§1. Tasks

283. Authorities who are competent to enforce a judgment or decision on their own initiative, include an enforcement officer, the court of enforcement, and the first instance court hearing the case. These agencies are collectively known as enforcement agencies. A court of enforcement is a single judge who has subject-matter jurisdiction over issuance of court orders and disposition regarding enforcement and matters of cooperation as statutes may require. A court of first instance is the trial court that heard the case from which the enforceable judgment is derived. The trial court is involved in enforcement procedures only when a judgment is enforced in particular manners.

284. An enforcement officer is an independent agent that performs enforcement of enforceable titles, service of court documents and other duties as stipulated in statutes (§55(2) COA, §2 EOA). As a public official, if an enforcement officer commits a tort in the course of his/her official duties, the State is liable to compensate the victim for the loss or injury.[51] Enforcement officers are not paid salaries by the State. Instead, they charge fees for their services (§19 EOA).

285. With regard to the enforcement of judgments against property, there is a distinction between "moveable" and "immovable" property. Moveable property roughly refers to personal property and immovable property refers to real property. However, some properties defined as movable in the Civil Act are treated like immovable in enforcement procedures. For example, ships, motor vehicles, construction machinery, and airplanes are movables in the Civil Act, but the right to these properties is registered just like immovables, and the enforcement provisions of the Civil Execution Act pertaining to immovables apply to this type of property.

286. Enforcement officers have functional jurisdiction over enforcement of judgments that might require use of physical force and that are procedurally simple. Such enforcements include enforcement of monetary claims against movable property (§2 CEA); enforcement of the delivery or surrender of immovable or movable property (§§257,258 CEA); enforcement of pre-judgment seizure against movables (§296 CEA); and judicial auctions of movable property based on security interests (§§272,274(1) CEA).

287. The enforcement agency which enforces a monetary judgment against immovables is the court of enforcement. An enforcement officer investigates the status and condition of the realty and submits a report and undertakes a judicial sale of

51. Supreme Court Decision 2002Da65929 decided on February 11, 2003.

the property according to an order of the court of enforcement. Enforcement officers also carry out service of documents and articles pursuant to court orders, enforcement of fines, sale of confiscated items, and enforcement of warrants (§6 EOA).

§2. Appointment and Supervision

288. The President of a District Court appoints enforcement officers from among public officials of courts or the prosecutors' offices, who have served for at least ten years (§3 EOA). The term of office for enforcement officers is four years, and they cannot be consecutively reappointed. The retirement age for enforcement officers is 61 (§4 EOA).

289. An enforcement officer's income varies depending on the number of enforcement cases assigned to him/her and his/her workload. Because of the relatively high income from this position, there is intense competition to become an enforcement officer. As a result, most high-ranking officials are appointed to this position. The number of enforcement officers within each judicial district is regulated by the Regulation of the Supreme Court. As of February 23, 2017, the sanctioned number of enforcement officers stands at 432 nationwide (§2 REO). Enforcement officers are supervised by the President of the relevant District Court (§7 EOA).

§3. Performance of Duties

290. A judgment creditor may request an enforcement officer to levy execution of an enforceable title. Enforcement officers may not refuse any such request without justifiable grounds (§14 EOA). When an enforcement officer accepts the request for enforcement from a creditor, a fiduciary relationship is created between them.

291. A judgment creditor may cancel the request or limit the scope of enforcement. However, an enforcement officer performs his/her duty independent of the creditor in accordance with the Civil Execution Act.

292. If deemed necessary for the purpose of enforcement, an enforcement officer may search a residence, warehouse and other places, and unlock doors of facilities in the control of the debtor (§5(1) CEA). He/she may request assistance from the police or military forces in the face of physical resistance put up by the judgment debtor or others (§5(2) CEA). Prior permission from the court of enforcement is necessary to levy execution at night or on holidays (§8(1) CEA).

293. Enforcement of a monetary claim against movables is commenced by a seizure (§188(1) CEA). The process of seizure is completed when an enforcement officer takes actual and physical possession or control of the items to be seized. After effectuating the seizure, the enforcement officer conducts a judicial sale of the seized goods by a public auction (§199 CEA). The proceeds of the sale are paid first for the costs of the enforcement procedure, and then distributed to the creditors in order of priority (§201 CEA). Any balance is delivered to the judgment debtor.

294. Compulsory enforcement of delivery or surrender of immovables and movables is within the enforcement officer's area of competence. If the debtor is required to surrender movables, the enforcement officer may recover them by force and hand them over to the creditor. If the debtor is required to surrender immovable property, the enforcement officer must take possession of the property and give possession to the creditor (§§257,258 CEA).

Part II. Jurisdiction

Chapter 1. Domestic Jurisdiction

§1. Introduction

I. Definition and Meaning of Jurisdiction

295. Jurisdiction is the authority given to the judicial system by the State to adjudicate a case. This authority comes from the sovereignty of a nation. There are three aspects of jurisdiction: personal jurisdiction, territorial jurisdiction and subject-matter jurisdiction. When a party to a civil case is a Korean citizen, the case is subject to adjudication in Korean courts because Korea has personal jurisdiction over its citizens. Territorial jurisdiction refers to the exercise of judicial authority over a case in which a party or legal relationship is connected to a place within Korean territory. There could be a conflict or overlap of jurisdictions in relation to personal jurisdiction or territorial jurisdiction between multiple countries, which raises a question of international jurisdiction.

296. Subject-matter jurisdiction is distinguished from personal jurisdiction or territorial jurisdiction in that the former concerns the division of the adjudicating function of the State among various courts in Korea. The judicial authority of the State is exercised by the Supreme Court, High Courts, District Courts, Family Courts, the Patent Court, the Administrative Court, and the Bankruptcy Court. Each of these courts has its own subject-matter jurisdiction as set out in relevant statutes. Thus, subject-matter jurisdiction is the authority of a court to hear cases of a particular type related to a specific subject-matter.

297. In a District Court, a Family Court and the Bankruptcy Court, there are single judges and judicial panels. When adjudicating a case, each judge or panel operates independently from other judges or panels, even though, for administrative purposes, they are under the leadership of the President of a court, hear the same kinds of cases, and share all the support staff and facilities. Cases are assigned to single judges or judicial panels according to the amount in controversy and other statutory provisions.

298. Venue is the statutory limitation on where a lawsuit may be filed. While all courts in different judicial districts have jurisdiction over a case, for example, which, among all District Courts, is the appropriate place to file a lawsuit, is a question of venue. However, the decision between filing in a District Court or a Family Court is determined by statutes pertaining to subject-matter jurisdiction.

299. In Korea, "jurisdiction," or "*guan-hal,*"' refers to the authority of a specific court to hear particular cases. This term encompasses subject-matter jurisdiction and venue. In the official English version of the Civil Procedure Act, the term "venue" is not used, instead the term "jurisdiction over the place" or "jurisdiction over the location" takes the place of "venue" (§§8,21,24 CPA). In addition, "subject-matter jurisdiction" generally denotes the adjudicating authority of a single judge or that of a judicial panel in relation to the amount in controversy.

II. Division of Jurisdiction and Venue

A. Jurisdiction by Statute, Designation, Agreement, or by Oral Statement

300. If jurisdiction of a court or courts is articulated in statutes, it is called statutory jurisdiction or jurisdiction by statute. This type of jurisdiction is further divided into subject-matter jurisdiction based on specialized areas, the amount in controversy and appellate jurisdiction.

301. When a court cannot adjudicate a case because of a legal or physical obstacle, or when it is uncertain about which court is competent, an immediate higher court of the relevant courts designates the court to hear the case. The decision of the higher court creates jurisdiction and proper venue.

302. The parties to a dispute may designate the court to hear their case by agreement regarding subject-matter jurisdiction based on the amount in controversy or agreeing on venue. In addition, if a plaintiff files a lawsuit with a court that does not have jurisdiction based on amount in controversy or in the venue that is not proper, but the defendant makes an oral statement at a hearing on the merits, the court becomes competent to hear the case.

B. Exclusive Jurisdiction and Noncompulsory Jurisdiction

303. Jurisdiction is classified as exclusive and noncompulsory jurisdiction based on statutory provisions. A case subject to exclusive jurisdiction can be tried only in a specific competent court. On the other hand, the Civil Procedure Act also provides for noncompulsory jurisdiction. Here the focus is on individual interests, convenience and fairness to the parties. Consequently, the parties are allowed to determine certain aspects of jurisdiction by agreement and shift jurisdiction to a different court. Subject-matter jurisdiction based on the amount in controversy is noncompulsory.

and a court of enforcement issues orders necessary to enforce the trial court's judgment in that same case. Functional jurisdiction is compulsory and exclusive because it is closely related to public interest.

II. Trial Court and Court of Enforcement

315. A trial court is the court in which a lawsuit is pending or was finalized; or in which a lawsuit is to be filed. It hears on the merits and renders a judgment. By contrast, a court of enforcement is a District Court which exercises authority to enforce judgments within its judicial district (§3(1) CEA).

316. In this context, a District Court functions as both a trial court and one of the enforcement agencies. When it exercises jurisdiction as a court of enforcement, its functional jurisdiction lies in a single judge. A court of enforcement is the enforcement agency in enforcing monetary claims against immovable property and a debtor's claims (§§79,224 CEA), and it has authority to rule on objections against the disposition by an enforcement officer (§16(1) CEA).

317. In respect of specific enforcement matters, the trial court, not the court of enforcement, is the enforcement agency. Procedures for the preservation of evidence (§376 CPA), prejudgment seizure or injunction regarding the object of the litigation (§§278,303 CEA), enforcement by substitute (§260(1) CEA) and indirect compulsory enforcement (§261(1) CEA) fall under the jurisdiction of the trial court.

318. Enforcing a judgment can itself generate additional lawsuits. Some of these cases are subject to the jurisdiction of the trial court; some to the jurisdiction of a court of enforcement and others are treated like ordinary civil cases not related to enforcement procedures.

319. Thus, a lawsuit seeking issuance of the court certificate of enforceability (enforcement clause) for a judgment (§33 CEA), a lawsuit to oppose an issuance of a certificate of enforceability (§45 CEA) and a lawsuit raising an objection to the claim being enforced (§44(1) CEA) are under the jurisdiction of the trial court that issued the judgment. A third party action against an enforcement is under the jurisdiction of the relevant court of enforcement in principle. However, when the amount in controversy exceeds the jurisdictional amount of a single judge, jurisdiction is transferred to a judicial panel of the same District Court (§48(2) CEA). A lawsuit to oppose the distribution plan in a judicial sale is subject to the jurisdiction of the District Court where the court of enforcement is situated (§156(1) CEA). This case is treated as an ordinary civil litigation case. Therefore, the subject-matter jurisdiction based on amount in controversy is determined in accordance with general principles of civil procedure.

III. Judicial Panels and Single Judges of a District Court

320. Irrespective of amount in controversy or provisions of the Civil Procedure Act pertaining to subject-matter jurisdiction based thereon, there are statutes that designate a specific court to hear particular cases. Proceedings for settlement prior to filing of lawsuit (§§385,386 CPA), summary proceedings for a payment order (§§462,474 CPA) and pretrial mediation proceedings (§3(1) JCCDA) are examples of specific jurisdiction of single judges based on statutory provisions.

321. A judicial panel of the District Court has jurisdictional authority to adjudicate lawsuits seeking correction of a press report (§26(5) APAR); a petition for judicial disqualification of, or challenge to a judge of the District Court (§32(1) COA); insolvency cases brought up in the district where a Bankruptcy Court is not seated (§3(1) DRBA); and cases of securities-related class actions (§4 SRCAA) and consumer class actions (§71 FAC).

IV. Appellate Jurisdiction

322. Appellate jurisdiction refers to the scope of authority for an appellate court to hear appeal cases from a lower court. Appellate jurisdiction is compulsory and exclusive. Filing a lawsuit with a High Court or appealing a judgment of a single judge in a District Court to a High Court is not allowed, because such cases are outside of the appellate jurisdiction of a High Court.

323. Korea has a three-tiered justice system. As for civil and criminal cases, courts of first instance are judicial panels and single judges of District Courts. The intermediate appellate courts are the High Courts and District Court judicial panels. Thus, in addition to hearing cases as a trial court, judicial panels in the District Court also hear appeal cases from single judges of the same court. The District Court panels that hear appeals are called appellate panels. The High Court hears appeal cases from the judicial panels of District Courts seated in its judicial district. The Supreme Court, as the court of last resort, hears appeals from High Courts and appellate panels of District Courts.

§3. Subject-Matter Jurisdiction Based on Amount in Controversy

I. Concept

324. In civil litigation, the jurisdiction of the District Court, sitting as a trial court, is divided between judicial panels and single judges depending on the amount in controversy. Subject-matter jurisdiction based on the amount in controversy is noncompulsory.

II. Jurisdiction of a Judicial Panel

A. Cases Whose Amount in Controversy Exceeds KRW 200 Million

325. The economic value at stake in a lawsuit is related to its public importance and weight. If it exceeds the KRW 200 million threshold amount prescribed by the Civil Procedure Act, the case is heard by a three-judge panel, rather than a single judge. However, there are exceptions and certain cases exceeding KRW 200 million may still be subject to jurisdiction of a single judge.

B. Lawsuit Based on Noneconomic Claims

326. A lawsuit based on noneconomic relationships is not directly related to economic interests and it is impossible to calculate the exact value of a claim. Examples of this type of lawsuit include those seeking affirmation of membership in a nonprofit organization, affirmation of nullity of dismissal by an employer, prohibition of infringement on the right to name and portrait rights, and corporation-related lawsuits under the Commercial Act.

C. Lawsuit Based on Property-Related Claims Whose Value Is Indeterminable

327. There are occasions where calculating value of a claim is difficult although it is based on a property relationship. Examples of such cases include prohibitions against; infringement on the right to light, using a business name (§23 ComA), operating a competitive business by a transferor of a business (§41(1) ComA), actions by a director that are prejudicial to a company (§402 ComA); and affirmation of a successful bidder status.

328. The amount in controversy of such lawsuits is deemed to be KRW 50 million (r.4-2 RSACL) when calculating the amount of judicial stamp to be attached to a complaint. However, this provision does not relate to subject-matter jurisdiction based on amount in controversy.

D. Cases That the Judicial Panel Decides to Adjudicate by Itself

329. Notwithstanding the amount in controversy, a judicial panel in a District Court and a Branch Court, can decide to assign a case to a judicial panel even though the amount in controversy is below the panel threshold (§32(1) COA).

330. Each District Court has a judicial panel in charge of assigning cases based on jurisdictional amount and the nature of the case. The District Court may designate an existing judicial panel to perform this task, or form a separate panel composed of one presiding judge and two member judges. Cases assigned to a judicial panel in this manner are called "panel cases by decision." These cases include: (a) cases where there is no precedent or relevant precedents are contradictory; (b) cases having factual or legal complexities; (c) multiple cases of the same type that require unified and exemplary proceedings and rulings, but are assigned to different judicial panels and single judges; and (d) other cases that deserve consideration by a judicial panel in light of their character and importance.[57] These considerations also apply to a small claims case that might otherwise be assigned to a single judge, but that is nevertheless assigned to a judicial panel.

III. Jurisdiction of a Single-Judge Court

A. Cases Except Those under the Jurisdiction of a Judicial Panel

331. A single District Court judge hears all civil cases except those assigned to a judicial panel of a District Court or a Branch Court (§7(4) COA). Thus, this Court is a court of general jurisdiction. If statutes refer to a District Court regarding subject-matter jurisdiction, it is understood that this refers to a single-judge court. When a statute intends to confer jurisdiction to a judicial panel, it says so.

B. Routine Cases

332. Straightforward and routine cases whose amount in controversy exceeds KRW 200 million are nevertheless heard by a single judge. These cases include those based on claims arising from promissory notes and checks; those seeking repayment of loan, indemnity, and payment of a guaranteed debt where financial institutions are the plaintiffs; and those pursuing damages for loss from accidents involving motor vehicles, trains and the workplace (r.2 RSMJCFC).

C. A Judicial Panel's Decision to Move Jurisdiction

333. A judicial panel may decide that a case under its subject-matter jurisdiction based on amount in controversy should be heard by a single judge (r.2 RSMJCFC). The President of a District Court can also refer simple and straightforward cases, which would otherwise be heard by a judicial panel according to amount in controversy, to the panel in charge of assigning cases to panels or single judges so that it can move jurisdiction to a single judge.

334. A panel to which a case is distributed may have a judge on that panel adjudicate the case as a single judge, or may, by its own decision, refer the case to the panel in charge of changing subject-matter jurisdiction.

---

57. *Court Practice Summary Civil Procedure (I)* 45 (National Court Administration, 2017).

IV. Amount in Controversy

A. Concept

335. The amount in controversy, or jurisdictional amount denotes the amount at stake in a lawsuit. It is the monetary value of the economic interest that the plaintiff would obtain if entirely successful (r.6 RSACL). It serves as the standard for determining the amount of judicial stamp (court filing fee) to be attached to the complaint when filing a lawsuit as well as the standard by which subject-matter jurisdiction is determined.

B. Computation of Amount in Controversy

336. Amount in controversy is based on claims in a lawsuit and is the value of the object of the dispute. It can be equal to the value of a claim or less than that. If a plaintiff filed a lawsuit seeking payment of the purchase price for the item he sold to the defendant for KRW 2 million and asserts only KRW 1 million in the prayer for relief, the amount in controversy is KRW 1 million . When the plaintiff seeks payment of KRW 2 million in exchange for the delivery of the sold item, the price of the item should not be subtracted and the amount in controversy is still KRW 2 million. Amount in controversy is computed at the time the complaint is filed (r.7 RSACL). The following are the specific criteria for calculating the amount in controversy.

1. Lawsuit Based on Monetary Claims

337. The monetary amount asserted in the complaint is amount in controversy. When the plaintiff seeks periodic payments, the amount in controversy is the aggregate amount of money that the defendant failed to pay on the due dates, combined with the amount to be paid for one year from the filing date of the lawsuit (r.12 RSACL).

2. Lawsuit Based on Claims Regarding Tangibles

338. For the purpose of calculating the jurisdictional amount, the value of a plot of land is 50% of the price published every year by the Ministry of Land, Infrastructure and Transport. A building is priced at 50% of the value computed using the criteria set out by the Ministry of the Interior and Safety. The value of a ship, machine, car, airplane, or other similar property is the equivalent to the value on a company's balance sheet, if any, or fair market value at the time the lawsuit is filed. The value of securities traded on a stock exchange is the previous day's closing price (rr.9,11 RSACL).

339. In a lawsuit seeking delivery of tangibles or prohibition of interrupting rights thereto based on ownership, superficies or lease, the amount in controversy is 50% of the value thereof (r.12(5) RSACL). In a case seeking registration of ownership transfer, the jurisdictional amount equals the value of the tangibles to be registered. As for pursuing registration for transfer, creation and termination of security interests, the amount in controversy is the same as the face value of the secured claim (maximum amount in case of a revolving mortgage) up to the market value of the collateral (r.13 RSACL).

C. *Amount in Controversy and Joinder of Claims*

340. Where a single plaintiff has more than one separate, unrelated claim against a single defendant, the value of each claim is cumulated (§27(1) CPA; r.19 RSACL). When economic interests of such joined claims are identical or overlapping wholly or partially, only the independent parts of the claims are summed up in the amount in controversy (r.20 RSACL).

341. In cases of alternative or contingent joinder of claims; alternative or contingent joinder of parties; claims against multiple obligors jointly and severally liable; and claims against both principal obligor and the surety; only the main claim or one of the claims counts in computing the jurisdictional amount.

342. Provided that one claim is a substitute for another claim, only one of them is taken into account. If one claim serves as a tool for the other claim, only the latter counts toward the amount in controversy. For example, when the plaintiff pursues demolition of a building on the land owned by him/her and surrender of the plot based on his/her ownership, two claims are joined but the claim for demolition of the building is a tool to have the plot returned with (r.21 RSACL).

343. Claims for contractual interest, interest as damages, penalty for breach of contract, and costs incidental to the principal or main claim are excluded in computing jurisdictional amount (§27(2) CPA). However, where these kinds of claims are the only damages sought in a lawsuit, they are not incidental and their value is included in the amount in controversy.

§4. Venue

I. Concept

344. The Act on the Establishment and Jurisdiction of Courts of Various Levels sets out the judicial districts across the country. It is the regional area within which judicial authority is exercised. In Korea, the terms "venue," "territorial jurisdiction" and "regional jurisdiction" are used interchangeably among legal professionals. In each district, there is a District Court or its Branch Court which has its own judicial district separate from that of the District Courts. In this sense, a District Court and its Branch Court are equal in their judicial functioning. However, the President of a District Court supervises the administration of the Branch Court. Branch Courts do not have judicial appellate panels. A City Court or a Town Court is established, if needed, in a city or a town geographically remote from a District Court or a Branch Court within the same judicial district. They have limited subject-matter jurisdiction.

345. When parties to a case or the legal relationship that is at the center of the case are related to a certain site within a judicial district, the District Court or the Branch Court in that district has the authority (or jurisdiction) to hear the case. The geographic site that connects a case to a judicial district is referred to as *jaepanjeok*. Domicile, a place of business, an office address, the place a tort occurred, etc. are collectively called *jaepanjeok*. The meaning of *jaepan* is judicial adjudication or trial, and *jeok* is defined as address. *Jaepanjeok* is distinguished from "venue," just as domicile is a geographical site, and venue is a city, town or district. Since I find no English equivalent of *jaepanjeok* I would like to coin the term "judicial address" to be used instead of *jaepanjeok*.

*346. Jaepanjeo*k or judicial address, in this context, is divided into general judicial addresses and special judicial addresses. The former commonly applies to all cases and the latter applies only to certain types of cases. Also, judicial addresses can be categorized as personal judicial addresses and claim-related judicial addresses. The former relates to the parties to the litigation, especially the defendant and the latter is connected to the claims or circumstances of a case.

347. General judicial addresses and several special judicial addresses can be involved in the same case. In such a case, a plaintiff can choose the venue to file the case. In principle, determination of venue is noncompulsive.

II. General Judicial Addresses

A. Natural Person

348. General judicial addresses apply to all civil litigation. The Civil Procedure Act sets general judicial addresses in a defendant-centered way. When the defendant is a natural person, the venue is determined by his/her domicile. When the defendant's domicile is not located in Korea or is unknown, the general judicial address is the location of his/her residence. And if the place of residence is unsettled or unknown, his/her last domicile is the general judicial address (§3 CPA).

349. For an ambassador, a vice ambassador or other diplomats, who are stationed abroad without a domicile or residence in Korea and who enjoy diplomatic immunity in the receiving states, their general judicial address is deemed to be the place where the Supreme Court of Korea is seated (§4 CPA).

B. *Legal Person and Organization Without Legal Personality*

350. The general judicial address for a legal person, or any other organization without legal personality is the place where its principal office or place of business is located. For those without an office, it is the domicile of the person responsible for its general management (§5(1) CPA). The general judicial address for a foreign legal entity is the place where its principal office or place of business is located in Korea. For those without such office, its judicial address is the domicile of the person responsible for its general management in Korea (§5(2) CPA).

C. *State*

351. The general judicial address for the State is the seat of the government agency which represents the State in litigation or the Supreme Court (§6 CPA). As the Minister of Justice represents the State in litigation and the Ministry of Justice is located in Gwacheon City which belongs to the judicial district of the Anyang Branch Court of the Suwon District Court, the Anyang Branch Court is the court of proper venue for cases brought against the State. In addition, the Supreme Court is seated in Seocho-Gu, Seoul, which is within the judicial district of the Seoul Central District Court. Therefore, the Seoul Central District Court is also the court of proper venue for such cases.

D. *When Determination of General Judicial Address Is Impossible*

352. When the general judicial address cannot be determined pursuant to the Civil Procedure Act, the Seoul Central District Court whose judicial district covers the seat of the Supreme Court, is deemed to be the court of appropriate venue (r.6 RCP). Such lawsuits include those in which a foreign nation, a foreign national without domicile or residence in Korea, a foreign legal person, or a Korean citizen without a known domicile, etc. is a defendant.[58]

III. Special Judicial Addresses

A. *Workplace*

353. When a person who works continuously in an office or place of business is sued, the location of his/her workplace is a special judicial address (§7 CPA).

---

58. *Ibid.*

B. Place of Residence or Place of Performance of an Obligation

354. Concerning a lawsuit based on economic or proprietary claims, the defendant's place of residence or the place where an obligation is performed is a special judicial address (§8 CPA). "Place of residence" means the place where the defendant stays and conducts day to day activity for a significant period of time.

355. The defendant's place of residence serves as the secondary general judicial address when his/her domicile is nonexistent or unknown in Korea. However, in this type of litigation, the defendant's place of residence is a special judicial address even when his/her domicile is known to exist in Korea.

356. The place where an obligation is to be performed becomes a special judicial address when the plaintiff seeks performance of an obligation in the complaint. The obligation may arise from property rights, contracts, unilateral acts, and others. This principle also applies to a lawsuit for declaratory judgment seeking confirmation of an obligation.

357. If the place of performance is undeterminable or the parties have not agreed thereon, the obligation, other than the delivery of a specific thing, should be performed at the present domicile of the creditor. However, an obligation arising from commercial transactions should be fulfilled at the creditor's present place of business (§467(2) CA).

358. According to case law, in a litigation seeking rescission and restitution for a fraudulent act by a debtor (§406(1) CA), the place of performance is not determined by the contract to be rescinded, but in accordance with the obligation to be created by the rescission. If the obligation is to register a title cancellation as a means of restitution, the place of the registry becomes the place of performance.[59]

C. Place of Payment of Promissory Notes or Checks

359. In a lawsuit concerning promissory notes or checks, the place of payment is the special judicial address (§9 CPA). In such cases, the place of payment is also the place of performance.

D. Place of Home Port or Military Installation

360. In a lawsuit based on a proprietary right against a commercial seaman, a special judicial address is the registered home port of the ship on which he/she

59. Supreme Court Decision 2002Ma1156 decided on May 10, 2002.

works. The owner of a Korean ship must designate its home port and register the ship with the Regional Office of Oceans and Fisheries in charge of the port (§§7,8 SA).

361. When a case is against someone in the military or a civilian working for the military, venue is established by the place of the main military installation or the home port of the naval vessel (§10 CPA).

E. Place of Property

362. In a lawsuit based on proprietary rights, venue can be determined by the location of the object of the claim, or the collateral therefor, or the location of the defendant's property that can be seized. This is true when the defendant is not domiciled in Korea or his/her domicile is nonexistent or unknown (§11 CPA). In a lawsuit seeking transfer of a claim, the general judicial address of the third-party debtor is a special judicial address.[60]

F. Place of Office or Business

363. When the defendant has an office or place for business, and the lawsuit is based on the commercial activities of that business, the place of his/her office or business is a special judicial address (§12 CPA).

G. Place of Home Port

364. For claims against the owner or operator of a ship concerning the ship or a voyage, the registered home port of the vessel is a special judicial address (§13 CPA). Matters "concerning a ship" refers to the rights and obligations with respect to the ship itself and use of the ship. Such lawsuits can include disputes about ownership of a ship, the transfer of ownership registration, a lease, shipping charges or wages of seamen.

365. Matters "concerning a voyage" refers to rights and obligations arising from such matters as purchasing supplies, repair of the ship, hiring seamen, and transportation of passengers and cargo.

60. Sang-won Kim et al., *supra* n. 46, at 163.

H. Place Where a Ship Is Located

366. A lawsuit based on a maritime lien or other claims secured by a ship may be brought in the district where the ship is located (§14 CPA). The location of a ship is where the ship is anchored at the time the lawsuit is filed.

I. Place of the General Judicial Address of a Company or Other Association

367. In lawsuits involving a company or associations and its members, a general judicial address of the business or association is a special judicial address. Thus, lawsuits by a business or association against their partners or members or vice versa and lawsuits among members or partners may be brought in the judicial district where the business or association is located.

368. Lawsuits by the creditors of a company or association against the partners or members, based on their role as partners or members, may also be raised in the judicial district where the company or association is situated (§§15(1),16 CPA). The same applies to lawsuits by an association or foundation against their directors or auditors; and by a company against its incorporators or inspectors (§17 CPA).

J. Place of Tort

369. A tort lawsuit may be filed in the judicial district where the tortious act took place (§18(1) CPA). However, in respect of a lawsuit for damages due to the collision of ship or aircraft, or any other accident, the place where the ship or aircraft involved in the accident first arrived, not the place where the accident occurred, is a special judicial address (§18(2) CPA).

370. Such lawsuits include claims for damages against a tortfeasor (§750 CA); claims for the damage caused by an employee's tort against his/her employer (§§755,756 CA); claims against the possessor or owner of the facility for damage caused by defects in the construction or maintenance of a facility (§758 CA); claims for the damage caused by animals against their possessor or owner (§759 CA); claims for the damage caused by a driver's negligence in a car accident against the owner of the vehicle (§3 GAACA); and claims for damages against the State or a municipality based on torts committed by public officials (§2 SCA).

371. There is a question whether the statutory provisions pertaining to tort lawsuits and the venue for such suits, apply to lawsuits seeking compensation for a loss caused by the nonperformance of contractual obligations. Opinions favoring the application of these provisions are based on the grounds that nonperformance of an obligation is included in the broad meaning of an unlawful act which constitutes a tort as set out in Section 750 of the Civil Act. Furthermore, the Civil Procedure Act includes the place of tort in the special judicial addresses for the benefit of the victim-plaintiff. This allows the plaintiff to easily obtain and use evidence, and this consideration should be given to the person damaged by the nonperformance of a contractual obligation for the same reason.[61]

372. According to contrary opinions, nonperformance of an obligation is, by its nature, different from a tortious act. Moreover, nonperformance is not always part of a tortious act.[62]

373. Reviewing these opinions, I agree that nonperformance of a contractual obligation is different from a tort. Liability for breach of contract arises from the failure to perform a duty required by the contract. The plaintiff just has to prove the nonexistence of the desired state articulated in the contract to be successful. However, in a tort case, the plaintiff must also assert and prove the legal elements of a tortious act. That is, the plaintiff must prove the wrongdoer's illegal conduct, his/her malice or negligence, the damage sustained by the plaintiff, and general causation between the wrongdoer's act and the damage. Therefore, material facts giving rise to contractual liability and liability for a tort are different, and the legal rights of each are separate and independent. In addition, it is difficult to determine the place of nonperformance, contrary to the place of tort.

K. Place of Salvage

374. Complaints regarding claims arising from rescue operations for a ship may be filed in the place of salvage or the port where the salvaged ship first arrived (§19 CPA).

L. Place Where Immovable Property Is Located

375. A lawsuit concerning immovable property may be brought in the place where it is located. According to the Civil Act, immovable property is land and any other property that is fixed to the earth such as a house or building (§99(1) CA).[63] There are also properties that are deemed immovable by statute. These include factory assets (§12(1) FMAMA), mining assets (§54 FMAMA), mining rights (§10(1) MIA), and fishery rights (§16(1) FA). However, ships, cars, construction machines, and airplanes are not immovable properties for purposes of venue.

376. Lawsuits concerning immovable property include those based on claims arising out of property rights or obligatory claims. However, if the object of a dispute is not immovable property, its location is not considered in the determination of proper venue, even though the claim is closely related to the property. For

61. Sang-won Kim et al., *supra* n. 46, at 173.
62. Si-yoon Lee, *supra* n. 8, at 104.
63. In Korea, a house or a building is not a fixture, but an immovable property separated from the land on which it is built.

instance, venue in lawsuits seeking payment of the purchase price, payment of rent, return of a lease deposit is not determined by the location of the property.

M. Place of Registration

377. Acquisitions of, losses of and changes in property rights over an immovable take effect when the same is entered in the registration record of the immovable property. Property rights to be registered are ownership, superficies, servitude, mortgage, lease right, etc. On the other hand, ships of more than 20 gross tonnage, cars, construction machinery and airplanes are treated as real properties in respect of registration. Changes in intellectual property, mining rights and fishery rights are also recorded in the register.

378. The District Court, the Branch Court or the Registry keeps the registers of real properties located in the relevant district and the registers of ships whose home port is therein. A Registry is established in the area where a District Court or a Branch Court does not sit.

379. With respect to registration of motor vehicles and construction machines, metropolitan municipal governments including the Soul Special Metropolitan City, Metropolitan Cities, and Provinces are in charge of such matters (§7 MVMA, §7 CMMA). For airplanes, the Ministry of Land, Infrastructure and Transport serves as the registration office (§7 ASA); for patent rights, it is the Korean Intellectual Property Office (§85(1) PA); for mining rights, it is the Ministry of Trade, Industry and Energy (§28(1) MIA); and for fishery rights, basic municipalities such as a City, Town and *Gu* handle these matters (§17 FA).

380. A lawsuit seeking registration for creation, transfer or extinction of a property right over an immovable property may be brought in the District Court or the Branch Court in the district where the relevant register is maintained (§21 CPA). For a lawsuit seeking registration of a property right over other property treated as an immovable, the proper venue is determined by the place of the relevant registration office.

N. A Deceased's General Judicial Address

381. A lawsuit concerning inheritance, a bequest and other juristic acts that become effective by death may be brought in the place where the general judicial address of the deceased was located at the time of his/her death (§22 CPA).

382. Inheritance cases are those based on disputes over the scope of inherited property; priority or share of inheritance; and recovery of inherited property from a fake heir. Lawsuits concerning juristic acts that become effective by death include claims based on rights and obligations from gift effective upon death (§562 CA);

legal reserve of inheritance (§1112 CA);[64] formation of a foundation through a will (§47 CA); and a trust created through a will (§3(1) TrA).

O. Functional Jurisdiction Concerning Intellectual Property Rights

383. Lawsuits concerning patent rights, utility model rights, design rights, trademark rights and plant variety rights are subject to exclusive jurisdiction of a District Court in the district where a High Court sits. In such cases, proper venue is first determined by the relevant judicial addresses. When the District Court of proper venue is seated in the city where a High Court sits, the District Court has exclusive jurisdiction over these cases. If there is no High Court in the district where the District Court of proper venue is located, the District Court in the city where the High Court which covers the proper venue is seated has exclusive jurisdiction (§ 24(2) CPA). At the same time, the Seoul Central District Court has concurrent jurisdiction over these cases (§24(3) CPA). Thus, the plaintiff of such cases may choose between the District Court in the city where an appropriate High Court is located or the Seoul Central District Court.

384. A lawsuit concerning intellectual property rights, except patent rights, utility model rights, design rights, trademark rights and plant variety rights; and international transactions may be brought in the place which is determined by the judicial addresses and optionally in the place where the High Court whose judicial district covers the former place is seated (§24(1) CPA).

385. Ruling on intellectual property rights and international transaction cases requires expertise and experience in these subject areas. In the large metropolitan areas where a High Court sits, the District Courts operate specialized judicial panels. By concentrating such cases in these specialized panels, procedural efficiency of justice would be enhanced and more unified treatment of cases could be realized.

IV. Judicial Address by Joinder: Trying Related Cases Together

386. When several claims are joined in a lawsuit, and one of their general or special judicial addresses is located in the place where the lawsuit was filed, the judicial address of that claim is deemed the judicial address for other claims (§25(1) CPA). This means that a special judicial address called "judicial address by connection" is created by one claim and applies to other claims in accordance with this provision. Joinder in this context includes joinder of independent, alternative or contingent claims.

387. The principle of judicial address by connection applies limitedly to joinder of parties. When claims and obligations are shared by claimants or defendants

64. The legal reserve is the minimum share of the inheritance prescribed in the Civil Act, which cannot be withheld from an heir.

jointly, severally or in the alternative, or when they arise out of the same transactions or instances, parties may join or be joined in a lawsuit. Such a lawsuit may be brought in the place which is proper venue for one of the parties.

388. Joinder of parties is permissible when: (a) the claims or obligations of a lawsuit are common to multiple parties, (b) the claims or obligations of a lawsuit are derived from the same factual or legal causes, or (c) the claims or obligations of a lawsuit are of the same sort, and are derived from the same sort of factual or legal causes. The principle of judicial address by connection applies only to examples (a) and (b). In cases of necessary joinder of parties, joinder of alternative parties, and joinder of contingent parties, a special judicial address can be created by connection.

§5. Subject-Matter Jurisdiction and Venue by Agreement

I. Specification by Agreement

A. Concept

389. Subject-matter jurisdiction based on amount in controversy or proper venue may be designated by agreement between the parties (§29(1) CPA). If both parties to a dispute agree to try their case before a judicial panel or a single judge in a specific District Court or Branch Court, that court is empowered to preside over the lawsuit. Subject-matter jurisdiction or venue created in this manner is referred to as jurisdiction by agreement or venue by agreement.

390. The agreement on subject-matter jurisdiction based on amount in controversy or proper venue is a procedural act or a procedural agreement, and parties to this agreement are required to have capacity to contract. Therefore, minors lack this litigation capacity and cannot validly agree on jurisdiction or proper venue even with the approval of their statutory agent.

391. As a procedural act, an agreement on jurisdiction or proper venue is governed by the Civil Procedure Act. Thus, such agreement is independent from the contract which contains it. In many cases, the parties elect which court will have the authority to adjudicate disputes under the contract by including a jurisdiction clause or venue clause in their contract. If at some later date, this contract is rescinded for some other reason, the jurisdiction clause or venue clause remains effective. Considering that the parties' purpose for inserting such a clause is to designate a certain court to decide possible future disputes, this interpretation is in conformity with the intention of the parties.

392. In practice, jurisdictional clauses based on amount in controversy are not used because parties are mainly interested in the place to sue or to be sued rather than subject-matter jurisdiction based on amount in controversy.

B. Requirements

393. Parties can only agree upon jurisdiction which is noncompulsory or on proper venue. When statutory provisions prescribe compulsory jurisdiction, jurisdiction is exclusive and contrary contractual jurisdictional clauses are void (§31 CPA). In addition, an agreement selecting a specific panel or judge is unenforceable because it concerns the distribution of cases among panels or single judges, not the question of jurisdiction or venue.

394. The agreement must be in writing and apply to a specific legal relationship (§29(2) CPA). If parties agree upon jurisdiction or venue for any dispute that might occur in the future, it is void. The requirement of a written agreement is for the sake of clarity and because the parties are agreeing to jurisdiction or proper venue outside of a court even though it is a procedural act.

395. According to case law, a venue selection clause is void when it gives one party the right to unilaterally choose the place for a lawsuit because such an agreement is unfair and against public policy.[65] A jurisdiction clause or venue clause contained in the general terms and conditions of a contract is void if it is unduly disadvantageous to consumers (§14 ARTC).

C. Types of Venue Selection Clauses

396. An agreement on venue can be exclusive or nonexclusive. An exclusive venue clause requires the specified lawsuits to be brought only in a specific district. On the contrary, a nonexclusive venue clause confirms that the lawsuits may be raised in a specific district but does not preclude a party from commencing the proceedings in other districts as provided by the Civil Procedure Act. When a clause is ambiguous, an agreement selecting one among multiple statutory venues is construed as exclusive, while selecting another venue other than ones determined by the venue statute is interpreted as nonexclusive.[66]

D. Effects of Venue Selection Clause

397. A nonexclusive venue clause creates additional places where venue is proper. An exclusive clause precludes venue other than the one mandated by the venue clause.

398. Even if a venue selection clause is exclusive, it is not mandatory, and the parties can change venue by a new agreement. If a lawsuit is filed with a court in

65. Supreme Court Decision 77Ma284 decided on November 9, 1977; Supreme Court Decision 2009Ma1482 decided on November 13, 2009.
66. Supreme Court Decision 63Da111 decided on May 15, 1963.

violation of an exclusive venue clause and the defendant appears and makes a statement on the merits in a hearing without objecting to venue, the court where the case is pending becomes the court of proper venue.

399. An agreement on selection of venue is binding on the parties and their respective successors and assignees. When a party to a contract containing a venue selection clause assigns his/her claim, or when a third party assumes a party's contractual obligation, the assignee or the transferee is bound by the venue selection clause. This is because a venue selection clause forms part of the contract, and transfer of the contractual claims or obligations carries all the terms attached to them at the moment of the transfer.[67]

400. But note that according to case law, where the parties entered into a mortgage contract with a venue selection clause and the mortgagor later sold the reality; the buyer and new owner is not bound by the venue selection clause, because he/she is neither an assignee of a contractual claim nor a transferee of a debt.[68]

II. Jurisdiction or Venue by Oral Statement

A. Definition and Meaning

401. If a plaintiff files a lawsuit in an improper venue or before a court without subject-matter jurisdiction based on amount in controversy, the court can adjudicate the case if the defendant appears on a trial preparation date or the trial date and argues the case on the merits without raising an objection to the court's jurisdiction or venue. The venue or jurisdiction created in this manner is called jurisdiction by oral statement or venue by oral statement (§30 CPA). That is, participation in a case on the merits and the failure to object to jurisdiction based on the amount in controversy or venue is construed as an oral statement agreeing to the otherwise faulty basis for jurisdiction or venue. The same is true when claims in a case pending before a single judge are expanded or additional claims are joined so that jurisdiction should lie with a judicial panel.

B. Requirements

402. The defendant or his/her counsel is required to appear in person at a hearing and assert orally on the merits. Therefore, when the statement is deemed to be made by the defendant at a hearing based on his/her briefs submitted to the court in advance (§148(1) CPA), the requirement of an oral statement is not satisfied.[69]

67. Supreme Court Decision 2005Ma902 decided on March 2, 2006.
68. Supreme Court Decision 94Ma536 decided on May 26, 1994.
69. Supreme Court Decision 80Ma403 decided on September 26, 1980.

403. An oral statement must be made arguing the merits of a case without lodging an objection to the propriety of venue or subject-matter jurisdiction, irrespective of whether the defendant is aware of the question concerning competence of the court.[70]

C. Effects

404. Jurisdiction or venue gained by oral statement applies only while the case is pending. Jurisdiction or venue does not survive if the lawsuit is withdrawn and a new lawsuit is filed based on the same claims.

§6. Resolution of Jurisdiction Conflicts

I. Designation of a Court with Jurisdiction or a Court of Proper Venue

A. Definition and Meaning

405. When a court is legally or practically unable to exercise its judicial authority over a case or the proper judicial district is indeterminable, the immediate superior court designates the court to hear the lawsuit at the request of the lower court or on petition by a party (§28(1) CPA). Jurisdiction or venue determined in this way is called jurisdiction by designation or venue by designation. Such designation of a court is different from the decision by a judicial panel to change subject-matter jurisdiction from a single judge to a judicial panel and vice versa.

B. Requirements

1. When a Competent Court Is Unable to Exercise Its Judicial Authority

406. The legal obstacles that keep an otherwise competent court from ruling on a case include judicial disqualification, challenge, and self-recusal of a judge or judges. Practical obstacles include illness or natural disasters.[71] The Court Organization Act has provisions to appoint acting judges in these situations. The Chief Justice of the Supreme Court may appoint an acting judge from other courts (§6(1) COA). The Presidents of a High Court or a District Court may also appoint a judge as an acting judge under their administrative authority (§6(2) COA).

---

70. Sang-won Kim et al., *supra* n. 46, at 217.
71. Sang-won Kim et al., *supra* n. 46, at 205.

407. When any court is unable to hear a case, the Chief Justice or the President of a relevant court should immediately appoint an acting judge. So, the provisions pertaining to designation of a court to hear a case by upper court for said reasons would be of little use.

2. When the Judicial Districts of Courts Are Uncertain

408. Judicial districts are related to the administrative districts. The boundary line of adjacent administrative districts can be uncertain when place of a tort or the location of immovable property is situated near the boundary. On the other hand, the location of an actionable event itself might be indiscernible, for instance, when a tortious act has been committed in a vehicle traveling near the boundary line of judicial districts.

C. Procedure

409. A court or a party may request the immediate superior court for a decision on the appropriate court to hear the case (r.7(1) RCP). If the Daejeon District Court or the Suwon District Court are the relevant courts, the immediate superior courts would be the Daejeon High Court and the Suwon High Court. The Supreme Court is the immediate superior court to the High Courts. Thus, in such a case the Supreme Court designates the court to hear the case.

410. A petition for designation may be raised before or after filing of a lawsuit. When a motion for designation is filed after commencement of the lawsuit, the court where the case is pending should stay the proceedings until a decision is rendered (r.9 RCP).

411. The common upper court designates a court to adjudicate the case provided the petition is well-grounded, if not, the petition is denied (r.8(1) RCP). Once the decision designating a competent court is issued, a newly proper venue is created. This decision is unappealable (§28(2) CPA).

II. Appeal Based on Lack of Jurisdiction or Improper Venue

A. Lack of Noncompulsory Jurisdiction or Wrong Venue

412. Parties may not appeal the final judgment of a trial court only on the ground that the court lacked subject-matter jurisdiction based on amount in controversy or proper venue (§411 CPA). Also, an appellate court may not reverse the judgments of a lower court on these matters. It is the same even when a party raised a timely objection to jurisdiction or the propriety of venue in the trial court. This means that such procedural defects are deemed cured by rendering the final judgment.

B. *Lack of Exclusive Jurisdiction*

413. Courts can address the lack of exclusive jurisdiction at any stage of litigation. Parties may appeal the judgment of a lower court for lack of exclusive jurisdiction (§411 CPA). Also, lack of exclusive jurisdiction is one of the absolute causes for appeal to the Supreme Court (§424(1) CPA). Because jurisdictional questions should be investigated *sua sponte* by the court, an appellate court examines whether the lower court lacked exclusive jurisdiction irrespective of the reasons for the appeal.

414. When an appellate court reverses the judgment of a lower court on account of lack of exclusive jurisdiction, the higher court transfers the case to the competent court by its judgment (§419 CPA). Where an intermediate appellate court renders a judgment on the merits of a case, overlooking the fact that the court of first instance lacked exclusive jurisdiction, the Supreme Court reverses both judgments and transfers the case to the court of first instance that has exclusive jurisdiction.[72]

III. Transfer of a Lawsuit

A. *Definition and Meaning*

415. When a lawsuit is filed in the wrong court, that court can transfer the case to the appropriate court. Such a transfer better serves the public interest by promoting procedural economy. Also, the parties can enjoy benefits such as the suspension of statutory limitation period.

416. When there is more than one proper venue for a case, the court in which the lawsuit was filed may transfer venue by a decision on its own motion or on motion of a party provided the other venue is deemed more appropriate for the purpose of a speedy trial and convenience of the parties.

B. *Requirements*

1. Transfer Based on Lack of Jurisdiction or Propriety of Venue

417. One of the reasons for transferring a case is lack of jurisdiction or the wrong venue (§34(1)CPA). Such lack of jurisdiction includes lack of compulsory and noncompulsory jurisdiction.

418. Transfers based on jurisdiction or venue usually occur at the trial level. However, the Civil Procedure Act's provisions pertaining to transfers also apply to

72. Supreme Court Decision 2010Ma1001 decided on June 30, 2011.

appellate jurisdiction. A notice of appeal must be submitted to the court which rendered the judgment being appealed. The presiding judge examines procedural requirements of the appeal on the face of the notice (§399(1) CPA). When there is a procedural defect, the presiding judge of the lower court dismisses the notice of appeal without prejudice by an order which is appealable (§§399(2),(3) CPA). According to case law, such an order by the presiding judge comes from the judicial authority of the lower court. A petition to appeal the trial court presiding judge's order must be filed with the intermediate appellate court. If such a petition is filed with the Supreme Court, it ought to be transferred to the competent appeals court, instead of dismissing it.[73]

419. Statutory provisions regarding transfer of cases also apply to functional jurisdiction. If an administrative law case subject to jurisdiction of the Seoul Administrative Court is filed with a District Court, the latter court transfers the case to the former court.[74] Similarly, a Branch Court of a District Court transfers the case under exclusive jurisdiction of the Seoul Family Court to that same court.[75]

420. If a court does not have jurisdiction over all of the claims in a suit, it is when part of the claims are under the exclusive jurisdiction of another court. In this case, the current court separates proceedings for the relevant claims and transfers them to the competent court, while the remaining claims stay in the court where the suit was initially filed.

2. Transfer by Discretion

421. A single judge of a District Court may transfer all or part of a case under its jurisdiction to a judicial panel in the same District Court by a decision on its own motion or on motion of a party. Small claims cases regulated by the Trial of Small Claims Act are subject to jurisdiction of the single judge. However, even though the trial proceedings for these cases are streamlined and simple, they may also be transferred to a judicial panel of a District Court.[76]

422. A single judge considers transferring a case when a related case is pending before a three-judge panel and consolidation of the proceedings is deemed necessary for a unified solution of the related cases, or when its judgment appears to conflict with those of other single judges of the same District Court in similar cases.

---

73. Supreme Court Decision (*en banc*) 94Ma1961 decided on January 20, 1995.
74. Supreme Court Decision 2011Du20321 decided on July 12, 2013.
75. Supreme Court Decision 80Ma445 decided on November 25, 1980.
76. Supreme Court Decision 74Ma71 decided on July 23, 1974.

3. Transfer to Avoid Disadvantage or Delay

423. Even when venue is proper, the court may transfer all or part of a case to another court of proper venue upon motion of a party or by its own authority, if it finds it necessary to avoid substantial disadvantage to a party or delay in the proceedings (§35 CPA).

424. A majority of jurists interpret "disadvantage" to concern the defendant's individual interest, whereas "delay" is related to the interests of justice or the public interest. Case law holds that a court should not transfer venue only based on burdensome litigation costs or inconvenience for the defendant. Rather the court should take into account the costs to be borne by both parties, the convenience of both parties and the court, and other circumstances concerning a transfer.[77]

425. Where a plaintiff who was serving a prison sentence filed a lawsuit against the State in a court of proper venue but was far away from the prison, the defendant-State moved to transfer the case to another court of proper venue closer to the prison. The Supreme Court reversed the decision granting the motion to transfer venue. The Court reasoned that the personnel and material costs incurred to escort the plaintiff-prisoner to and from the court should be borne by the State as such, not as a defendant.[78]

426. Regardless of the reasons explained by the courts, in practice, it is hard to find a Supreme Court precedent granting a motion to transfer venue. This is understandable considering that Korea is not geographically large, and the transport infrastructure is well-developed.

4. Transfer of a Lawsuit Based on Intellectual Property Rights

a. A Lawsuit Based on Patent Right, Utility Model Right, Design Right, Trademark Right and Plant Variety Right

427. Lawsuits over intellectual property rights are subject to the exclusive jurisdiction of the District Court in the district where the High Court sits (§24(2) CPA). In addition, the Seoul Central District Court also has concurrent jurisdiction over such cases (§24(3) CPA).

428. When a lawsuit based on intellectual property rights was filed before a District Court with exclusive jurisdiction or the Seoul Central District Court with concurrent jurisdiction, these courts may transfer the case to another court with proper venue as determined by general or special judicial addresses. A court can consider such a transfer to avoid substantial disadvantage to a party or delay in the proceedings, upon motion or by its own authority (§36(3) CPA).

---

77. Supreme Court Decision 2007Ma346 decided on November 15, 2007.
78. Supreme Court Decision 2010Ma215 decided on March 22, 2010.

429. The jurisdiction described here seems to be a legislative error in the Civil Procedure Act. For it states the exclusive jurisdiction of this type of intellectual property case on one hand and authorizes courts with such "exclusive jurisdiction" to transfer venue or the Seoul Central District Court to have a "concurrent jurisdiction" on the other hand. The Act should have approached this issue from the perspective of venue rules, rather than jurisdictional standards.

b. A Lawsuit Based on Other Intellectual Property Rights and International Transactions

430. When such a lawsuit is brought in the place determined in accordance with judicial addresses, the current court of proper venue may transfer the case on its own motion or on motion of a party to the District Court in the district where the High Court which covers said judicial addresses is seated, unless the transfer is likely to substantially delay the trial or the current court has exclusive jurisdiction over the case (§§36(1),(2) CPA).

5. Transfer Caused by Counterclaims

431. If the defendant in a lawsuit pending before the single judge files a counterclaim that raises the amount in controversy and makes the case eligible for jurisdiction before a three-judge judicial panel, the single judge transfers the case, including the counterclaim, to a panel on its own motion or on motion of a party.

432. However, as subject-matter jurisdiction based on the amount in controversy is noncompulsory, the single judge may retain jurisdiction provided the plaintiff makes an oral statement on the merits of the counterclaim (§269(2) CPA). In this case, a counterclaim is a new lawsuit filed by the defendant against the plaintiff. Therefore, if the original plaintiff, who is the defendant in the counterclaim, orally defends against the counterclaim, jurisdiction by oral statement is created. Of course, the single judge who has jurisdiction by oral statement may nevertheless transfer the case to a judicial panel for good reasons (§34(2) CPA).

IV. Transfer Procedure

A. Transfer due to Lack of Jurisdiction or Improper Venue

433. As jurisdiction and proper venue are matters to be determined by the court, if either is not proper, the court transfers the case to the court that has jurisdiction or to proper venue. A decision to transfer a case is subject to an immediate appeal (§39 CPA).

434. The Supreme Court opined that a motion by a party to transfer a case by reason of lack of jurisdiction or impropriety of venue is legally meaningless and the court need not respond to such a motion because matters concerning competence of a court should be examined by its own authority, Moreover, when the court dismisses such a motion unnecessarily by a decision, the decision is void and an appeal of that decision is also void.[79]

435. The judgment rendered by the court which lacks exclusive jurisdiction may be appealed for that reason. However, parties may not appeal the judgment of a trial court solely on the basis that it lacked noncompulsory jurisdiction, or it was not the court of proper venue. In this context, the interpretation of the Supreme Court regarding a motion to transfer for said reasons is not prejudicial to a party, but effectively bars the defendant from using such a motion to delay proceedings.

B. Transfer for Other Reasons

436. As mentioned before, a party may file a motion asking the current first instance court of proper venue to transfer the case to another venue for compelling reasons. When such a motion is filed, the current court gives both parties an opportunity to state their positions and renders a decision on the motion (r.11(1) RCP). A party may lodge an immediate appeal against the decision irrespective of whether it grants or denies the motion (§39 CPA).

V. Effects of Decision to Transfer

A. Binding Effects

437. A court decision ordering transfer of a case is binding on the court receiving the case when it becomes final and unappealable (§38(1) CPA). The court to which a case is transferred may not return it or transfer it again to another court or venue (§38(2) CPA). This is true even when a case is transferred to a court which has no jurisdiction or proper venue.

438. However, since the lack of exclusive jurisdiction is one of the absolute grounds for an appeal to the Supreme Court (§424(1) CPA), there have been debates on whether the binding force of the decision to transfer overrides the absolute grounds for a final appeal. A majority of jurists placed a higher priority on the finality of a transfer decision. They reasoned that the transferred case might be adrift among the courts if the court receiving the case is allowed to transfer it again and that a party may appeal the decision to transfer and have that decision reviewed by an appellate court.[80]

439. However, the Supreme Court makes an exception to this rule where a case is transferred to the court which does not have appellate jurisdiction. The Court held

79. Supreme Court Decision (*en banc*) 93Ma524 decided on December 6, 1993.
80. Sang-won Kim et al., *supra* n. 46, at 241.

that if the decision to transfer a case to a higher court is binding on the court receiving the case, it would violate the parties' right to appeal. When the court receiving the case is the Supreme Court whose task is limited to determine whether the law was applied correctly, it does not have authority to find the facts to decide the case. This results in a violation of the parties' right to a trial. Therefore, the appeals court should transfer the case to a competent lower court.[81]

B. The Time when a Lawsuit Was Filed

440. When the decision for transfer becomes final and unappealable, the lawsuit is deemed to have been filed when it was initially filed in the court transferring the case (§40(1) CPA). Accordingly, the question of whether a lawsuit was filed within the statutory period is determined according to the date when the complaint was filed with the court transferring the case; and the procedural acts taken in the transferring court remain effective.[82]

441. For instance, a plaintiff filed a complaint for retrial of a case in the court of first instance, even though the appellate court has exclusive jurisdiction over this retrial case because the reasons for the retrial lay in the proceedings of the appellate court. The court of first instance transferred the case to the appellate court. In this case, whether the lawsuit for retrial was brought within the statutory period should be decided according to the date when the complaint was incorrectly filed in the court of first instance.[83] This precedent was also applied when an administrative law case was incorrectly filed in a District Court and then transferred to the Seoul Administrative Court.[84]

442. On the other hand, the Supreme Court took an approach deserving of attention in dealing with a notice of appeal. In appealing a court judgment, the appellant must submit the notice of appeal to the court which rendered the judgment (§§397(1), 425 CPA). However, the appellant erroneously submitted the notice to the Supreme Court instead of the Daegu High Court which delivered the judgment. The Supreme Court transmitted the notice of appeal to the Daegu High Court after the statutory two-week period to file an appeal. The Supreme Court held that the appeal was filed at the time the Daegu High Court received the notice of appeal from the Supreme Court. The Supreme Court opined that transmitting a notice of appeal to the court where it should have been submitted is distinguishable from transferring an appellate case to another court.[85] This opinion is understandable because the Supreme Court to which the appellant appealed had appellate jurisdiction over this case and it did not transfer it. The Court only transmitted the notice of appeal, which is distinguished from transferring a case.

---

81. Supreme Court Decision 94Ma1059, 1060 decided on May 15, 1995.
82. Sang-won Kim et al., *supra* n. 46, at 244.
83. Supreme Court Decision (*en banc*) 83DaKa1981 decided on February 28, 1984.
84. *Supra* n. 74.
85. Supreme Court Decision 81Nu230 decided on October 13, 1981.

Chapter 2. International Jurisdiction

§1. Definition and Meaning

443. The authority of the State, as a sovereign, to adjudicate civil cases is referred to as civil jurisdiction. Civil jurisdiction is exercised within the limits of the Constitution, statutes, international treaties and international customary law. Jurisdictions of more than one nation can compete or overlap when parties to a case are citizens of different countries; when claims are connected with multiple nations; or when property is owned by a foreign national. International jurisdiction refers to the judicial authority of a nation over civil cases which also involve the jurisdiction of foreign countries.

§2. Persons Who Are Exempted from Civil Jurisdiction

444. There are individuals residing or staying in Korea, who are exempt from the criminal, civil and administrative jurisdiction of Korean courts. This privilege is called extraterritoriality or diplomatic immunity. The following are examples of persons with this exemption.

I. Diplomats

445. The United Nations Vienna Convention on Diplomatic Relations ("Vienna Convention of 1961") regulates the diplomatic exemption from jurisdiction of the courts in the receiving country. The Vienna Convention of 1961 was signed on April 18, 1961, at the United Nations Conference on Diplomatic Intercourse and Immunities and took effect on April 24, 1964. In Korea, after approval from the National Assembly on December 28, 1970, the Convention took effect on January 27, 1971.

446. In principle, diplomats enjoy immunity from the civil jurisdiction of the receiving country. However, diplomatic immunity does not extend to lawsuits involving private immovable property situated in the receiving country and in lawsuits relating to inheritance in which the diplomat is personally involved as an executor, administrator, heir or legatee. In cases relating to any professional or commercial activity personally exercised by the diplomat, they are also not exempted (§31 VCD). The family members of a diplomat forming his/her household enjoy the same privileges and immunities (§37(1) VCD). Members of the administrative and technical staff of the diplomatic mission enjoy the similar immunities but the scope thereof is narrower (§37(2) VCD).

II. Consular Officers

447. A consul usually performs his/her duty out of the embassy in a receiving nation to protect the interests of people from his/her nation. The UN Vienna Convention on Consular Relations ("Vienna Convention of 1963") provides for consular relations of the relevant nations and consular immunity. The Vienna Convention of 1963 was signed on April 24, 1963 at the United Nations Conference on Consular Relations and took effect on March 19, 1967. Korea joined the Vienna Convention of 1963 on December 26, 1976 and it took effect on March 7, 1977.

448. Consular officers and employees are not subject to the jurisdiction of the courts concerning performance of their consular duties in the receiving nation (§43(1) VCC). However, they could be sued in controversies arising from personal contracts or accidents caused by them while operating a vehicle, vessel or aircraft (§43(2) VCC).

III. Head of Foreign State

449. There is no statute or international treaty exempting heads of foreign states, their entourage and their family members from civil jurisdiction while visiting Korea. However, immunity from judicial authority has been accepted and acknowledged as a matter of international comity and international customary law. According to the Constitution, treaties duly concluded and promulgated, and the generally recognized rules of international law have the same effect as the domestic laws (Art. 6 Cons).

IV. Foreign Nation

450. Foreign sovereign immunity is rooted in the principles of customary international law. In *The Schooner Exchange v. McFaddon*, 11 U.S. 116 (1812), the U.S. Supreme Court established the theoretical background of a foreign nation's absolute immunity from civil jurisdiction. Thereafter until the mid-twentieth century, the doctrine of absolute immunity was the dominant view in international law. However, after World War II, as governments got more and more involved in commercial activities with the emergence of state enterprises, a new doctrine of restrictive sovereign immunity gradually took the place of absolute immunity. Under the restrictive theory, the immunity of a foreign state is limited to claims involving the foreign state's public acts. A foreign nation does not enjoy immunity from claims arising out of its commercial activities.

451. Korean courts followed the doctrine of absolute immunity until 1988.[86] However, in an *en banc* decision, 97Da39216 decided on December 17, 1998, the

86. Supreme Court Decision 74Ma281 decided on May 23, 1975.

Supreme Court adopted the doctrine of restrictive immunity. In this case, the plaintiff was employed by the United States Army and Air Force Exchange Service and worked at the Camp Casey for the U.S. Army Second Infantry Division. Alleging he was terminated without cause, the plaintiff filed a lawsuit against the United States seeking judgment affirming nullity of his termination and ordering reinstatement with payment of wages from the date of dismissal until the date of his re-employment.

452. The Seoul High Court dismissed the lawsuit on the basis of foreign sovereign immunity. However, the Supreme Court reversed the High Court's judgment and remanded the case. The Court reasoned that a dispute arising out of commercial activities undertaken in Korean territory by a foreign nation is not free from jurisdiction of domestic courts, unless they are part of, or closely related to, the exercise of sovereign power so that the adjudication of the dispute by a domestic court would interfere with sovereign or public acts by the foreign nation.

453. In defining the limits of restrictive immunity, case law recognizes immunity in enforcement of judgment cases which are closely related to the public policy of a foreign nation. In a case where the judgment debtor was employed at the U.S. Army Headquarters as a high-voltage electrician, a judgment creditor seized the debtor's wage and severance pay owed to him by the U.S. Army and filed a lawsuit against the United States seeking payment thereof after the court of enforcement issued an order authorizing debt collection. The Supreme Court upheld the judgment of the Seoul High Court which dismissed the lawsuit due to sovereign immunity. The Supreme Court held that, when issuing a decision for seizure of a monetary claim, the court of enforcement prohibits the third-party debtor from making any payment to the judgment debtor; that in this case, the United States was prohibited from paying its employee the wage and severance pay even though it is a third party; and that the decision for seizure certainly interfered with the exercise of sovereignty and the public policy of the United States.[87]

V. United States Armed Forces in ROK

454. The U.S.-ROK Status of Forces Agreement (SOFA) is intended to resolve legal disputes arising from the performance of official duties by the U.S. military stationed in Korea.

455. According to SOFA, in claims arising out of acts or omissions in the course of performing official duties by members or employees of the U.S. armed forces that cause damage to third-parties other than the Korean government, the ROK, as a legal person, becomes the defendant instead of the United States. The ROK compensates for the loss or injury in accordance with the State Compensation Act of Korea as if such acts were done by members of the Korean armed forces (§23(5)(a) SOFA). The United States is exempt from the civil jurisdiction of Korean courts to

87. Supreme Court Decision 2009Da16766 decided on December 13, 2011.

the extent of this provision of SOFA. However, the costs incurred by ROK to satisfy such claims are to be distributed between the two nations (§23(5)(e) SOFA).

456. In disputes arising out of contracts concerning the procurement of materials, supplies, equipment, or services; the United States does not enjoy sovereign immunity and can be sued by the Korean claimants (§23(10) SOFA). Claims based on tortious acts or omissions by members or employees of the U.S. armed forces in the performance of official duty are dealt with in the same way when the United States is a party to a commercial contract.[88]

§3. Factors for Determining International Jurisdiction

I. Definition and Meaning

457. International jurisdiction is the judicial power of a sovereign nation to adjudicate a case which has foreign elements. A civil dispute has foreign elements when the parties have domiciles, main offices or places of business in the different countries; or their domiciles, location of properties, the place to perform an obligation, or the place of tortious acts are situated in multiple countries. Note that international jurisdiction is distinguished from the choice of law provisions. A different set of rules determines which country's substantive law is applied in international civil disputes.

II. Debate on the Standard Determining International Jurisdiction

A. Debate

458. There have been two legal theories regarding the standard by which jurisdictional questions in transnational civil disputes are decided. Some courts applied domestic statutes and rules concerning venue and if any domestic court had proper venue, the forum state was deemed to have international jurisdiction over the case. Other courts balanced the reasonableness of asserting jurisdiction in a particular case, the burdens placed on an alien defendant and the convenience of the plaintiff. In addition, the pendency of a lawsuit should not offend "traditional notions of fair play and substantial justice." This theory is generally accepted among scholars.[89]

459. Case law was traditionally in line with the domestic law approach,[90] but recent precedents tend to combine both approaches.[91] According to a decision by

88. Supreme Court Decision 95Da29895 decided on December 12, 1997.
89. Sang-won Kim et al., *supra* n. 46, at 116-117.
90. Supreme Court Decision 87DaKa1728 decided on October 25, 1988 [Purchase price of goods] A lawsuit concerning property rights against a person whose domicile is not in the Republic of Korea

the Supreme Court, the provisions pertaining to venue by oral statement apply to international jurisdiction. The Supreme Court reversed the judgment by the Seoul High Court which dismissed the lawsuit for lack of international jurisdiction and remanded the case. In this case, both the parties were foreign nationals and three separate monetary claims were joined. Two of the claims were subject to jurisdiction of Korean courts because they were substantively related to Korea, however, a claim was not. The defendant argued the case on the merits at a trial court hearing without objecting to international jurisdiction. The Supreme Court applied the principle of venue by oral statement and held that international jurisdiction over one of the claims was created by the defendant's oral statements. In addition, the Court also balanced the interests of the parties. It reasoned that applying the principle of venue by oral statement to a question of international jurisdiction is not likely to create unfairness to the parties and that resolving all three claims at once serves the purpose of procedural efficiency and economy.[92]

B. Substantive Relationship

460. The Act on Private International Law was revised to legislatively settle jurisdictional issues in cases having foreign elements in 2001. Section 2 of the Act stipulates as follows:

(1) When a party or the matter in dispute is substantively related to the Republic of Korea, a court in ROK shall have international jurisdiction. In judging the existence of substantive relations, the court shall take into account reasonable principles compatible with ideologies concerning the allocation of international jurisdiction.
(2) A court shall judge whether or not it has the international jurisdiction in light of venue provisions of domestic laws and shall take full consideration of the unique nature of international jurisdiction in light of the legislative intention of the provision of Subsection (1).

461. The Act on Private International Law deems "substantive relations" the most important factor in solving jurisdictional issues. Venue statutes in domestic laws and other considerations are additional factors. "Substantive relations" may be interpreted the same as "the relationship among the defendant, the forum, and the

---

or is unknown, may be brought in Korea provided the objects of the claim, its collateral, or any seizable property is located in Korea although the defendant is a foreign national (§9 CPA). Korea's jurisdiction over the lawsuit is justified because in such a case a winning plaintiff can enforce the judgment against the property.

91. Supreme Court Decision 91Da41897 decided on July 28, 1992.
92. Supreme Court Decision 2012Da7571 decided on April 10, 2014.

litigation" in the U.S. case law.[93] The attitude of the Supreme Court in interpreting the jurisdictional clause of the Act is in accordance with the balanced interest approach.[94]

462. The Supreme Court has interpreted "substantive relations" under Section 2 of the Act as a new standard to determine international jurisdiction. That case was a wrongful death case where the plaintiffs were Chinese and family members of a flight attendant who was killed when a Boeing 767 of Air China crashed in Korea. The defendant was a company incorporated in China and operated the doomed passenger plane. The Supreme Court held that this lawsuit had "substantive relations" with Korea considering the venue provisions of the Civil Procedure Act with respect to the place of a tort occurred (§18 CPA), the individual interests of the parties, the interests of the court, and fairness in relation to other victims in the crash. Thus, Korean courts had international jurisdiction over this case.[95]

III. Agreement on International Jurisdiction

463. A forum selection clause is usually included in international contracts to designate one or more courts which will adjudicate disputes between the parties. These clauses can be exclusive or permissive. An exclusive forum selection clause requires that all lawsuits concerned with the contract be brought only in a specific forum. A permissive clause is more flexible.

464. In Korea, issues concerning forum selection are mainly focused on the validity and enforceability of such a clause. The first question is whether a forum selection clause is valid when it designates a forum which has nothing to do with the legal relationship between the parties. The second issue is raised when a party files a lawsuit in a country which has international jurisdiction over the case in accordance with its domestic law but it is contrary to a contractual forum selection clause.

465. The Supreme Court has applied very strict standards in determining the validity of a forum selection clause. The requirements set out by the Court are satisfied when the contract claims are not under the exclusive jurisdiction of another

---

93. *Shaffer v. Heitner*, 433 U.S. 186, 204 (1977)

94. Supreme Court Decision 2006Da17539 Decided July 12, 2013 [Damages] International jurisdiction is determined based on the fundamental principle of achieving equity between the parties, as well as the public's interest in judicial propriety, expedition, and economy. Specifically, courts should balance the personal interests, such as equity, convenience, and predictability between the parties, as well as the state's broader interests in judicial propriety, expedition, efficiency and the effectiveness of the judgment. The selection of the protected interests out of this diverse pool shall be reasonably determined based on the objective criteria of substantial relation between the court's location and the parties, and between the court's location and the issues in individual cases. Especially in product liability cases against manufacturers making and selling the goods, the court where the loss occurred has international jurisdiction if there is a substantial relation between a manufacturer and the loss, to such an extent that the manufacturer can reasonably anticipate a lawsuit at that court.

95. Supreme Court Decision 2010Da18355 decided on July 15, 2010.

country; the designated forum has jurisdiction over the case in accordance with forum state's law regulating international jurisdiction; the designated forum has reasonable relations with the case; the forum selection clause is not unreasonable or against public policy and the forum selection agreement was made in writing.[96] Many jurists are critical of these requirements for being too restrictive, especially the "reasonable relations" requirement.[97]

466. The Supreme Court considered a case whether a contract venue clause had any effect in determining international jurisdiction. This case involved a loan contract with venue selection clause between two Japanese citizens who were domiciled in Japan. The venue clause exclusively designated the Tokyo District Court as the proper venue. Later, the loan creditor assigned the claim to a Korean citizen residing in Seoul. The Korean assignee creditor then sued the debtor in the Seoul Central District Court, seeking the payment of the debt. The defendant objected to international jurisdiction in Korea. The Supreme Court held that the exclusive venue agreement was made on the premise that a lawsuit based on the loan contract would be brought in Japan. The parties did not anticipate that a lawsuit might be filed in a country other than Japan. Therefore, international jurisdiction over this case should be determined by the Korean law. Without regard to the venue clause, the Seoul Central District Court was the proper court to hear the case.[98]

96. Supreme Court Decision 2001Da53349 decided on March 25, 2004.
97. Si-yoon Lee, *supra* n. 8, at 113.
98. Supreme Court Decision 2006Da68209 decided on March 13, 2008.

Part III. Lawsuits and Claims

Chapter 1. Lawsuits

§1. Definition and Meaning

I. Concept

467. A lawsuit is a plaintiff's request for the court to adjudicate a dispute with the defendant. The act of filing a lawsuit is a procedural act in a court. Because a lawsuit is a legal proceeding to decide a dispute, it ends with a final judgment. By filing a lawsuit, litigation proceedings commence. The main elements of a lawsuit are the participants and the subject-matter.

468. Participants of the proceedings are the court, the plaintiffs, and defendants. The subject-matter is the claim asserted by the plaintiff. Because a claim for relief is the most important component of a lawsuit, "lawsuit" and a "claim for relief" are oftentimes understood as having the same meaning. Accordingly, joinder of lawsuits and joinder of claims are interchangeably used in Korea. However, a claim and a lawsuit are not the same. The claim or the subject-matter is but one component of a lawsuit.

469. The subject-matter denotes a legal right or obligation in dispute between the plaintiff and the defendant. The extent of legal rights or obligations falling under the rubric of "subject-matter" varies depending on legal theories. According to substantive-law approach which is adopted by the Supreme Court, the subject-matter is the legal right or legal relationship established by substantive law.

470. In a lawsuit, the subject-matter is distinguished from the object of the suit. For example, when a plaintiff filed a lawsuit seeking delivery of land, the subject-matter is the claim for delivery of land or the legal status of the plaintiff to request the defendant to deliver the land, whereas the object is the specific land itself.

II. Types of Lawsuits

A. *Lawsuit for Performance*

1. Concept

471. In a lawsuit for performance, the plaintiff requests the court to render a judgment confirming his/her claim against the defendant for performance of a specific obligation asserted in the complaint and ordering the defendant to fulfill that obligation. Such claims and obligations are defined in substantive law including laws relating to individual relationships (private law) and laws that affect the relation between an individual and the state (public law). Legal rights established by public law can be realized by filing a civil lawsuit provided the dispute is private in nature. Claims here encompass those based on real rights as well as obligatory claims.

472. Generally, in lawsuits for performance, the plaintiff pursues payment of money, delivery of things or a declaration of intent to perform an act, or certain or other acts or inactions. A declaration of intent is a personal obligation of the defendant to make plain his/her intent to perform a certain act. This intent forms or alters a legal relationship in favor of the plaintiff. Such a lawsuit is unique in that at the moment the judgment ordering a statement of intent becomes final and binding, the defendant is deemed to have done the required act, leaving no room for its compulsory enforcement (§389(2) CA). For example, where the purchaser-plaintiff of real property brings a successful lawsuit against the seller-defendant, seeking registration of title transfer, and then submits the enforceable judgment to the registry, the registrar enters the title transfer in the registration record of the real property as if the defendant applied for such registration.

473. Lawsuits seeking declaration of intent include those praying for registration of ownership transfer, cancellation of a registration as void, registration of real rights including establishment of a mortgage, notification to the obligor that a claim has been transferred, etc. Claims for performance of a positive obligation include pursuing correction of a press report, demolition of a building, etc. Regarding performance of negative personal obligations, the transferee of a business may sue the transferor seeking prohibition of running a competitive business. Also, prohibition of digging or constructing a building close to an adjacent property, and prohibition of obstructing legitimate passage through a property are examples of this category.

2. Lawsuits for Immediate Performance and Future Performance

474. A lawsuit may be filed seeking immediate performance as well as future performance. Usually the person who benefits from the performance (the obligee) sues the obligor (the person required to perform) when the time for performance has passed. If due date has not arrived until the hearing is closed and the defendant raises an affirmative defense based on the fact, the claim would be dismissed. However, if the obligor shows his/her intention in advance not to perform the obligation on the due date, the obligee may file a lawsuit for future performance (§251 CPA). This rule would be applied, for instance, where a debtor disputes the existence of a debt. As such, whether a lawsuit is for immediate performance or for future performance depends on the date specified for performance and the date the hearing closes.

3. Effects of Judgment

a. Enforceability

475. A final and binding judgment for performance is enforceable. Enforceability means the judgment is suitable to be enforced by enforcement agencies. To enforce a monetary judgment, enforcement agencies sell or dispose of the debtor's properties and use the proceeds to satisfy the judgment. Enforcement agencies might also commence a compulsory administration procedure and collect earnings from real property to be paid to the judgment creditor.

476. Compulsory enforcement for the delivery or surrender of immovable property is carried out by an enforcement officer. The enforcement officer takes possession of the property from the obligor and hands it over to the obligee (§§257,258 CEA). This type of execution is called a direct compulsory enforcement.

477. If an obligation may be fulfilled by a third party because there is no difference depending on who carries out the obligation, the enforcement agency performs such acts at the cost of the debtor (§389(2) CA, §260 CEA). For such enforcement by substitutes, the enforcement officer usually hires workers to perform the obligation.

478. With respect to any obligation for an inaction or an action that depends exclusively on the willingness of the debtor, enforcement is carried out by levying a coercive penalty on the judgment debtor (§261(1) CEA).

b. Preclusive Effects

479. The principle of preclusive effects confirms that rights and obligations of the parties to a lawsuit are completely and finally decided in the lawsuit. Therefore, once a judgment favoring a plaintiff's claim for performance becomes final and binding, the existence of the claim cannot be disputed any more between the parties. On the other hand, a judgment dismissing the plaintiff's claim precludes the plaintiff from asserting the claim against the defendant again.

B. Declaratory-Judgment Lawsuit

1. Concept

480. A declaratory-judgment lawsuit is brought to resolve legal uncertainty over the existence or nonexistence of the legal rights, obligations, status or any other legal relationships between the parties. Because the court affirms only the legal relationship, the lawsuit seeking affirmation of facts or factual truth is, in principle, not permitted. However, a lawsuit for declaratory judgment may be filed to determine the authenticity of a document that purports to evidence legal relationships (§250 CPA).

2. Types

481. A lawsuit for declaratory judgment may be filed by someone seeking a court decision to show the existence or nonexistence of a legal relationship. Examples of this type of lawsuits include those for affirmation of: the nonexistence of a debt, a void termination or a void disciplinary measure, the nonexistence of a person's status as a representative, membership, a void board of directors' resolution, the status as a successful bidder, and a void contract. Suits to quiet title are the same.

482. A special type of declaratory judgment is an interlocutory declaration. When resolution of a lawsuit depends on whether a legal relationship between parties is valid, either party may join a new claim seeking a declaratory judgment on the disputed legal relationship (§264 CPA). For example, if the plaintiff filed a lawsuit seeking surrender of a house based on his/her ownership and the defendant disputed the ownership of the plaintiff the decision on this controversy is premised on the ownership of the house; however, the preclusive effect of the judgment is limited to the existence of the plaintiff's claim for surrender, not the ownership of the house. In th is case, the plaintiff may join a claim or the defendant may lodge a counterclaim to quiet title to the house, which is referred to as a claim for interlocutory declaration.

3. Effects of Judgment

483. A final and binding declaratory judgment has preclusive effects affirming the existence or nonexistence of the legal relations in the judgment. A judgment dismissing a case on the merits, with prejudice, affirms the legal relationship counter to the claims asserted by the plaintiff. A declaratory judgment has preclusive effects but cannot be an enforcement title.

C. Lawsuit for Formative Judgment

1. Concept

484. A formative judgment creates, alters or extinguishes legal rights, status or relationships of the parties. This type of remedy is available only if the law specifically allows it. When a court judgment upholding a claim for revocation of a resolution at a shareholders' meeting become final and binding, it has an *erga omnes* effect and the resolution becomes invalid henceforth. This judgment is formative in that no one can dispute the existing legal relationship until a formative judgment becomes final and binding, and no one can dispute the new legal relationship formed by a formative judgment due to its *erga omnes* effect. If a co-owner demands partition of a parcel of jointly owned land and the co-owners fail to agree on the method for doing so, any co-owner may file a lawsuit seeking partition with a court (§269 CA). In such a case, provided the court renders a judgment ordering partition, each co-owner becomes an independent owner of the partitioned land at the moment the judgment becomes final and binding.

485. As a general matter, parties have the right to alter legal relationships and form new relationships. However, such a right is distinguished from the lawsuit for a formative judgment. For instance, parties can revoke or terminate a contract (§543 CA); void a declaration of intent (§140 CA); ratify unauthorized representation (§130 CA); and a lessee can demand the purchase of a building on the leased land (§643 CA), etc. To exercise the right to alter these kinds of legal relationships, the relevant party has only to manifest his/her intention to the other party in a proper way and need not file a lawsuit. Of course, a party to a lawsuit may exercise this right in the litigation proceedings.

486. However, a lawsuit for a formative judgment, as a subset of lawsuits that alter legal relationships, is allowed only when it is provided by statutes. Usually the legal relationships that can be created through a formative judgment, the prerequisites and the parties to such a lawsuit, and the statutory period are prescribed in relevant statutes.

2. Types

a. Lawsuit for Formative Judgment under Substantive Law

487. Such a lawsuit aims to change a legal relationship under substantive laws. Examples under family law include lawsuits seeking revocation of a marriage, a divorce, revocation of adoption, reversal of adoption, among others. Under corporate law, lawsuits filed for nullification of incorporation, nullification of a merger, nullification or revocation of a resolution at a shareholders' meeting, removal of directors, and nullification or revocation of a resolution to elect directors all belong to this category.

488. There have been debates on whether a judgment affirming the nullity of a resolution at a shareholders' meeting and the nonexistence of a resolution is declaratory or formative. However, the Commercial Act revised in 1995 stipulates that these judgments are effective as to all who deal with the corporation (§§380,190 ComA). Thus, it is construed as formative.

b. Lawsuit for Formative Judgment Based on Perfunctory Causes

489. This type of lawsuit seeks change of a legal right or status like other suits for a formative judgment. However, statutes do not specify the legal elements for this type of claim. Here, the court exercises a wide judicial discretion to award equitable remedies and the content of the judgment is not strictly bound by the complaint. Examples of this type of lawsuit include claims for partition of jointly owned properties (§268 CA), claims for settling land boundary lines, and claims for determining rent to be paid by the superficiary in case of legal superficies (§366 CA).

490. For example, the legal elements of a claim to revoke a resolution at a shareholders' meeting in the Commercial Act include the fact that the procedures for the convocation of the shareholders' meeting or the methods for adopting resolutions violate the statutes or the articles of incorporation, or are substantially unfair; or the details of the resolution are contrary to the articles of incorporation (§376 ComA).

491. By contrast, claims for partition of jointly owned land do not have such legal elements, and may be filed by a co-owner based on his/her status as such. The court uses its discretion to draw dividing lines of the plots to be owned by each co-owner after partition.

c. Lawsuit for Formative Judgment under Procedural Law

492. This type of lawsuit pursues changes to legal effects regulated by procedural law. Examples include a lawsuit seeking modification of a final and binding judgment ordering compensation by periodic payments (§252(2) CPA), a lawsuit for a retrial (§451 CPA), a lawsuit for a quasi-retrial (§461 CPA), a lawsuit for setting aside an arbitral awards (§36 AA), and a complaint on appeal to rescind a judgment of exclusion (§490 CPA).

493. Jurists have different opinions on the nature of a lawsuit raising an objection to the claim being enforced (§44 CEA) and a third-party lawsuit against enforcement (§48 CEA). The Supreme Court views such lawsuits as those for formative judgments in that enforceability of a prior judgment is excluded when the judgment upholding a plaintiff's claim becomes final and binding.[99] However, such a judgment has a binding effect only on the parties.

---

99. Supreme Court Decision 2015Da224469 decided on October 26, 2017; Supreme Court Decision 96Da37176 decided on November 22, 1996.

3. Effects of Judgment

494. The judgment dismissing a lawsuit for a formative judgment on the merits is a declaration and has preclusive effects regarding the nonexistence of the claim for such relief. On the other hand, a formative judgment favoring the plaintiff alters the existing legal relationships or status as asserted in the suit, and has preclusive effects regarding existence of the claim for such relief.

§2. PROCEDURAL PREREQUISITES

I. Definition and Meaning

495. There are four stages a plaintiff must pass to obtain a judgment upholding his/her claim. Procedural prerequisites are tested in the first two stages.[100]

496. Initially, the presiding judge of a judicial panel or a single judge examines the formality of the complaint. Mandatory items must be stated in the complaint and the correct amount of judicial stamp must be attached. When the complaint, on its face, lacks these prerequisites, the judge may issue an order to dismiss the complaint, which means the court rejects filing of the complaint and pendency of the lawsuit does not occur.

497. In the second stage, the court examines further procedural requirements, jurisdiction and venue. It may dismiss the case without prejudice or transfer the case to a competent court when the current court lacks jurisdiction or the venue is improper.

498. In the third stage of proceedings, the plaintiff should plead facts sufficient to constitute a cause of action. Even if the asserted facts in the pleadings are admitted by the defendant, if they are not sufficient for the court to grant judicial relief, the court dismiss the case on the merits without oral argument.

499. In the fourth stage, the facts must be established by evidence or admitted by the defendant. Provided, however, the defendant does not raise a successful affirmative defense.

500. Procedural prerequisites are requirements that must be satisfied for a lawsuit to be properly before a court. There are requirements with respect to courts, parties, claims, and special lawsuits. Each prerequisite is derived from provisions of the Civil Procedure Act.

501. Prerequisites for lawsuit are distinguished from the validity of procedural acts. When a single procedural act is invalid, the act does not give rise to the desired

100. Si-yoon Lee, *supra* n. 8, at 205-206.

legal effect. However, if a lawsuit lacks a procedural prerequisite prescribed by the Civil Procedure Act, the lawsuit itself is unlawful and may be dismissed for that reason.

II. Types of Prerequisites for a Lawsuit

A. As for the Court

1. Personal Jurisdiction and International Jurisdiction

502. Lawsuits filed against persons who are exempt from civil jurisdiction in Korean courts are unlawful. Diplomats, consuls, the head of a foreign state, and the like who are performing their official duties in Korea fall into this category. A foreign sovereign state is also free from the civil jurisdiction of Korea with some exceptions.

503. Whether Korean courts have authority to hear the case with issues that relate to foreign nationals or states is determined in accordance with Section 2 of the Act on Private International Law and general principles of international jurisdiction.

504. When a lawsuit, filed in Korea, is not subject to the jurisdiction of Korean courts, the court dismisses the case without prejudice.

2. Subject-Matter Jurisdiction, Functional Jurisdiction and Venue

505. The court in which a lawsuit is filed must have jurisdiction to hear the case and must be a court of proper venue. If not, the case is transferred to a court with jurisdiction or to a proper venue.

B. As for the Parties

1. Capacity to Be a Party

506. Capacity to be a party to court proceedings denotes a legal status to become a plaintiff, defendant, or participant in litigation proceedings. This concept corresponds to the legal capacity to hold private rights under the Civil Act. Anyone with legal capacity has the capacity to be a party. However, an association without legal personality or a foundation without legal personality can also be a party to a civil lawsuit (§52 CPA).

507. The State, a municipality, a foreign nation, or a company incorporated in a foreign country is capable of becoming a party. If the plaintiff or the defendant lacks capacity to be a party, the lawsuit is unlawful. Accordingly, a lawsuit filed by a person representing animals is dismissed without prejudice.[101] Also, because a partnership under the Civil Act does not have capacity to be a party, all the partners should be parties to a lawsuit regarding assets of the partnership.[102]

508. An unborn child is deemed to have been already born with respect to tort damages (§762 CA), inheritance (§1000(3) CA), and bequest (§1064 CA). There are two different approaches in interpreting the legal status of an unborn child in such cases. According to the theory of "condition subsequent," the unborn child has the capacity to be a party but such capacity terminates retrospectively if it is stillborn.[103] A second theory, the theory of "condition precedent," states that because the legal capacity of a person begins at the time of birth, the unborn child does not have the capacity to be a party; and that, however, in applying the above statutory provisions, a person is deemed to have been born at the time of a tort, inheritance or bequest.[104]

509. Case law says that a deceased person cannot be sued. If the defendant dies before a copy of the complaint is served upon the defendant, the lawsuit is unlawful and the judgment rendered in such a case is void.[105] However, if the plaintiff corrects the name of the defendant from the deceased to the successor to the deceased defendant during the pendency of the case in the court of first instance, the suit is deemed lawful from the time the complaint was filed initially.[106] When a party dies after the service of the complaint, the proceedings are interrupted until resumed by a court decision upon petition by a successor or the other party (§241 CPA).

2. Litigation Capacity

510. Litigation capacity refers to the competency of a party to a civil proceeding to sue or to be sued in his/her own name. Litigation capacity corresponds to the capacity to contract in the Civil Act. Litigation capacity is regulated by the Civil Act and other substantive statutes (§51 CPA), and a person incapable of contracting does not have litigation capacity.

511. Minors, adult wards, and limited wards do not have litigation capacity unless statutes allow them to take procedural acts in special circumstances. A lawsuit filed by a person who lacks litigation capacity, rather than by a guardian on his/her behalf, is void.

---

101. Supreme Court Decision 2004Ma1148,1149 decided on June 2, 2006.
102. Supreme Court Decision 2008Da79340 decided on January 30, 2009; Supreme Court Decision 2012Da44471 decided on November 29, 2012.
103. Sang-won Kim et al., *supra* n. 46, at 296-297.
104. The Supreme Court opinions adopt the latter theory. Supreme Court Decision 76Da1365 decided on September 14, 1976.
105. Supreme Court Decision 2014Da34041 decided on January 29, 2015.
106. Supreme Court Decision 2010Da99040 decided on March 10, 2011.

3. Standing and Proper Party

a. Definition

512. The term "standing" refers to the status of a plaintiff as the right person to bring a lawsuit. "Standing" usually requires that the plaintiff suffers from the adverse effect or harm if the dispute remains unresolved. When a legal dispute originates from relationships between specific persons, generally those persons have standing to sue in order to settle the dispute. However, in some exceptional cases, statutes grant plaintiffs the right to assert, in their own name, the rights of third parties. A bankruptcy trustee is a good example. He/she has standing to be a party in civil procedures concerning the debtor's properties and obligations. The bankruptcy trustee acts in his/her own name, in the interest of the bankruptcy estate.

513. A proper party is a person or entity who has an interest in the subject-matter of a legal dispute and, for that reason, can bring a lawsuit or be sued. A proper plaintiff has standing to sue the proper defendant.

b. Proper Parties

(1) In a lawsuit for performance

514. Where a plaintiff files a lawsuit for performance, contending that he/she has a claim against the defendant under substantive law, in principle, the issue of standing or proper party is absorbed into the determination whether the plaintiff would prevail on the merits. For example, in a lawsuit seeking surrender of an immovable property based on ownership, if the plaintiff is not the owner of the property, the court dismisses the case on the merits, not for lack of standing.

515. However, in a lawsuit pursuing cancellation of ownership registration due to voidness, the person who is the registered owner is the proper defendant. If this lawsuit is filed against a person other than the registered title holder, it is unlawful.[107] The Supreme Court also held that if, during the course of a lawsuit seeking payment of purchase price, the plaintiff's creditor seizes the claim for the purchase price and obtains a decision authorizing debt collection by a court of enforcement, the plaintiff ends up lacking standing to sue and the lawsuit should be dismissed without prejudice.[108]

(2) In a lawsuit for a declaration

516. In a lawsuit for a declaration, the plaintiff has standing when he/she has a legal interest to petition the court to clarify his/her rights or obligations, and a proper defendant is the one who is creating legal uncertainty by disputing the plaintiff's rights or obligations. For instance, in a lawsuit to declare the nonexistence of a debt, the alleged debtor has standing to sue the person who alleges he/she owes the debt.

---

107. Supreme Court Decision 93Da39225 decided on February 25, 1994.
108. Supreme Court Decision 2011Da98426 decided on October 31, 2013.

In a lawsuit to affirm the nullity of a resolution to elect the representative of an association, case law says that the proper defendant is the association, not the elected representative. This is because the lawsuit concerns the validity of the resolution itself.[109]

(3) In a formative judgment lawsuit

517. A formative judgment lawsuit is allowed only when it is provided for in statutes. The statutes allowing formative lawsuits stipulate standing to sue but are usually silent on the requirements for a proper defendant. For example, statutes define standing to sue in the following cases: either spouse in a contested divorce (§840 CA), a creditor seeking to rescind a fraudulent act by a debtor (§406(1) CA), a shareholder, director or auditor in a lawsuit seeking revocation of a resolution at a shareholders' meeting (§376(1) ComA), and shareholders who hold no less than 3% of the total number of shares in a lawsuit seeking removal of a director due to inappropriate activities or a grave violation of any statute or the articles of incorporation (§385(2) ComA).

518. However, these statutes do not have any provisions regarding defendants. In most cases, a person or entity whose interest would be directly affected by a judgment and who is most closely related to the subject-matter of the lawsuit is a proper defendant. Thus, proper defendants are the spouse who is not the plaintiff in a divorce case or the beneficiary or the subsequent purchaser in a fraudulent act lawsuit and the company in the above corporate law cases.

c. Third-Party Standing

519. As mentioned above, third-party standing is granted by statutes that prescribe when one party may file a lawsuit or raise a defense in his/her own name in the interest of a third party. Such third-party standing includes an obligee exercising subrogation rights by filing a lawsuit in order to preserve his/her own claim (§404 CA), shareholders in a derivative lawsuit (§403 ComA), a rehabilitation trustee in a lawsuit involving the debtor's properties (§78 DRBA), a bankruptcy trustee in a lawsuit involving the bankruptcy estate (§359 DRBA), an executor of a will in a lawsuit involving inherited property (§1101 CA),[110] an administrator in a lawsuit involving inherited property when it is unknown whether an heir exists (§1053 CA), an appointed party from among parties who share common interests (§53 CPA), and the judgment creditor who obtained an order authorizing the judgment creditor for debt collection (§229(2) CEA).

520. When the legal relationship between the creditor and the debtor, which is the basis of third-party standing, turns out to be nonexistent, the lawsuit filed by the creditor against the third party becomes unlawful. For instance, a lawsuit filed by a

109. Supreme Court Decision 2006Da86597 decided on September 25, 2008.
110. Supreme Court Decision 97Da57733 decided on November 26, 1999.

creditor exercising subrogation rights against a third-party debtor will be dismissed without prejudice if the creditor-plaintiff fails to prove a claim to be preserved against the debtor.

C. *As for the Subject-Matter of Lawsuit*

1. Specifying the Claim and Its Causes

521. The subject-matter of a lawsuit which is a legal right or obligation in dispute should be clearly specified in the pleadings. If the dispute is not clearly defined, the court cannot tell what to adjudicate, a judgment upholding such a vague claim is likely to be unenforceable and the defendant cannot effectively defend against it.

2. Prohibition of Duplicative Lawsuits

522. A lawsuit filed during the pendency of another lawsuit based on the same cause of action is duplicative and invalid (§259 CPA). The following are elements of a duplicative lawsuit.

a. Filing a Subsequent Lawsuit

523. The distinction between a previous lawsuit and a subsequent lawsuit is determined based on when a copy of a complaint is served on the defendant. It is the same whether or not the subsequent lawsuit is filed with the court where the previous lawsuit is pending. Even when the previous lawsuit lacks procedural prerequisites, the subsequent lawsuit based on the same subject-matter is duplicative and unlawful unless the previous lawsuit is withdrawn or dismissed for lack of procedural prerequisites by the close of the hearing for the subsequent lawsuit.[111]

b. Identical Parties

524. If the judgment in a previous case would have binding effect on a person who is a party in a subsequent lawsuit, assuming that a court would adjudicate the case on the merits, the party in the second case is deemed identical with a party to the previous case (§218(1) CPA).

525. For example, persons who share common interests may appoint, from among them, one or more persons to act as a plaintiff or defendant on their behalf (§53(1) CPA). After a suit is filed, a group of parties may do the same (§53(2) CPA). In such cases, only the appointed party has standing to sue or is a proper defendant. The persons who appoint them automatically lose their status as a party. However, the appointing persons or parties and the person appointed are deemed identical.

111. Supreme Court Decision 97Da45532 decided on February 27, 1998.

526. When a creditor exercises subrogation rights in order to preserve his/her own claim by filing a lawsuit against a third-party debtor (§404 CA), the plaintiff-creditor is deemed to be identical to the debtor to be subrogated. The Supreme Court opines that a lawsuit is unlawful as a duplicative when it is filed based on a subrogation right during the pendency of a previous subrogation lawsuit brought by another creditor.[112] The lawsuit filed by a creditor to exercise subrogation rights is also duplicative when the debtor to be subrogated has already filed a lawsuit asserting his/her claim against the third-party debtor and the case is pending.[113]

c. Identical Subject-Matter

527. If the subject-matter of a lawsuit is different from that of a previous lawsuit, the subsequent lawsuit is not duplicative. The subject-matter denotes a legal right or obligation in dispute between the plaintiff and defendant. For example, an action to declare the termination of one's employment void and an action seeking payment of one's salary on the grounds that the termination was void, have different subject-matters even though they are both based on the same employment contract. In addition, a quiet title lawsuit for real property and a lawsuit seeking surrender of the property based on ownership, do not have subject-matter in common.

528. Raising an affirmative defense that could in itself be the subject-matter of a lawsuit is not considered a duplicative lawsuit; nor would a counter suit based on that defense. For instance, where the seller of an item files a lawsuit asking for payment of the purchase price, the defendant-purchaser may assert an affirmative defense of simultaneous performance based on his/her claim for delivery of the item and, at the same time, may lawfully file a lawsuit seeking delivery of the goods. Also, where a plaintiff files a lawsuit pursuing payment of money and the defendant has a monetary claim against the plaintiff, the defendant may plead a setoff as a defense and, while this lawsuit is pending, may file a separate lawsuit seeking payment of the debt owed by the plaintiff. The subsequent lawsuit is not duplicative because raising the defense of a setoff is not the same as filing a lawsuit.[114]

529. A plaintiff may sue for a portion of a claim without any restrictions. However, there are debates over whether the plaintiff may bring a second suit for the balance. Some commentators suggest that the second suit is duplicative and unlawful whereas other commentators argue that the second suit is lawful. According to case law, if the plaintiff asserts in a pleading that the amount or quantity prayed for is a portion of a claim, the subject-matter is separated into two and he/she may file a second lawsuit for the remaining part. If not, the second lawsuit is duplicative.[115]

---

112. Supreme Court Decision 94Da12517, 94Da12524 decided on November 25, 1994.
113. *Supra* n. 177.
114. Supreme Court Decision 2000Da4050 decided on April 27, 2001.
115. Supreme Court Decision 84Da552 decided on April 9, 1985.

3. Prohibition of Repetitive Lawsuit

530. The plaintiff may withdraw a lawsuit with or without the defendant's consent after rendition of a judgment until it becomes final and binding. Should the lawsuit be withdrawn, it is considered as if it was not filed and the judgment which have not yet become final and binding, is ineffective (§267(1) CPA). Provided, however, the plaintiff may not file the same lawsuit when the withdrawal is made after a final judgment on the merits is rendered (§267(2) CPA).

531. Even in an appeals court, the plaintiff may amend the cause of action insofar as the new cause of action is based on the same general set of facts as were set forth in the original pleadings. In such a case, the claim based on the previous cause of action, which was superseded by the new one, is considered to have been withdrawn after the judgment was rendered in the prior court and filing a lawsuit for the same claim in the original pleadings is prohibited.[116]

532. For a subsequent lawsuit to be prohibited as repetitive, the parties and subject-matters of the previous lawsuit and subsequent one are required to be identical. Whether the parties and claims are identical is determined by the same criteria as explained above regarding the prohibition of overlapping lawsuit.

533. A legitimate interest to take legal action should be taken into account in deciding whether a lawsuit is repetitive. For instance, a plaintiff filed a lawsuit seeking prohibition of trespass to his land and the court rendered a judgment favoring the plaintiff, which was appealed by the defendant. The plaintiff then withdrew the case, believing the defendant's promise not to trespass again while the case was on appeal. Thereafter, the defendant violated his promise and again trespassed. In such a case, the plaintiff may lawfully file a lawsuit based on the same causes of action with the withdrawn one. Also, where the plaintiff withdrew a lawsuit in accordance with a settlement agreement but the defendant violated the agreement, a second lawsuit for the same claim is lawful and nonrepetitive.[117]

4. Legitimate Interest to Sue

534. For a lawsuit to be lawful, the plaintiff is required to have a legitimate interest to sue. That is, a plaintiff must have reasonable grounds or necessity to obtain a judgment to resolve a dispute. The grounds for a legitimate interest to sue include the following.

(a) The dispute must be about a specific legal right or legal relationship that can be resolved by a judicial decision. For a claim to be justiciable and enforceable, there must be a dispute over a specific right or legal relationship, and that claim must be in regard to a current legal relationship.

116. Supreme Court Decision 68Da1798 decided on May 27, 1969.
117. Supreme Court Decision 2000Da46399 decided on December 22, 2000.

(b) There must be no cause that prohibits filing a lawsuit. If there is an agreement between the parties not to file a lawsuit, a legitimate interest to sue is absent.
(c) There must be no legal obstacle to filing of a lawsuit. If there are other statutory procedures in place to resolve a specific type of dispute, a lawsuit ignoring or bypassing these procedures lacks a legitimate interest to sue.
(d) The remedy requested by the plaintiff should be the best fix to resolve the dispute. If the prayer for relief asserted in the complaint is granted, the dispute should be resolved conclusively. For example, where the defendant refuses to surrender a commercial space contending that he/she has the right of retention, the plaintiff does not have a legitimate interest in an action seeking a declaratory judgment confirming the nonexistence of the right of retention. Rather, an action seeking surrender of the commercial space is more appropriate in resolving the dispute.[118]
(e) A claim must not contradict the principle of good faith. For more discussion on this principle, refer to "§3. Litigation against Principle of Good Faith" in this chapter.

D. Special Prerequisites for a Lawsuit

1. Joinder of Action

535. A plaintiff may assert two or more claims against the same defendant in a lawsuit, even though they are based on different causes if the same court has jurisdiction over both claims and they may be dealt with in the same proceedings. Adding claims in an action is referred to as objective joinder. It includes joinder of independent claims, joinder of alternative claims, and joinder of primary and contingent claims. For a lawsuit to be lawful, prerequisites of each type of joinder must be met.

536. There may be multiple plaintiffs or defendants in one lawsuit, which is called subjective joinder of action or co-litigation. There are four types of co-litigations: joinder of independent parties, necessary joinder of parties, joinder of parties in the alternative, and joinder of primary and contingent parties. Each type of co-litigation requires a certain relationship between co-litigants. Co-litigation which lacks such a relationship is unlawful.

537. A counterclaim is an action filed by the defendant against the plaintiff in the same lawsuit. For a counterclaim to be lawful, it must be related to the claim set forth in the complaint or the reply, and must be filed by the time the hearing for oral argument is closed without substantially delaying the court proceedings (§269(1) CPA).

---

118. Supreme Court Decision 2010Da84932 decided on April 10, 2014.

2. Class Action

538. Class actions were first adopted in 2004 when the Securities-related Class Action Act was promulgated in order to efficiently provide remedies for collective losses arising in the course of trading securities. In 2008, consumer class actions were introduced, which allows consumer organizations to bring claims on behalf of consumers. In 2011, class actions related to personal information were allowed. Under the Personal Information Protection Act, consumer organizations and other nonprofit organizations have standing to sue to prevent or suspend infringement on the rights of data subjects by the information controller. Class action statutes regulate standing to sue and other procedural requirements, and they prohibit *pro se* legal representation for such lawsuits.

3. Statutory Period for Filing a Lawsuit

539. For some cases prescribed in statutes, filing a lawsuit within the statutory period is a procedural prerequisite. For example, a lawsuit seeking rescission of a fraudulent act must be brought within one year from the time the creditor became aware of the fraudulent act and within five years from the time the debtor engaged in such an act (§406(2) CA). A lawsuit based on the right to claim recovery of an inheritance must be filed within three years from the date the plaintiff becomes aware that the inheritance right has been infringed and within ten years from the time the inheritance commenced (§999(1) CA). A lawsuit filed after the lapse of the statutory period is unlawful.

E. Positive and Negative Prerequisites

540. Positive prerequisites are requirements that must exist for a lawsuit to be lawful. Examples include matters such as jurisdiction, capacity to be a party, litigation capacity, and standing. Negative prerequisites are ones whose existence makes a lawsuit unlawful. Duplicative lawsuits, repetitive lawsuits, an agreement between parties not to file a lawsuit and an arbitration clause belong to this category.

541. In principle, the court must examine, *sua sponte,* procedural prerequisites before ruling on the merits. However, there are also prerequisites that the court examines only when the defendant raises a procedural defense. Without a defendant's challenge, defects in such prerequisites do not have any procedural effect. A venue selection clause and an arbitration clause are the examples of prerequisites that must be affirmatively asserted (§29 CPA, §9(1) AA).

III. Examination of Prerequisites for a Lawsuit

542. The court examines facts *sua sponte* with respect to procedural prerequisites. Even though the defendant asserts a deficiency in the prerequisites in a pleading, it is nothing more than a reminder to the court to take notice of the procedural issue. However, in practice, the court rules on the defendant's procedural defenses by means of interlocutory judgments (§201 CPA) or explains the legitimacy of the lawsuit denying the defense in a judgment on the merits.

543. With respect to procedures in examining evidence to prove procedural prerequisites or defects, some commentators suggest, the rules of evidence must be strictly followed.[119] However, the majority opinion supports the view that the court may examine such evidence in ways deemed necessary and appropriate.[120]

544. Legitimacy of a lawsuit is determined as of the time when the hearing for the case is closed. Therefore, an unlawful suit at the time of filing a complaint becomes lawful provided the procedural insufficiency is cured by the close of the hearing. In some cases, a lawsuit satisfying all the procedural prerequisites can become unlawful later if procedural deficiencies take place while the lawsuit is pending. For example, if a house on land owned by the plaintiff is burned down while a lawsuit seeking its demolition is pending, the plaintiff no longer has a legitimate interest to sue and the suit becomes unlawful. This is also true, if, while a lawsuit seeking repayment of a loan is pending, the plaintiff's creditor (judgment creditor) seizes the claim against the defendant and obtains court order authorizing the judgment creditor for debt collection, the plaintiff loses standing in the lawsuit.

545. When the court finds that there is a procedural deficiency which is curable, the presiding judge orders the plaintiff to correct it. If the plaintiff fails to correct the error or the defect is uncorrectable, the court dismisses the case without prejudice. Lack of international jurisdiction is deemed uncorrectable. However, the court transfers the case to a competent court when it does not have domestic jurisdiction.

§3. Litigation Against Principle of Good Faith

I. Definition and Meaning

546. Section 1 Subsection 2 of the Civil Procedure Act stipulates that the parties and participants in a lawsuit shall perform the litigation in good faith. The principle of good faith was adopted in the Act with the amendment in 1990. Although some scholars were skeptical of this legislative measure because the term "good faith" is inconsistent with the adversarial nature of litigation and such an indefinite legal concept should not be employed in procedural law. However, since long before 1990,

119. Dong-yoon Chung et al., *supra* n. 7, at 395.
120. Si-yoon Lee, *supra* n. 8, at 210.

courts held that if a lawsuit is filed in bad faith or constitutes an abuse of rights, the litigation lacks a legitimate interest and is unlawful.

II. Types of Violation of Principle of Good Faith

A. Unjust Formation of Legal Relationships

547. A party might form legal relationships for a hidden purpose in bad faith, which are advantageous to him/her but is disadvantageous to the other parties, and later exploit these legal relationships in a lawsuit.

548. For example, just after a creditor's financial situation deteriorated to the point of default and the price of the financial instruments issued by him/her sharply dropped, the debtor bought up the promissory notes issued by the creditor *en masse* at less than 40% of the face value. Then, the debtor claimed a setoff based on these deflated promissory notes. Thereafter, the debtor filed a lawsuit seeking declaratory judgment affirming nonexistence of the prior debt to the creditor. The court held that the plaintiff did not have a legitimate interest to sue and the lawsuit was unlawful.[121]

B. Litigation Inconsistent with Prior Acts (Promissory Estoppel in Litigation)

549. Parties engaged in a legal relationship must exercise rights derived from that relationship equitably, in good faith and with due regard for the other party's interests. In order for a party to deny the exercise of a right for violation of the good faith principle, there must be circumstances that show that the party caused the other party to put trust in him/her or the other party is justified in having such faith from an objective perspective, and the exercise of such right against the other party's faith should rise to the level which is intolerable in light of the principles of fairness and justice.[122]

550. For example, the plaintiff contributed his land to the defendant-company as an in-kind investment. The plaintiff completed the ownership transfer registration but the investment-in-kind was not entered in the articles of incorporation. The plaintiff participated in the management of the company for fifteen years. However, as disputes arose between the plaintiff and a co-founder, the plaintiff filed a lawsuit asking for the cancellation of the ownership transfer registration on the grounds that his investment-in-kind was not in the articles of incorporation and therefore invalid. In this case, the Supreme Court held that there was not a legitimate interest in filing the lawsuit and it violated the principle of good faith.[123]

---

121. Supreme Court Decision 2002Da59481 decided on April 11, 2003.
122. Supreme Court Decision 2009Da68941 decided on February 10, 2011.
123. Supreme Court Decision 2013Da88829 decided on March 20, 2015.

C. Lapse of the Right to File a Lawsuit

551. If a party to a legal relationship neglects to exercise a right for a long time and acts as if he/she would not file a lawsuit against the other party, and the latter has a justifiable expectation that the right holder will not exercise that right by way of a lawsuit; then a lawsuit filed by the right holder is unlawful.

552. For example, a person sustained a loss due to a tortious act committed by a civil servant and the victim sued the State. In the lawsuit, the State raised an affirmative defense based on the statute of limitations. This was denied on the ground that the defendant's defense constituted abuse of right because the State obstructed the plaintiff from filing a lawsuit for damages. The state lost the case and paid the judgment. Thereafter, the State sued the civil servant to recover the judgment amount it paid based on the right of indemnity. The Supreme Court held that the State's lawsuit should be dismissed without prejudice. The Court opined that the State's suit violated a principle of good faith absent evidence that the defendant-civil servant played an active role in making the State's defense inadmissible as an abuse of right in the previous lawsuit.[124] It is interpreted that the civil servant's expectation that the statute of limitations expired for the victim's claim for damages was justifiable.

D. Abuse of Right to File a Lawsuit

553. It is an abuse of the right to file a lawsuit based on a statutory right to achieve a goal, which runs counter to the legislative intent. According to case law, where it is apparent that a patent will be invalidated due to lack of nonobviousness even prior to a judgment, filing a lawsuit for an injunction against infringement or damages based on the patent can constitute an abuse of right. This is true even though a previous lawsuit seeking to invalidate the patent has not yet been decided.[125]

554. In another case, a shareholder transferred shares in payment of a debt, but delayed delivery of the stock certificates falsely claiming to the transferee that they were not yet issued. The transferee and other shareholders held a temporary meeting of shareholders and elected board members and an auditor. Later, the transferor-plaintiff filed a lawsuit against the company-defendant seeking affirmation of nonexistence of the resolution at the meeting of shareholders on the ground that the transferee was not a shareholder as required in the Commercial Act. The Supreme Court held that the plaintiff's claim based on that defect violated a principle of good faith because it was caused by the plaintiff's nonperformance of an obligation.[126]

124. Supreme Court Decision 2015Da217848 decided on June 10, 2016.
125. Supreme Court Decision (*en banc*) 2010Da95390 decided on January 19, 2012.
126. Supreme Court Decision 90DaKa1158 decided on December 13, 1991.

III. Effects

555. If a plaintiff's claim violates the principle of good faith or constitutes an abuse of right, he/she does not have a legitimate interest to sue and the court dismisses it by judgment without prejudice as unlawful. When a defendant's affirmative defense does the same, the court does not consider such a defense.

556. The court may determine whether a party's claim or affirmative defense is contrary to this principle on its own authority, even if a party does not raise it.[127] This is because a legitimate interest in filing a lawsuit or raising a defense is a procedural prerequisite.

127. Supreme Court Decision 88DaKa17181 decided on September 29, 1989.

Chapter 2. Claims and Defenses

§1. Subject-Matter of a Lawsuit

I. Functions

557. The concept of subject-matter serves important functions from commencement of the proceedings until the final resolution of a case. In the commencement phase, the subject-matter is one of the factors in determining the court's jurisdiction and proper venue. The scope of adjudication by the court is confined to the subject-matter specified in the plaintiff's pleadings. The interruption of the limitation period by filing a lawsuit or the statutory period to sue has a bearing only on the subject-matter asserted in the complaint. In the course of litigation, joinder of claims, modification of a claim, and duplicative lawsuits are defined with regard to the subject-matter of the pending lawsuit. In the conclusion phase, prohibition of repetitive lawsuits after withdrawal of a suit or the preclusive effect of a judgment is relevant only to the subject-matter of the previous lawsuit.

II. Criteria for Determining the Scope of the Subject-Matter

558. Two theories on the criteria to separate one subject-matter from another are the substantive law approach and the procedural law approach.

559. The substantive law theory distinguishes subject-matter by the legal right or legal relationship established by substantive law. Application of a different statutory provision gives rise to a different legal right which is a separate subject-matter.[128]

560. Procedural law theory suggests that subject-matter should be determined by procedural law, excluding substantive law.[129] This approach is based on the grounds that a plaintiff asserts a claim for relief and facts, and the court applies substantive law to the established facts. However, subject-matter must be fixed in a pleading before the application of law and this is the job of the court. The procedural law theory further holds that the prayer for relief determines subject-matter and subject-matter is considered in very broad terms. A third tenet suggests that subject-matter is decided by the prayer for relief plus the facts alleged by the plaintiff.[130]

561. Case law is in line with the substantive law approach. For example, where cargo was damaged due to the negligence of seamen employed by a shipping company, a claim against the shipping company for damages in tort and a claim for a

128. Hong-yup Kim, *Civil Procedure* 287 (Parkyoungsa 5thed. 2014).
129. Si-yoon Lee, *supra* n. 8, at 249.
130. Dong-yoon Chung et al., *supra* n. 7, at 274.

money damage award based on breach of the transportation contract are two separate subject-matters. And in this case, if the plaintiff joins both claims in one lawsuit, it must be joinder of alternative claims.[131]

562. Also, the Supreme Court opines that each of the following claims are two separate subject-matters: a claim for surrender of a building based on ownership and a claim for surrender based on possessory rights;[132] a claim for ownership transfer registration based on an agreement of substitute performance and the same claim based on completion of acquisitive prescription;[133] claims of retrial based on each cause prescribed in Section 451 of the Civil Procedure Act;[134] and a claim of unjust enrichment against a person who has possessed land owned by the plaintiff without legal cause and a claim for damages in tort based on the illegal occupation of land.[135]

563. In a lawsuit seeking payment of damages in tort for personal injury or wrongful death, claims for actual damages, damages for loss of working capacity and damages for pain and suffering are separate subject-matters. Therefore, when a party appeals a judgment awarding damages, the rule prohibiting disadvantageous modification to the appellant applies to each category of damages.[136] In a lawsuit asking for loan repayment, principal and interests or damages for delayed repayment are all separate subject-matters.[137]

564. On the other hand, according to case law, in a lawsuit pursuing cancellation of ownership transfer registration based on the allegation that the registration is void and the plaintiff is the owner of the registered property, the subject-matter is the claim for cancellation of a void registration based on ownership. The reasons why the registration is void, such as cancellation of expression of intent or the revocation of the underlying contract for nonperformance, are just the facts of the case.[138] Under the substantive law theory, in an action seeking return of unjust enrichment, the claim itself is the subject-matter and each cause for it is also merely a factual assertion.

III. Joinder of Claims (Objective Joinder of Actions)

A. Definition and Meaning

565. Joinder of claims refers to consolidating more than one subject-matter between the same parties in a single lawsuit. It may occur at the commencement of

131. Supreme Court Decision (*en banc*) 82DaKa1533 decided on March 22, 1983.
132. Supreme Court Decision 94Da53006 decided on June 14, 1996.
133. Supreme Court Decision 88DaKa19002,19019 decided on January 15, 1991.
134. Supreme Court Decision 69Da1888 decided on January 27, 1970.
135. Supreme Court Decision 2013Da45457 decided on September 13, 2013.
136. *Supra* n. 29.
137. Supreme Court Decision 2009Da12399 decided on June 11, 2009.
138. Supreme Court Decision 97Da54024 decided on September 17, 1999.

the proceedings or during the pendency of a lawsuit by joining additional claims. A lawsuit having one subject-matter with numerous causes of action is not a joinder of claims.

B. Types of Joinder

1. Joinder of Independent Claims

566. Joinder of claims includes consolidation of independent claims, alternative claims, and primary and contingent claims. The plaintiff may join all independent claims against the defendant even though they are unrelated. The claimant may join claims or file separate lawsuits based on each claim as he/she desires. In a personal injury lawsuit, actual damages, damages for loss of working capacity and damages for pain and suffering are independent claims that are joined. Thus, the plaintiff may file separate lawsuits seeking each of them.

2. Joinder of Alternative Claims

567. In joinder of alternative claims, when a claim is satisfied, the other claims are extinguished. Considering the nature of the relationship between alternate claims, the court grants only one claim and does not adjudicate other claims when at least one claim is established. However, when the court renders a judgment dismissing the case, it should adjudicate all the claims and dismiss each of them.

568. Examples of this type of joinder includes consolidating a claim for damages in tort and a claim for money damage award based on breach of contract arising from the same instance.[139] Also, where a promissory note was issued for payment of the purchase price for an item, a claim for payment of the purchase price and claim for payment of the debt on the promissory note may be alternatively joined.[140]

3. Joinder of Primary and Contingent Claims

569. In the joinder of contingent claims, the plaintiff asserts multiple claims which are incompatible and designates the order of claims to be adjudicated. The court should consider the primary claim first. When the court renders a judgment favoring the plaintiff on the primary claim, it does not adjudicate the contingent

139. Supreme Court Decision 2004Da44506 decided on September 28, 2006.
140. Supreme Court Decision 98Da2051 decided on June 26, 1998.

claim. However, when the court dismisses the primary claim, it adjudicates the contingent claim and renders judgment granting or dismissing that claim. Since both claims derive from identical legal relationships, the dispute can be completely resolved.

570. For example, a claimant sued for delivery of an item as a purchaser when the seller refused delivery alleging that the contract for sale was revoked. If the contract for sale is not valid, the claim would be to recover the purchase price paid. Therefore, the claimant's lawsuit consolidates the primary claim for delivery of the item and a contingent claim seeking return of the purchase price if the contract for sale is not valid. Here, the two inconsistent claims are joined. The court could render three different judgments: granting the primary claim with the contingent claim remaining unadjudicated, dismissing the primary claim and granting the contingent claim, and dismissing both the claims.

C. Alteration of Action

1. Definition and Meaning

571. Alteration of action refers to changes to the subject-matter of a lawsuit in the course of litigation by quantitatively or qualitatively expanding or superseding a claim originally specified by the plaintiff. Substituting between actions seeking judgment for performance and actions for declaratory judgment based on an identical claim is included here. While keeping the prayer for relief unchanged, the original claim may be replaced by new one insofar as the latter is based on the same general set of facts as the original claim. For instance, during the pendency of a lawsuit seeking payment for damages in tort, the plaintiff may join a claim in the alternative for money damages based on a breach of contract arising from the same incident or replace the former with the latter.

2. Replacement and Supplement

572. Alteration of action includes replacement and supplementing of claims. In the replacement of claims, the new claim supersedes the original claim asserted in the complaint. It is legally interpreted as a combination of withdrawal of the existing claim and filing a lawsuit for a new claim. An alteration by supplement of claims is to join a new claim with the existing claims or to expand the latter. After supplementing claims, the lawsuit takes the form of joinder of claims, including joinder of independent, alternative and contingent claims.

3. Prerequisites

573. The original claim and new claim must be based on the same general set of facts. An alteration must be made by the time the trial is closed. In addition, the trial schedule must not be seriously delayed by an alteration (§262(1) CPA). Because the court of second instance is a trial court, alteration of action is allowed in such a court as well.

574. In the replacement of claims, as mentioned above, the existing claim is deemed to have been withdrawn. For this reason, there was a debate whether consent of the defendant is required in this type of alteration if it occurs after the defendant files an answer or makes an oral statement on the merits. The Supreme Court has held that consent of the defendant is not a prerequisite because alteration of an action is based on the same factual grounds and so infringement on the defendant's right of defense is not likely to take place.[141]

D. Counterclaim

1. Definition and Meaning

575. The defendant may set forth his/her claims against the plaintiff by way of a counterclaim as part of his/her defense in the same proceedings. The plaintiff in the principal lawsuit becomes the defendant in the counterclaim. The counterclaim must be related to the claim that is the subject-matter of the principal action or to the allegations and evidence for the defense (§269(1) CPA). It serves procedural economy and both parties' individual interests since all the claims based on the same general set of facts are to be resolved in one lawsuit. This is why alteration of an action or counterclaims are provided for in the Civil Procedure Act.

2. Simple and Contingent Counterclaims

576. A simple counterclaim is independent from the disposition of the principal action. If the principal lawsuit is withdrawn, a simple counterclaim remains an independent lawsuit. A contingent counterclaim is brought on condition that the plaintiff's claim is granted or dismissed in the pending principal lawsuit. For example, where the plaintiff claims for registration of ownership transfer based on a contract for sale of a house in the principal lawsuit, the defendant may dispute validity of the contract and file a counterclaim asking for payment of the purchase price if the court grants the plaintiff's claim. In this case, if the court renders judgment dismissing plaintiff's claim, it leaves the counterclaim unadjudicated.

3. Prerequisites

577. A counterclaim must be related to the claim or defense asserted in the principal lawsuit (§269(1) CPA). The claims of the principal lawsuit and counterclaims

141. Supreme Court Decision 2017Da21411 decided on May 30, 2018.

are required to have factual and legal grounds in common or counterclaims must be based on the allegations in the defense. A counterclaim should be brought by the time the hearing for the principal case is closed and must not result in a substantial delay of the trial schedule.

578. Since a court of second instance is a trial court, a counterclaim may be filed while the principal lawsuit is on appeal. Provided, however, the opposing party stipulates to lodging the counterclaim or it is deemed not prejudicial to his/her right to appeal (§412(1) CPA).

§2. Joinder of Parties

I. Definition and Meaning

579. Multiple plaintiffs or defendants may be joined in a lawsuit. This serves the goal of procedural economy and prevents inconsistency and contradictions among different court decisions if disputes among the multiple parties arising from common legal relationships or facts are resolved in one lawsuit.

580. Multiple parties may be joined in a complaint or later by participations during the pendency of a lawsuit. Parties can be joined by a simple joinder, necessary joinder, joinder of parties in the alternative and joinder of primary and contingent parties.

II. Simple Joinder of Parties

581. The parties who join, or are joined, may sue or be sued separately. They may conduct litigation jointly or severally for the convenience of themselves or the opposing party. Parties may join or be joined in one action if: (a) claims or obligations that form the subject-matters of the lawsuit are common to the parties, (b) such claims or obligations are based on the same factual or legal cause, or (c) similar claims or obligations form the subject-matters in dispute and such claims are based on an essentially similar factual and legal cause (§65 CPA).

582. For example, a creditor-plaintiff may join the principal and surety, or joint and several obligors as co-defendants (type (a)). An injured party may file a lawsuit seeking payment of damages against multiple tortfeasors (type (b)). A landlord may sue multiple tenants in his/her building for the unpaid rents in a lawsuit (type (c)).

583. In principle, joined parties may conduct litigation independently without intervening or influencing other co-parties (§66 CPA). Thus, admission of material facts by a co-party does not have any binding effect on the other co-parties. It is the same regarding the interruption or suspension of the litigation process, the nonappearance at a hearing, the lapse of a statutory period, or filing an appeal.

584. However, evidence submitted by one of the co-parties serves as evidence for other co-parties as well. This principle promotes procedural economy, which is the reason for allowing simple joinder of parties in the first place.

III. Necessary Joinder of Parties

585. When the claims and obligations in disputes among parties are so closely interconnected that each controversy cannot be separately resolved without prejudice to the material interest of other parties, joinder of all the parties is required so that all claims and liabilities can be determined comprehensively in one lawsuit (§67(1) CPA). Conduct of the litigation or the court decisions on the case should be unified among the co-parties. In this context, procedural acts by one party against one of the opposing co-parties has the same effect as to all of the opposing co-parties. By the same token, any procedural acts by one of the co-parties is effective only when it is in the interest of all the co-parties (§67(2) CPA).

586. A withdrawal of an action, settlement, waiver of a claim or acknowledgement of a claim by some of the co-parties does not take effect. On the other hand, if litigation procedures are interrupted or suspended for one of the co-parties, such interruption or suspension takes effect for all the co-parties (§67(3) CPA).

587. Necessary joinder involves joinder of indispensable parties and quasi-necessary parties. Indispensable parties are those whose interests in the subject-matter is so unavoidably involved that the court cannot adjudicate the case in their absence. For example, in a lawsuit concerning claims arising from partnership properties, all the partners must be joined. Provided, however, each partner may file a lawsuit to preserve a specific partnership property against anyone who infringes on the right to that property.[142]

588. If such parties are absent in the complaint, they may be joined by the time the hearing is closed in the first instance court (§68(1) CPA). If not, the lawsuit is dismissed as unlawful.

589. Quasi-necessary joinder involves parties who ought to join or ought to be joined because the judgment in a lawsuit will have binding effect on them. Joinder of all the parties has nothing to do with procedural prerequisites. The court may proceed without quasi-necessary parties but they may not file a different lawsuit for the same subject-matter. Once quasi-necessary parties are joined in a lawsuit, the statutory provisions applicable to indispensable parties apply to them with some exceptions.

590. For example, multiple shareholders as co-plaintiffs may file a lawsuit seeking revocation of a resolution at a shareholders' meeting. Some of the shareholders

142. Supreme Court Decision 96Da16896 decided on September 9, 1997.

may withdraw their claims but the proceedings by the remaining plaintiffs go forward without being affected by the withdrawal. It is true where multiple creditors sue a third-party debtor to exercise the rights belonging to the debtor in order to preserve their own claims against the debtor.

IV. Joinder of Parties in the Alternative and Joinder of Primary and Contingent Parties

591. When claims by or against multiple parties are incompatible or invalid when considered separately, the parties may be joined as co-parties in the alternative or as primary and contingent parties (§70(1) CPA). For example, a claimant may sue the agent and principal as co-defendants asking for performance of a contractual obligation and assert that the agent is obliged to perform the contract as an unauthorized agent (§135(1) CA), or if he/she had the authority to enter into the contract, the principal is liable for the performance. Here, the claimant may join the agent and principal in the alternative or as primary and contingent parties.

592. When the court renders a judgment granting a claim, it must dismiss the claims against the other co-parties (§70(2) CPA). The provisions of the Civil Procedure Act pertaining to necessary joinder apply to this type of joinder, with the exception of the waiver or acknowledgment of a claim, settlement and withdrawal of the lawsuit (§70(1) CPA).

§3. Pleadings

593. In a lawsuit, each party takes responsibility to assert material facts that he/she bears the burden of pleading. Material facts are facts giving rise to, impeding rise of, extinguishing, and impeding the exercise of legal rights. A plaintiff and defendant allege material facts advantageous to them and state their response to the facts alleged by the opposing party. The order of such pleadings is as follows.

I. Plaintiff's Pleading (Complaint)

594. A complaint is the first pleading which sets forth the prayer for relief and a set of facts constituting one or more causes of action. The plaintiff must assert the facts that fit the legal elements of a claim which are defined in the substantive law and which give rise to a right to relief. For example, the plaintiff claiming payment of the purchase price should state in the complaint that he/she entered into a sales contract with the defendant, specifying the date of the contract, the item that was sold and the contract price. In a claim for the repayment of a loan, a plaintiff must assert the facts of the loan agreement detailing the lender, borrower, date of the contract and the amount of money that the defendant-borrower received in the loan. The cause of action asserted in the complaint need not be sufficient to fit every element of a claim because the plaintiff may correct, supplement or amend pleadings later.

II. Defendant's Pleading (Answer)

595. The defendant may raise procedural defenses challenging the legitimacy of the legal proceeding. In general, procedural prerequisites of a lawsuit are matters to be examined, *sua sponte*, by the court but some procedural defects such as the presence of an arbitration clause are considered only on the motion of a party.

596. The defendant must answer the plaintiff's material allegations with a denial, admission, nonresponse or affirmative defense. If the defendant denies the material allegations of facts, the plaintiff must prove them or the court will dismiss the action on the merits. If the defendant admits the material facts alleged by the plaintiff, and does not lodge a successful affirmative defense, the court renders the judgment favoring the plaintiff. Any material allegation not expressly denied by the defendant is deemed to be admitted (§150(1) CPA).

597. The defendant may, in addition to or in lieu of a denial, plead affirmative defenses by stating facts impeding the rise of, or extinguishing or impeding the exercise of the right which is the basis of the plaintiff's claims. A sham transaction and illegality are examples of material facts that impede the rise of legal rights. Payment, the running of the statute of limitations, and a declaration of intent by deceit or unlawful duress and a declaration of avoidance are facts that extinguish legal rights. The defense of simultaneous performance of a bilateral contract, the right of retention and the exception of prematurity are facts that hinder the exercise of a legal right. If the defendant's affirmative defense is upheld, the case is usually dismissed on the merits. However, if the defense of simultaneous performance or right of retention is well-founded, the court renders judgment ordering the defendant to perform his/her obligation in exchange for the opposing party's counter-performance.

III. Repleadings

598. To the defendant's affirmative defense, the plaintiff may respond with a denial, admission, nonresponse or affirmative defense. Where the defendant raises an affirmative defense, the plaintiff may replead an affirmative defense. For example, if a defendant pleads the running of the statute of limitations, the plaintiff may replead the interruption of the statutory limitation period based on the defendant's act of acknowledgment of the claim. In some cases, the defendant may file a subsequent pleading to the plaintiff's affirmative defense.

599. Once pleadings and repleadings are exhausted, the court examines the material allegations and supporting evidence presented in the trial stage by stage and decides the case in the final stage where a pleading of either party is affirmed. As a result, the party who filed the last pleading upheld by the court wins the case partially or wholly.

Chapter 3. Sanctions on Procedural Irregularities

§1. Judicial Stamp and Service of Complaint

600. If the precise amount of judicial stamp is not attached to the complaint, the presiding judge issues an order to correct the defect. If the plaintiff fails to comply with the order, the presiding judge dismisses the complaint without prejudice *sua sponte* by an order (§§254(1),(2) CPA).

601. The court clerk serves a copy of complaint on a defendant. If it is not possible to serve the complaint, the presiding judge dismisses the complaint without prejudice (§255 CPA).

§2. Time Limits

I. Date and Period

A. Date

602. "Date" denotes the designated time for procedural events. Examples include the date for oral argument, the date for trial preparation, the date for the examination of evidence and the date for rendition of a judgment. Dates are designated by the presiding judge. The delegated member of a three-judge panel or a commissioned judge sets the dates for tasks assigned to him/her (§165(1) CPA). The court must notify the parties and relevant persons of the dates (§167 CPA).

603. At the designated time and location, the procedural events commence by calling out the case and names of the parties (§169 CPA). Dates may be changed only in compelling circumstances (r.41 RCP). However, the first date for an oral hearing or for the preparatory proceedings may be changed without cause if agreed by the parties (§165(2) CPA).

B. Period

604. The Civil Procedure Act sets forth certain periods for various procedural acts to maintain a stable litigation schedule and to protect the procedural rights of the parties. There are two types of periods: statutory periods and periods specified by the court or the presiding judge.

605. Statutory periods include the following: a period for completion of procedural acts where the party, for good reason, could not complete an act (§173(1) CPA), a period for service by publication to become effective (§196 CPA), a period for an objection to a decision setting the terms of settlement for resolving the pending case (§226 CPA), a period for submission of an answer (§256(1) CPA), a period for filing an appeal (§§396,425 CPA), a period for submission of a statement of reasons for a final appeal (§427 CPA), and a period for filing a complaint for retrial (§456(1) CPA). Periods specified by the court or the presiding judge include a period for correction of defects in capacity to be a party (§59 CPA) and a period for submission of allegations and evidence (§147 CPA).

606. The Civil Procedure Act designates some periods as fixed. The rest are extendable. The former is a period expressly stated as such in statutes. Examples of a fixed period are: the time frame for an objection to a decision setting forth the terms of settlement for resolving the pending case; the time frame for filing an appeal; the time frame for filing a complaint for retrial. The latter is a time limit for the submission of a statement of reasons for a final appeal. The court may extend or shorten an extendable period but it may not do so for a fixed period (§172(1) CPA). However, for a fixed period, the court may provide additional time for a person whose residence is far away from the court (§172(2) CPA).

607. Where a party was unable to observe a fixed period due to any cause beyond their control, they may complete the task within two weeks after the cause for the delay ceases to exist. Provided, however, for a party who is in a foreign country, the period for completion of a procedural act is thirty days (§173(1) CPA).

II. Nonobservance of a Date or Period

A. *Judgment Without Hearing*

608. A defendant should submit an answer within thirty days from the date a copy of the complaint was served (§256(1) CPA). Where the defendant fails to do so after receiving the complaint by means other than service by publication, the court may deem the defendant to have admitted the material allegations of facts in the complaint and render a judgment without holding a hearing (§257(1) CPA). However, if the defendant files an answer disputing the facts stated in the complaint prior to a judgment without a trial, the court must proceed with an ordinary trial (§257(1) CPA).

B. *Constructive Withdrawal of Lawsuit*

609. If both parties fail to appear on the date for oral argument on two occasions and neither of them files a petition for designation of a new hearing date within one month, the lawsuit is deemed to have been withdrawn (§268(2) CPA). The lawsuit faces the same fate when parties fail to appear once again after a petition for designation of a new date (§268(3) CPA). This rule also applies to the pretrial hearing

(§286 CPA). If both parties fail to make oral statements at a pretrial hearing or hearing for oral argument, they are deemed absent.[143] The failures to make an appearance need not be consecutive.

610. The two nonappearances by both parties in the same kind of proceedings are required to deem a lawsuit withdrawn. Therefore, a nonappearance on the date for trial preparation and another on the date for oral argument do not meet the number of failures required for the constructive withdrawal of a lawsuit.[144]

C. Dismissal of Belated Allegations and Evidence

611. The court may dismiss any untimely allegations and evidence on its own motion or on motion of a party, if admitting them would delay processing of the legal dispute and further provided that the untimely submission is intentional or due to gross negligence (§149(1) CPA).

612. Allegations and evidence that have not been submitted until the close of the pretrial hearing may be submitted later only when they meet the following requirements: the trial schedule is not substantially delayed by their submission, the untimely submission is not the result of any grave negligence, or they are matters to be examined *sua sponte* by the court (§285(1) CPA). Otherwise, the belated submission of allegations and evidence are dismissed by a court decision. The presiding judge may set the period to submit allegations and evidence regarding specified matters (§147(1) CPA). Submissions after the lapse of this period are not permitted.

D. Burden of Litigation Cost for Delayed Proceedings

613. If a lawsuit has been delayed due to a party's failure to submit allegations or evidence in a timely manner, nonobservance of the litigation schedule or any other causes attributable to the party, the court may impose all or part of the litigation costs incurred from the delay on the offending party even where he/she wins the case (§100 CPA).

E. Court Order for a Party to Be Represented by an Attorney

614. The court may prohibit a party or an agent from making statements before the court when they are unable to present material allegations of facts clearly (§144(1) CPA). In this case, the court may order that the party be represented by an attorney (§144(2) CPA) and designate another trial date. If the party fails to obtain an attorney by the next trial date, the court may dismiss the case without prejudice (§144(4) CPA).

---

143. Supreme Court Decision 2001Da60491 decided on July 26, 2002.
144. Supreme Court Decision 2004Da69581 decided on October 27, 2006.

Part IV. Proceedings

Chapter 1. Proceedings in First Instance

§1. Adversary Proceedings

I. Introduction of the Claim

A. Instituting an Action

1. Form of the Complaint

615. In a complaint, the parties, the statutory agent, the prayer for relief and the cause of action must be stated (§249(1) CPA). A party who lacks litigation capacity must be represented by a statutory agent. Parents are the statutory agents of a minor (§909 CA). Where there is no parent or parents, or they are unable to exercise parental authority, the guardian of the minor is the statutory agent (§928 CA). An adult ward is represented by an adult guardian (§929 CA), and a limited ward is represented by a limited guardian (§959-2 CA).

616. A legal person or an organization without legal personality must specify its representative. When an attorney files a lawsuit on behalf of a plaintiff, the attorney must be set forth as well (§274(1) CPA).

617. The prayer for relief is a statement of the remedy that the plaintiff is seeking. If the plaintiff wins the case entirely, the operative provisions of the judgment should be identical to the prayer for relief. In an action for performance, the prayer for relief must show the form and content of the judgment asked for, for example, "Defendant shall pay Plaintiff KRW 100,000,000." In an action seeking a declaratory judgment, the prayer for relief must list a specific legal relationship to be affirmed and declared by the court, such as "This Court declares that Plaintiff has ownership of the building listed in the attachment." In an action for a formative judgment, the prayer for relief must state a legal relationship to be altered and the result of its alteration, such as, "This Court revokes the resolution at the shareholders meeting of Defendant Company on May 1, 2018, regarding the matters listed in the attachment."

618. The complaint must contain a statement of facts supporting the prayer for relief. A majority of jurists suggest that the plaintiff must state facts sufficient to describe the subject-matter in the complaint, but need not assert all facts of a claim completely.[145] It is also desirable that the complaint alleges facts that constitute the cause of action. But the plaintiff is allowed to supplement the facts omitted in the complaint in later pleadings.

619. In theory, the role of the court is to apply the law to facts asserted by the parties. However, the material facts that must be alleged by the parties are inferred from the provisions of substantive law. Therefore, a party has to point out statutory provisions to be applied when they are not readily apparent from the alleged facts.

2. Filing of the Complaint

620. Generally, a lawsuit begins with filing a complaint in a court of first instance (§248 CPA). A plaintiff may file a complaint by submitting a written statement of claim. He/she may also file a lawsuit by uploading a complaint form on the court website according to the "Act on the Use, Etc. of Electronic Documents in Civil Litigations, Etc." of 2010.

621. In small claims cases, a plaintiff may file a complaint orally (§4(1) TSCA). The oral statement is made in the presence of a court clerk who transcribes the statement. This transcript serves as a complaint (§§4((2),(3) TSCA). However, in practice, filing of a lawsuit by an oral statement is seldom used.

3. Receipt and Examination of the Complaint

a. Receipt

622. The formality of a complaint and the amount of judicial stamp are reviewed by the court clerk. When the court clerk finds any defects in the formality of the complaint or insufficient stamp, he/she may advise the plaintiff or the plaintiff's agent to correct the defects but may not refuse to receive the complaint for that reason (r.5(1) RCP).

623. Where a complaint is mailed to the court, there is no way to recommend corrections. In such a case, the court clerk attaches a note on the relevant part of the complaint or other documents concisely describing the defects and forwards the complaint and documents to the judicial panel or single judge in charge of the case.

b. Allocation of Cases

624. The President of a court or the Chief of a branch court assigns tasks to judicial panels and single judges reflecting the recommendations by the Judges' Council of the relevant court and administrative practices (r.4(2) GDTC). When a new

145. Si-yoon Lee, *supra* n. 8, at 265.

case is received, it is assigned to a judicial panel or a single judge according to the case distribution schedule set in advance in the court. Where there is more than one judicial panel or single judge that has responsibility to deal with a certain type of case, it is randomly distributed by a computer program.

c. Presiding Judge's Examination of the Complaint

625. A court clerk associated with the judicial panel or single judge in charge of a case inspects the formality of a complaint and advises the plaintiff to correct any defects or informs the presiding judge. Thereafter, the case record is transmitted to the judicial panel or single judge.

626. The presiding judge who is the chief judge of a panel or a single judge examines the complaint before commencement of proceedings. If a complaint lacks required items such as parties, statutory agents, the prayer for relief and cause of action, or if the precise amount of judicial stamp is not attached, the presiding judge allows the plaintiff a reasonable time to correct the defects. If the plaintiff fails to timely correct the defects, the judge dismisses the complaint *sua sponte*. The presiding judge only reviews the formality of a complaint. Therefore, even though a party specified in the complaint lacks capacity to be a party or has deceased prior to the filing of the lawsuit, the presiding judge may not take any measure for that. In such a case, the court dismisses the case by judgment without prejudice for lack of a procedural prerequisite.[146] Also, insofar as the prayer for relief is stated, which is ambiguous and so the claim cannot be specified, the presiding judge may not dismiss the complaint.[147]

627. The court clerk serves a copy of the complaint on the defendant. If it is not possible to serve the complaint, the presiding judge dismisses the complaint without prejudice (§255 CPA).

628. The presiding judge can examine the causes for dismissal of a complaint until a copy of the complaint is served upon the defendant. A lawsuit is deemed to be pending upon the service of the complaint and is considered an adversarial proceeding. Thereafter, the court, not the presiding judge, dismisses the case by judgment without prejudice if causes for dismissal of a complaint are found.[148]

629. An immediate appeal may be filed against the order of the presiding judge to dismiss a complaint (§254(3) CPA).

---

146. Supreme Court Decision 70Ma103 decided on March 20, 1973.
147. Supreme Court Decision 2004Mu54 decided on November 24, 2004.
148. *Court Practice Summary Civil Procedure (II)* 640 (National Court Administration 2017).

B. Service of the Complaint

1. Service Agency

630. Service of the complaint and other court documents is conducted under the judicial authority of the court and is considered notice to the parties about the contents of a legal document. The complaint and answer or other documents are served as a certified copy. As service is performed by the court, an original document must be submitted to the court with the necessary number of copies to be served. The court clerk files the original in the case record and sends the copies to the parties and relevant persons.

631. The court clerk is in charge of administrative affairs related to service (§175(1) CPA). He/she may entrust service of a specific document to a court clerk or enforcement officer of the District Court that sits in the area where the place of service is located (§175(2) CPA). The presiding judge of the court hearing the case effects service in a foreign country. The presiding judges send the documents to the Korean ambassador, minister or consul stationed in the foreign jurisdiction or the competent government agency of such country (§191 CPA).

632. In Korea, actual service is implemented by a postal employee or enforcement officer (§176 CPA). The court clerk may also effect service by publication, service by placement in the court service box, and service by delivery directly to a person who has appeared before the court. When service has been made, the postal employee or enforcement officer making service must promptly submit a return of service. If service has failed, a return of no service must be reported. A return of service must set forth the date, time, place and manner of service, the identity of the person served and any other facts necessary for the court to determine whether proper service has been accomplished (§193 CPA).

2. The Person to Be Served

633. Service of a document must be made on a person whose name is listed as the addressee. The addressee is usually a party or any other person who is required to be served in the Civil Procedure Act. In some particular circumstances, the party to a case and the addressee are not identical.

634. In the event an individual party to be served lacks litigation capacity, service should be made on his/her statutory agent (§179 CPA). Where an attorney of record is retained by a party to be served, service may be made on the attorney. If there are multiple attorneys, it suffices to effect service upon any one of them (§180 CPA).

635. When a party to a lawsuit is the State, legal documents must be served on the Chief of the District Public Prosecutors' Office in the district where the lawsuit was brought. If there is a High Public Prosecutors' Office, service must be made upon the Chief of the High Public Prosecutors' Office (§9(1) ALSP). However, where a litigation performer is designated or an attorney of record is hired for the State, documents must be served on them (§9(2) ALSP).[149]

636. Service on a person residing in a military barracks or military vessel must be effected on the head of the facility or vessel (§181 CPA). If a person to be served is arrested, detained or imprisoned, service must be made on the chief of the institution where the person is held (§182 CPA).

637. A party or his/her attorney may file a report with the court designating a place of service other than the places prescribed by the relevant statutory provisions and may also designate a recipient of service at that place (§184 CPA). In such a case, the designated recipient is the person to be served.

3. Methods of Service

a. Personal Delivery

(1) Place of service

638. A process server effects service by handing the documents to the legitimate recipient at the place of service. Service should be made at the domicile, residence, any office or usual place of business of the person on whom service is to be made. Service on a statutory agent may be effected at the office or usual place of business of the principal (§183(1) CPA).

639. Provisions applicable to the statutory agent apply to the representative of a legal person or organization without legal personality (§64 CPA). Thus, when an association or foundation is a party, the domicile, residence or any office or usual place of business of its representative, as well as any office or usual place of business of the party, is the place for service.

640. If the places for service specified above are unknown or service cannot not be effected there, service may be made at the workplace where the person to be served is working based on employment, entrustment, or any other legal transaction (§183(2) CPA).

641. As mentioned above, when a party has notified the court of an alternative place of service, service should be made there.

149. The Minister of Justice may designate staff of the Ministry of Justice, public prosecutors of the prosecutors' office at each level or public-service advocates and have them perform the state litigation (§3(1) ALSP).

(2) Substituted service to persons at the place of service

642. When an individual party to be served is unavailable for personal service at the place of service other than his/her workplace, the document may be delivered to his/her employee, any other worker or a person that lives with him/her, provided such person has reasonable discretion concerning the receipt of documents (§186(1) CPA).

643. If the person to be served has been unavailable at the workplace, the document may be delivered to the employer or an employee at the workplace unless they refuse to accept the document (§186(2) CPA).

(3) Substituted service by leaving documents

644. If the person to be served refuses to accept delivery or he/she is unavailable at the place of service, and further provided the employee, any worker or a person that lives with him/her refuses to accept delivery of the document, service may be accomplished by leaving the document at the place of service. This method of service is allowed at the workplace only when the person to be served refuses to accept delivery there (§186(3) CPA).

(4) Service where encountered

645. Where the person to be served does not have a place of service within Korea or such a place is unknown, service may be implemented anywhere the person effecting the service finds him/her (§183(4) CPA). If he/she refuses acceptance of delivery, the server may perform service by leaving the document at that place.

646. On the other hand, service may be effected at any place if the person to be served accepts delivery of the document even when he/she has a place of service within Korea (§183(3) CPA).

b. Service by Mailing

647. In general, service of documents is performed by the postal service in the form of registered mail. If a postal employee hands the court document to the person to be served, it is service by personal delivery because the postal employee is functioning as a service agency of the court, rather than an employee in the postal service.

648. Service by mailing is distinguished from the personal delivery by a postal employee. It is allowed only when other means of actual delivery are exhausted. For service by mailing, the court clerk may send the document to the person to be served by registered mail (§187 CPA, r.51 RCP). The document is deemed served as soon as it is mailed, whether the person to be served receives it or not (§189 CPA). In addition, the court clerk may effect service by mailing when a party to a pending case fails to notify the court of a change of address (§185(2) CPA).

c. Service by Placement in the Service Box

649. For law firms, attorneys or any others that have numerous cases, service boxes are furnished in the courthouse. To have exclusive use of a service box, the applicant must have permission from the President of the court and pay a fee (rr.52(1),(2) RCP). The court clerk effects service by placing documents in the service box (§§188(1),(2) CPA). The document is deemed served three days after placement in the service box (§188(3) CPA).

d. Simplified Service

650. A court clerk may give notice to an attorney of record by phone, fax, e-mail or mobile phone text message in lieu of delivering documents (r.46(1) RCP). Where both parties retain attorneys of record, service is effected when a party's attorney directly delivers to the other party's attorney a copy of the document to be served or sends it by fax or e-mail and submits proof of service to the court (r.47(1) RCP).

651. In electronic litigation, a court clerk posts the electronic documents on an electronic data processing system and electronically notifies the person to be served (§11(3) AUEDC). In such cases, service is deemed made when the person to be served checks the posted electronic document or one week after such notification (§11(4) AUEDC).

e. Service by Publication

652. Service by publication is implemented by placing a notification on the bulletin board for the court or advertising it in an official gazette, official report, newspaper or court website while the court clerk retains the document to be served (§195 CPA, r.54(1) RCP). Service by publication is allowed if the place of service for the person to be served is unknown, or if it is not possible to serve the document abroad or such service is not likely to be successful (CPA § 194).

653. The court clerk may, either upon its own motion or upon the request of a party, make service by publication (§194(1) CPA). The presiding judge of the court hearing the case may issue an order directing service by publication or revoking such measures taken by the court clerk if deemed necessary (§§194(2),(3) CPA).

654. For the first service by publication, the document is deemed served two weeks after the notification is posted. Thereafter, subsequent services by publication on the same person takes effect the next day after the published notice (§196(1) CPA). In the case of service by publication in a foreign country, the time frame for the first service to take effect is two months (§196(2) CPA). For subsequent documents, service is deemed accomplished the next day.

655. Courts have held that the lack of prerequisites for service by publication do not have any adverse effect on the validity of the service. In this case, the party to be served may resort to subsequent completion of procedural acts (CPA §173) or an action for retrial of the case (CPA §451(1)).[150]

f. Service Abroad

656. Service abroad is regulated by the Civil Procedure Act, the Act on International Judicial Mutual Assistance in Civil Matters and the Convention on the Service Abroad of Judicial and Extrajudicial Documents in Civil or Commercial Matters ("Hague Service Convention"). The Hague Service Convention was signed in 1965, and Korea ratified it on January 13, 2000.

657. When the place of service is located in a foreign country, the presiding judge entrusts the document to the Korean diplomatic mission stationed there or the competent government authorities of the country to serve the document (§191 CPA). Court documents from a foreign country are served in Korea only when service of the documents comes through diplomatic channels (§12 AIJMA). The Minister of the National Court Administration receives the documents to be served in Korea as well as a written statement entrusting the service. The National Court Administration then transmits them to the court of first instance in the district where service of the documents should be effected (§13(1) AIJMA).

658. In addition, the Hague Service Convention states that each contracting state should designate or establish a central authority which receives requests for service coming from other contracting states (§2 Hague Service Convention). The authority or judicial officer competent under the law of the state in which the documents originate may request the central authority of the state where the place of service is located to serve the documents (§3 Hague Service Convention).

659. Each contracting state may effect service of judicial documents in foreign countries directly through its diplomatic missions. However, in a state which has declared opposition to such service, such service may be effected only on nationals of the state in which the documents originate (§8 Hague Service Convention). In Korea, the central authority for service is the National Court Administration. Korean courts have refused to recognize a foreign judgment if the foreign court had a consul stationed in Korea directly serve a Korean citizen, residing in Korea, on the ground that service of the documents in such a manner is unlawful and invalid.[151]

150. Supreme Court Decision 2011Da73540 decided on December 22, 2011.
151. Supreme Court Decision 92Da2585 decided on July 14, 1992.

II. Answer

660. The defendant must file an answer to the complaint with the court hearing the case within thirty days from the date of receiving a copy of the complaint (§256(1) CPA). In filing an answer, a copy for service on the plaintiff must also be submitted (§256(3) CPA).

661. The function of the answer is to avoid the plaintiff's claim by denying factual allegations in the complaint or by setting forth affirmative defenses. An answer must respond to the prayer for relief and include specific statements responding to the cause of action.

662. A simple general denial such as "Defendant denies all the allegations in the complaint" is not allowed. The defendant must go through the complaint sentence by sentence, admitting or denying each fact alleged by the plaintiff. In addition to or, in lieu of a denial, the defendant may plead any affirmative defense and the facts supporting the defense. Also, the answer must state the evidence to prove the defendant's allegation or rebutting evidence, as well as a declaration regarding the evidence designated by the plaintiff in the complaint (§274 CPA, r.65(1) RCP).

III. Trial Preparation Proceedings

A. Definition and Meaning

663. Trial preparation proceedings are in place to clarify issues and evidence, so the trial is carried out in an efficient and speedy manner (§279(1) CPA). In the trial preparation proceedings, the presiding judge sorts out contested facts, admitted facts, legal issues and the necessary evidence to be examined to make the trial speedy and fair. The parties should cooperate with such efforts (r.70(1) RCP). Korean civil procedure law does not adopt discovery procedures which are widely used in common law countries for trial preparations.

664. Parties must notify the opposing parties of the material allegations of facts to be made or designation of evidence to be examined at the trial by way of preparatory briefs. The matters not contained in the preparatory briefs may not be asserted in the hearing (§276 CPA). Preparatory briefs must be submitted in such a way that the other party may have sufficient time to investigate and respond to the matters as stated (§273 CPA). Trial preparation proceedings are before the presiding judge or a member of the judicial panel hearing the case (§§280(2),(3) CPA).

665. In order for trial preparation proceedings to be fruitful, the parties have a responsibility to fully investigate the facts and evidence before the trial preparation proceedings (r.69-2 RCP). In the trial preparation proceedings, the parties may discuss procedural matters and the presiding judge may recommend an agreement about these matters (r.70(2) RCP).

B. Referring to Trial Preparation Proceedings

666. Trial preparation proceedings are initiated by the presiding judge's order (§258(1) CPA). Cases having complex issues and evidence are referred to this type of proceeding. The presiding judge issues such an order at his/her discretion after reading the pleadings. The presiding judge may refer a case to trial preparation proceedings even while the oral argument is underway (§279(2) CPA). This might occur where new factual or legal allegations are pleaded at the trial and these allegations are amenable to the trial preparation process.

C. Trial Preparation Proceedings by Preparatory Briefs

667. The presiding judge may direct the parties to submit preparatory briefs and other documents to be exchanged among the parties. The presiding judge may also allow the parties to apply for the examination of evidence within a specified period of time (§280(1) CPA). All the documents submitted to the court should have the necessary copies to be served upon the opposing parties (r.48(1) RCP).

668. Under the direction of the presiding judge, the court clerk may urge the parties in his/her name to submit briefs, applications for examination of evidence and other documents (r.70-3 RCP). The court clerk monitors whether the matters are prepared or arranged on time, and if not, prompts parties to perform tasks as prescribed by the order of the presiding judge (rr.73,30 RCP).

669. As exchange of claims, answers and defenses continue between the parties in complex cases, their allegations may go astray from the core issues. In such a case, the presiding judge may order each party to submit a summarizing brief prior to closing the trial preparation proceedings (§278 CPA).

D. Pretrial Hearing

670. The pretrial hearing is a conference called by the presiding judge or authorized member of a panel in order to clear up any issues and administrative matters prior to the beginning of a trial (§282 CPA). If a pretrial conference is deemed necessary in a case which was referred to trial preparation proceedings, the presiding judge sets the date. A pretrial hearing is held when trial preparation by briefs is insufficient due to the complexity of the case or there are some matters that are best resolved through face to face discussions between the judge and the parties.

671. Just as in a trial, a pretrial hearing begins with the presiding judge's introduction of the case and calling out the parties' names. When a party fails to appear at the hearing, in principle, the judge gives the attending party an opportunity to make statements on the case and closes the trial preparation proceedings (§284(1) CPA). However, the presiding judge may, at his/her discretion, set another date for the pretrial hearing.[152]

672. When both parties fail to appear at the hearing, the presiding judge designates another date and notify both parties (§§286,268(1) CPA). The provisions pertaining to constructive withdrawal of a lawsuit due to failure to appear at hearings apply to the pretrial hearing (§§ 286,268(2),(3) CPA).

673. In the pretrial hearing, a detailed plan for the trial is produced. This plan includes such matters as the approximate number of trial dates, the time frame for completion of the trial, the number of witnesses and methods of examining them, the length of time needed for witness examination, order of presentation of evidence, methods to secure appearance of witnesses, and methods to examine digital media evidence in the courtroom. The pretrial hearing may be held in camera because its function is to set the schedule of the trial, rather than to rule on the case.

674. The presiding judge may decide on the admissibility of each item of evidence (§281(1) CPA) if it serves the goal of an efficient and speedy trial. In exceptional circumstances, the judge may also have witnesses and parties examined at the pretrial hearing (§281(3) CPA).

675. New allegations and evidence submitted after the close of the pretrial hearing will be dismissed except when the trial schedule is not substantially delayed or late submission was not the result of grave negligence, or when they are the matters to be examined *sua sponte* by the court (§285(1) CPA).

E. Limitation, Separation or Consolidation of the Proceedings

676. The court may order limitation, separation or consolidation of the proceedings, or may cancel such an order (§141 CPA). Limitation or separation of the proceedings is aimed at streamlining the procedure to prevent delay in resolving complex cases. Consolidation of the proceedings is allowed when there is relevancy between cases and all or part of the evidence can be used in common. This is considered when related cases are pending before different judicial panels or single judges in the same court.[153]

677. The court may limit the proceedings to a specific matter in order for the parties to focus their allegations or production of evidence on that issue prior to turning to subsequent issues.

678. Separation of the proceedings is a decision to select a claim or parties in a lawsuit which has multiple claims or co-parties and to preside over the proceedings

152. *Supra* n. 57, at 1132.
153. *Supra* n. 148, at 1007.

as independent cases. For example, where some of the co-parties admit material facts and other co-parties deny them, the court may separate the proceedings for those who admit certain facts and render judgments based on such admissions.

F. Designation of Trial Date

679. As management of the litigation schedule is the responsibility of the presiding judge, he/she sets dates for trial considering his/her judicial calendar. Accordingly, a party's motion for designation of a trial date is merely to prompt the judge to do so. However, if both parties fail to appear on the date of the hearing on two occasions, filing a motion for a designation of another trial date within a month is required to keep the case pending (§268(2) CPA). In this case, such a motion has legal effects.

680. After examining the plaintiff's complaint and the defendant's answer, the presiding judge decides whether to refer the case to the trial preparation proceedings. For the cases not referred to trial preparation proceedings, the judge designates a trial date immediately (§258(1) CPA). In cases referred to trial preparation, the trial date is set when trial preparation proceedings are closed (§258(2) CPA).

681. The court is required to make an effort to avoid piecemeal trials and the parties must cooperate with this effort (r.69(2) RCP). A trial is required to be completed in one block of time for a case that has gone through trial preparation proceedings. If it takes a longer time, the trial dates should be designated consecutively without interruption until the hearing is closed. When a piecemeal hearing is unavoidable, the court should make the intervals between trial dates the shortest possible (r.72(1) RCP).

682. If agreed by the parties, a motion for rescheduling the first trial date is granted without cause (§165(2) CPA). However, trial dates other than the first one may be rescheduled only in compelling circumstances (r.41 RCP), and a party seeking the change must show a good reason and submit supporting documents (r.39 RCP).

683. When rescheduling, postponing, or continuing a trial, subsequent trial dates are designated immediately unless the litigation procedure is interrupted or suspended by statutory provisions, or where there are other special circumstances (r.42(1) RCP).

IV. Trial

A. *Summary of Trial Proceedings*

1. Cases Not Having Gone Through Trial Preparation Proceedings

a. The First Trial Date

684. The presiding judge designates a trial date for simple cases without referring them to preparation proceedings. The following is a summary of the proceedings for such a case.[154]

(a) The presiding judge outlines the case as he/she understands it after reading the documents submitted by the parties. Thereafter, the plaintiff states facts supporting the claim in the complaint. Then, based on the answer, the defendant responds to the plaintiff's allegation of facts by admitting or denying each of them. The defendant may also plead an affirmative defense and state supporting facts. Next, both parties submit documentary evidence. Where there is an item of evidence examined by the court prior to the trial, such as an expert report by a court-appointed examiner, the relevant party states the essence of that examination.
(b) The presiding judge points out ambiguous or inconsistent statements and requests clarification and asks questions about the evidence. The judge reviews the factual and legal allegations of both parties and delineates disputed facts, admitted facts and the legal issues.
(c) Both parties present arguments on the disputed issues. Each party points out inconsistencies in the other party's arguments and reasserts their points. At the end of the argument, the presiding judge offers an alternative resolution such as a settlement.
(d) The parties apply to examine the evidence. The presiding judge rules on the admissibility of evidence. When an item of evidence is inadmissible, the judge explains the reason. The judge discusses with the parties the date, order and methods for examination of the evidence.
(e) The presiding judge confirms the methods for the examination of the evidence and the trial schedule. He/she may announce a continuance of the trial and designates the second trial date.

b. Examination of Evidence

685. Examination of evidence should be conducted in one block of time. In general, such a concentrated examination of evidence takes place on the second trial date, mainly focused on the examination of witnesses and parties. Examination of documentary evidence is supposed to be performed on the first trial date. However, where authenticity of a document or its contents is disputed, it is examined together with witnesses on the second date.

---

154. *Supra* n. 148, at 1106.

686. Prior to witness examination, the presiding judge reminds both parties of the factual issues and instructs them to ask questions relevant to the contested facts and avoid irrelevant testimony.

687. In the ideal model, examination of evidence should be completed in one day or several consecutive days. However, in practice, there are many occasions where the trial date for examination of evidence needs to be continued, such as where a witness did not appear for a good reason or where new issues come up at the examination of evidence. In addition, parties may move the court for a continuance to submit a summarizing brief reflecting the results of the examination of evidence.

c. Arrangement for Amicable Resolution of the Dispute

688. After the close of proof, the presiding judge weighs the possibility of reaching an agreement between the parties to resolve the case amicably, including settlement or mediation. At this stage, the court is able to consider facts based on the examination of evidence and so may offer the appropriate terms of a settlement or issue a decision setting forth the terms of agreement (§225 CPA). If any party does not lodge an objection to this decision, it has the same effect as a settlement before the court.

d. Close and Resumption of Trial

689. At the close of proof, the presiding judge gives both parties an opportunity to provide an oral statement summarizing each party's case. The court closes oral arguments when it is deemed that the case has been heard and evidence examined sufficiently for the court to rule.

690. The close of a trial is made by a court decision and the presiding judge announces it to the parties. Because the claim preclusive effect of a judgment covers legal relations between the parties at the point in time when the trial is closed, thereafter submission of new allegations or evidence is barred unless the trial is resumed.

691. The trial may be resumed by court decision before rendering of a judgment if the court finds that arguments on a material issue were insufficient or inconsistent, or there were errors in the examination of evidence (§142 CPA). A decision to resume a trial is made by the court *sua sponte*.

2. Cases Having Gone Through Trial Preparation Proceedings

692. For cases that have gone through trial preparation proceedings, the presiding judge ensures that an expeditious examination of evidence is conducted on the first trial date, and that the parties cooperate with this effort (§287(1) CPA). Since the allegations of facts and issues were already considered in the trial preparation proceedings, and the court decided the admissibility of evidence, there is no difficulty in undertaking evidence examination on the first trial date.

693. The parties must present oral statements on the material facts and other issues at the trial even though they were already asserted orally or in writing in the trial preparation proceedings. This is because they are not deemed to have been stated orally at the trial. However, the parties may summarize the issues and the results of the evidence examination or the court can confirm such matters with the parties (§287(2) CPA).

B. Averment and Defense

1. Procedural Defense

694. While the court examines procedural requisites *sua sponte*, the parties may still need to draw the court's attention to procedural issues that the judge might easily overlook. There are also prerequisites, such as an arbitration clause (§9 AA), that are taken into account only when the parties raise them as a procedural defense.

2. Legal Allegation

695. In oral argument, parties must assert facts in the light of the substantive legal context of the case. This oral statement is not just to recite the pleadings. The parties should set forth a description of the facts and the application of legal theories and legal conclusions persuasively from their perspective. Legal terms of art are frequently used in asserting facts, and the parties may allege legal rights, liabilities and legal effects in such a way as to convince the court that the plaintiff is, for instance, the owner of a building, or that the defendant has an obligation to return unjust enrichment, or that the statute of limitations has expired.

696. In principle, the parties present allegations of facts. The application of the law and the legal conclusions that follow from the facts are up to the court. At the same time, the facts to be alleged and proved are defined by the substantive law and legal theories. From the perspective of the court, it is able to judge whether the alleged facts meet every element of the cause of action only after the applicable substantive law is specified by the parties.

3. Factual Allegation

a. Definition and Meaning

697. The plaintiff must state orally the material facts constituting the cause of action. The material facts to be alleged by the plaintiff are those which give rise to the claim for relief. The defendant may raise an affirmative defense together with statements of the facts that render the plaintiff's right void or extinguished or facts that hinder or limit the exercise of plaintiff's right.

698. Under the adversarial principle, courts may not find material facts unless they are asserted at the trial even when there exists enough evidence to support them.[155] Thus, oral argument is focused on statements of the material facts.

699. The parties may allege specific facts including material facts, basic facts and evidentiary facts depending on their legal implications. The cause of action or legal elements of an affirmative defense comprise a set of material facts. To be successful, the parties should state orally material facts that fit the legal elements.

700. Basic facts are used to infer the existence of a material fact based on common sense. For example, where the fact that the plaintiff's declaration of intent to terminate a lease agreement is material, the fact that the plaintiff sent a registered letter containing such a intent to the defendant can provide an inference that the defendant received notice of plaintiff's intent.[156] Evidentiary facts concern the admissibility or probative value of a piece of evidence. Because the adversarial principle does not apply to basic facts or evidentiary facts, courts may find such facts even if not alleged by the parties. In addition, an admission of such facts does not have any binding effect on the court.

b. Response to the Opposing Party's Factual Allegation

701. The opposing party's response to material allegations of facts by a party who bears the burden of pleading, can be classified as a denial, ignorance due to lack of information, an admission or a nonresponse.

702. A denial is a statement that a material fact alleged by the party who bears the burden of proof is not true. The simple denial is a statement that the factual allegation is untrue. An indirect denial is an allegation of a fact that is inconsistent with a factual allegation by the opposing party.

703. Ignorance due to lack of information is a statement that a party does not know whether the factual allegation of the opposing party is true or not. Such a statement is deemed to be a denial (§150(2) CPA). A party may not respond with a statement of ignorance to a factual allegation when he/she is alleged to have been involved in an incident unless he/she provides a reasonable explanation such as a blackout due to intoxication.

704. An admission is a statement that an allegation of a material fact by the opposing party is true. On the other hand, where a party does not specifically

155. *Supra* n. 32.
156. Supreme Court Decision 69Da2449 decided on March 25, 1969.

respond to a factual allegation, he/she is deemed to have admitted the fact unless his/her argument as a whole is construed to be contrary to the alleged fact (§150(1) CPA).

c. Affirmative Defenses

705. An affirmative defense is the allegation of a fact or a set of facts that defeats or mitigates the legal effects arising from the facts alleged by the other party. The facts alleged in an affirmative defense are consistent and compatible with the facts alleged by the other party in the complaint or his/her affirmative defense.

706. An affirmative defense may be raised in consecutive order between the parties. For example, in a lawsuit seeking the payment of the purchase price, the defendant may raise an affirmative defense by stating that the statute of limitations for the plaintiff's claim has expired. Responding to the defendant's defense, the plaintiff may bring an affirmative defense by asserting the suspension of the limitation period on the grounds that he/she executed a prejudgment seizure against the defendant's property. In response, the defendant may lodge an affirmative defense on the grounds that the prejudgment seizure was later repealed by a court.

d. Admission Before the Court and Constructive Admission

(1) Matters to be admitted

707. Admissions of alleged material facts for which the opposing party bears the burden of proof have a binding effect upon the court and the parties. Admissions of immaterial facts such as basic or evidentiary ones do not have such an effect. According to case law, if a party admits the genuineness of a document submitted as evidence by the opposing party, the admission is binding even though the facts regarding the authenticity thereof are evidentiary.[157] This is in line with Section 358 of the Civil Procedure Act which allows a lawsuit for declaratory judgment to determine the authenticity of a document that certifies a legal relationship.

708. There has been a debate on whether the admission of the nonexistence of a material fact is binding. A party must prove the existence of a material fact if he/she bears the burden of proof and he/she is exempted from the burden if the opposing party admits the fact. However, where a party denies a fact and the other party who has the burden of proof admits the nonexistence of the fact, the majority of jurists suggest that such an admission is not legally effective. Other opinions are that an admission that a fact does not exist is equally as binding as an admission that a fact does exist. Case law takes side with the latter opinion.[158]

157. Supreme Court Decision 2001Da5654 decided on April 24, 2001.

158. Supreme Court Decision 92Da24899 decided on September 14, 1993. [Confirmation of co-owner's share of realty] In this lawsuit to quiet title, the plaintiffs should prove the fact that the decedent completed ownership transfer registration for the real property. However, if the plaintiffs conceded that he has not been registered as the owner of the realty in its register and the defendant quoted

709. Admissions may be made on a portion of the facts that constitute the legal elements of a claim or affirmative defense. For example, where the defendant asserts that a sales contract was revoked due to the plaintiff's nonperformance, the material facts are that the plaintiff failed to perform an obligation within the agreed time frame, that the defendant gave the plaintiff additional time and requested him/her to perform the obligation, that the plaintiff failed to do so within the extended period, and that the defendant notified the plaintiff of his/her intent to revoke the contract. In this case, the plaintiff may admit some of the facts and deny the rest.

710. Finding and interpreting the applicable law are the sole responsibility of the court. Therefore, an admission on such matters is not legally effective. In addition, the evaluation of facts or conclusions of law on such matters as negligence, contributory negligence, reasonable cause, violation of public policy, impossibility of performance and the statutory order of debts to be paid may not be lawfully admitted.

(2) Types of admission

(a) Admission before the court

711. An admission of fact before the court is effected when both parties state the same material fact at the trial or the trial preparation hearing. The statement of the material facts may be made when one of the parties fails to appear at the hearing and so the preparatory brief submitted by the absent party is deemed stated.

712. Under the principle of statement for mutual interest, it does not matter which party states the material fact first concerning the burden of proof. For example, a plaintiff may admit material facts which the defendant has the burden to prove if the plaintiff believes that the defendant is sure to do so. In such a case, the plaintiff may reverse his/her statement. However, once the defendant recites or ratifies the plaintiff's statement, an admission of the fact is effectuated.[159]

(b) Constructive admission

713. When a party fails to clearly deny a fact alleged by the opposing party, he/she is deemed to have admitted that fact unless his/her statements are construed as contrary to the facts considered in their entirety (§150(1) CPA). It is the same if a party fails to appear at the trial or hearing for trial preparation without submitting a preparatory brief denying the facts alleged by the opposing party unless he/she was served by publication (§150(3) CPA).

714. If a defendant fails to file an answer within thirty days from the service of a copy of the complaint, the facts alleged in the complaint are deemed to have been

the plaintiffs' statement before the court, the admission has been effectuated on the nonexistence of the fact that the decedent completed ownership transfer registration therefor.

159. Supreme Court Decision 2018Da229564 decided on August 1, 2018.

admitted by the defendant and the court may render a judgment based on the complaint without holding a trial (§257(1) CPA). It is the same when the defendant submits an answer admitting the facts alleged in the complaint without raising an affirmative defense (§257(2) CPA).

(3) Effects of an admission

(a) Admissions before the court

715. An admission becomes effective at the time it is made. An admission is binding on the court and the parties only in the present action. An admitted fact is treated as if the fact were proved even though it is contrary to evidence. In principle, the parties may not withdraw or controvert an admission. However, an admission may be revoked when the revoking party proves that the admitted fact was not truthful and the admission was made based on an erroneous assumption (§288 CPA). Also, in a case where both the parties state a fact contrary to an admitted fact, the new admission prevails and the previous admission ceases to be effective.[160]

(b) Constructive admission

716. Unlike an admission before the court, a constructive admission becomes effective at the close of the hearing for oral argument. Even if a party failed to appear or did not clearly dispute a fact alleged by an opposing party at a hearing, he/she may appear and deny the facts at a subsequent hearing.

717. As the court of second instance is also a trial court, a party who lost in the first instance court due to a constructive admission may reverse the effect of that admission by denying the facts in the appellate court. However, such a denial might be dismissed on the ground that it was not submitted in due time (§149(1) CPA).

4. Exercise of the Right to Alter a Legal Relationship in Litigation

718. The substantive right to alter a legal relationship may be exercised out of court as well as in court. For example, a plaintiff may declare an intent to revoke a contract and seek return of things that were delivered to perform the contractual duty in the complaint. A defendant may counter this declaration of intent on the grounds of deceit or duress, or revoke the contract related to the plaintiff's claim in the answer or other preparatory briefs.

719. Where a substantive right to alter a legal relationship is exercised in a lawsuit and the lawsuit is later withdrawn or dismissed without prejudice, there is a debate on whether the legal effect of exercising such a right remains effective or not.

160. Supreme Court Decision 90DaKa20548 decided on November 27, 1990.

The Supreme Court held that if the plaintiff declared an intent to revoke the contract in a complaint and then withdrew the lawsuit, the revocation of the contract is not affected by the withdrawal of the lawsuit.[161]

720. However, the right to set off is an exception. According to case law, when the defendant pleads a setoff as an affirmative defense in an action, the setoff is effected, not at the time when the declaration is made, but when the court decides that both the claims set against each other are established and appropriate for setoff.[162] Likewise, if an affirmative defense of a setoff is raised together with other defenses, the court considers the defense of setoff last after denying all other defenses. Thus, where the defendant wins a case by making an affirmative defense of a setoff in the first instance court and then raises another defense based on the statute of limitations in the intermediate appellate court, the court should consider the statute of limitations first and then the defense of a setoff only if the former is groundless.[163]

C. Directing the Course of the Proceedings

1. Authority to Direct the Course of Proceedings

721. The court has the authority to direct the course of the proceedings from the commencement to the close of a case (§§140˜145 CPA). The court exercises this authority to render the proceedings fair, speedy and orderly. In practice, the presiding judge presides over specific proceedings on the date for trial preparation or the date for evidence examination while executing this authority (§135 CPA).

2. Authority to Ask for an Explanation

722. The presiding judge may ask questions of the parties in order to clarify matters in relation to the litigation and urge them to provide proof with regard to factual or legal matters (§136(1) CPA). When a party's allegations of fact are incomplete or the presentation of evidence is irrelevant due to lack of attention or litigation skills, the presiding judge may prompt the party to review the allegations and evidence to the extent that this does not infringe on the adversarial principle. For example, the presiding judge may not suggest that omitted material facts should be alleged or advise a party about an affirmative defense. Doing so would violate the adversarial principle.[164]

161. Supreme Court Decision 80Da916 decided on May 11, 1982.
162. Supreme Court Decision 2013Da95964 decided on June 12, 2014.
163. Supreme Court Decision 2011Da21556 decided on February 28, 2013.
164. Supreme Court Decision 2011Da60759 decided on July 11, 2013.

3. Prohibition of Making Statements

723. When a party, his/her agent or an attorney is unable to address matters related to the litigation, the court may prohibit him/her from making a statement before the court (§144(1) CPA). The person subject to this decision loses the capacity to present oral statements in the case. The court may continue the hearing and order that the relevant party be represented by an attorney or another attorney (§144(2) CPA). If the plaintiff or appellant in the appellate court fails to comply with such an order, the court may render a judgment dismissing the lawsuit or appeal without prejudice (§144(4) CPA).

724. The presiding judge may also permit a party or any others to speak or prohibit a person who does not comply with the judge's orders from speaking before the court (§135(2) CPA).

4. Maintenance of Order in Court

725. The presiding judge may exercise powers necessary to maintain order in the court (§58(1) COA). He/she may issue an order to prohibit any person who might endanger the dignity and order of the court from entering or staying in the courtroom, or to take other necessary measures to maintain order (§58(2) COA).

726. The presiding judge may direct the court personnel, prison officers in the courtroom, or national police officials to detain a person who is not complying with his/her orders (§61(2) COA). In addition, the court may impose an administrative detention order for not more than twenty days or an administrative fine not exceeding KRW 1 million (§61(1) COA).

727. The presiding judge may also prohibit photographing, broadcasting, audio or video recording, handwriting or drawing any part of a hearing or other proceedings in the courtroom. He/she may also allow this activity provided it is not likely to interfere with a fair and smooth judicial process (§59 COA).

V. Judgment

A. Types of Ruling

728. There are three types of rulings issued by a court: judgment, decision and order. The type of a ruling is prescribed in the Civil Procedure Act and other statutes depending on the matters to be adjudicated.

729. A judgment is a ruling which decides a case on the merits or dismisses a case on the procedural grounds conclusively and finally. An interlocutory judgment is an exception, which decides an issue in an intermediate stage while the main case is pending. The court must hold a hearing for oral argument prior to rendering a final judgment and the presiding judge must pronounce the operative provisions of the judgment and summarize the reasons in an open courtroom at the designated hearing date for rendition thereof. The judgment document must be made and served on the parties. The judgment is enforceable when it is final and binding.

730. A decision is a ruling by the court on procedural matters and other matters that need to be addressed expeditiously. The court may hold a hearing at its discretion prior to issuing a decision (§134(1) CPA). A decision document is not needed. The decision is notified to the parties in an appropriate manner as determined by the court. If the court announces the decision in the courtroom at a hearing, it takes effect immediately and the court clerk enters the decision in the record of the hearing. Examples include a decision to transfer a case to the court with jurisdiction or proper venue (§§34,35 CPA); a decision to limit, consolidate or separate the proceedings (§§141,142 CPA); a decision ordering a person to produce a document (§347(1) CPA), etc. A decision is enforceable as soon as it takes effect except as otherwise provided for in statutory provisions.

731. An order is issued by a judge including a presiding judge, a delegated judge of a judicial panel and a commissioned judge. Proceedings for an order are the same with a decision. An order is enforceable from the time it takes effect. Examples are an order to prohibit any person from entering or staying in the courtroom (§58 COA), an order to dismiss a complaint (§§254(1),(2) CPA), an order directing service by publication (§194(2) CPA), etc. Some decisions are referred to as an order, e.g., an order of prejudgment seizure and payment order (§462 CPA) but such a ruling is a decision issued in the name of a court.

B. Decision Conference and Writing of a Judgment

732. The single judge or members of the judicial panel that has heard a case must decide the case. When a three-judge panel hears a case, a decision conference is convened after the close of oral arguments. The case-management judge for the case states the factual and legal issues, conclusions of law, and his/her view of the case before the other two panel members.[165] A discussion follows and if they are unable to reach a unanimous conclusion, the decision is made by a majority (§66(1) COA).

733. The case-management judge writes the judgment reflecting the opinions expressed by the other judges in the decision conference. However, the vote taken at the conference may not be final because the judges on the panel, especially the case-management judge, may find defects in the decision with respect to the facts or the law while doing the further research or writing the judgment. Thus, a decision conference may be called again and the previous decision may be altered by the time the judgment is rendered in the courtroom.

165. A case management judge is a member of judicial panel, who is assigned the case prior to the commencement of the proceedings according to the internal rules of the court.

734. Under the principle of directness, only the single judge or the judges on the panel that has participated in the oral argument and the examination of evidence may rule on the case (§204(1) CPA). Oral arguments are those made at the final hearing. If a judge who took part in the final hearing is unable to participate in the decision conference, the hearing for oral argument must be resumed.

C. *Types of Judgment*

1. Interlocutory Judgment

735. If an independent allegation or any other issue in dispute must be decided first before arriving at a final judgment and the interlocutory dispute is ripe for a decision, the court may render an interlocutory judgment on that issue during the pendency of the main case. A material allegation of facts and an affirmative defense are examples of disputes that are resolved by an interlocutory judgment. Where a claim for damages is in dispute both on the existence of liability and its amount, the court may decide that the defendant is liable by way of an interlocutory judgment and then go forward with proceedings to determine the amount of the damages (§201 CPA). In such a case, if the court finds that the existence of the claim is not proved, a final judgment dismissing the case with prejudice must be handed down, instead of an interlocutory judgment.

736. In practice, interlocutory judgments are seldom used because judges take on additional work by rendering an interlocutory judgment. Another reason is that an interlocutory judgment is binding on the court and so the court may not reverse the decision even if it turns out to be wrong at the time a final judgment is rendered.

737. An interlocutory judgment is binding on the court and the parties as long as the case is pending in the same court. Therefore, the parties may not present factual or legal allegations contrary to the interlocutory judgment and the court may not render a contrary final judgment. A party may not appeal an interlocutory judgment. If a party is dissatisfied with an interlocutory judgment and appeals the final judgment, both judgments are reviewed by the appellate court.

2. Final Judgment

738. A judgment on the merits includes a performance judgment, declaratory judgment, and a formative judgment, respectively corresponding to an action for performance, action for declaration and action for formation. To be a final judgment, it must be final and complete, as to the entire subject-matter and all the causes of action. A final judgment can be classified into a procedural judgment and a judgment on the merits. The former includes a dismissal without prejudice, a dismissal of an appeal on procedural grounds or a declaratory judgment affirming the termination of an action. A judgment on the merits is rendered if a lawsuit satisfies all the procedural prerequisites. This includes judgments that grant a claim, dismiss a claim with prejudice, or partially grant and partially dismiss a claim.

739. In a case where the claims or parties are joined, the court usually enters a judgment that includes all the parties and claims. However, where only one of several claims or co-parties are ready for a final decision, the court may deliver a partial judgment on that portion of the case. To render a partial judgment, the proceedings for claims or co-parties must be separated. An additional judgment is rendered on the rest of the claims when proceedings have sufficiently developed to allow a judicial decision to be reached.

740. A partial judgment is not allowed in the joinder of alternative claims, joinder of a main claim and contingent claim, necessary joinder of parties, intervention as an independent party, joinder of parties in the alternative, and joinder of a primary party and contingent party.

741. Where the court unintentionally fails to adjudicate one of the claims between the same parties or a claim with regard to a co-party and this claim can be separated, the unaddressed claim remains pending before that court. In this case, the court renders a supplementary judgment on the remaining claim *sua sponte*. Therefore, an appeal based on the omission is unlawful provided the unaddressed claim was procedurally separable.[166]

742. On the other hand, if an omitted claim is procedurally inseparable and a partial judgment is not allowed, the court may not render a supplementary judgment. In this case, if a party appeals the judgment based on the omission, all the claims are reviewed by the appellate court.[167]

D. Content of a Judgment

743. The format of a judgment is regulated by the Guidelines on Format of Judgment Documents (Jaeil 2003-12) which is a litigation guideline of the Supreme Court. The content of a judgment is prescribed as follows.

(a) The court

744. The name of the court is set out at the top of the judgment document. When a judicial panel adjudicates a case, the name of the panel is below the name of the court, e.g., the first civil panel or the second panel. Because all judicial panels of the Patent Court, the Administrative Court or the Family Court respectively deal the same type of cases, the name of panel in these courts is simply stated as, "the first panel." A judgment rendered by a single judge does not set out the name of the judicial division.

---

166. Supreme Court Decision 94Da50274 decided on February 9, 1996.
167. Supreme Court Decision 96Da99 decided on July 24, 1998.

(b) Denomination of a judgment

745. A judgment is distinguished from a decision and an order. For this reason, on the judgment document, a judgment is labeled as such beneath the name of the court. A Judgment generally means a final judgment on all matters. Thus, when the court renders a partial judgment (§200 CPA), interlocutory judgment (§201 CPA), or a supplementary judgment (§212 CPA), the specific type of the judgment is to be specified.

(c) The number assigned to the action

746. A case number is given by the court but the case title is named by the plaintiff; e.g., "2011GaHap356 Loan." Here, "2011" means the year when the lawsuit was filed. The Korean alphabetical letters "Ga," "Na" and "Da" signify the level of the court. "Ga" represents the court of first instance; "Na," the intermediate appellate court; and "Da," the final appeal to the Supreme Court. "Hap" indicates a civil case that is to be processed by a judicial panel. "Dan" indicates a single judge. In this example, "356" is a sequential number to identify the case. Here "Hap356" means that a civil lawsuit was the 356th case filed in the year of 2011 and was heard by a judicial panel. "Loan" is the descriptive name of the complaint.

(d) Parties

747. The identification of the plaintiff and defendant are set forth, including the name, date of birth and domicile for a natural person, and the name and location of the principal office or place of business for a legal person.

748. Should there be co-parties, a serial number is given to each. In a counterclaim, the plaintiff is the defendant, and vice versa. In a judgment as to a claim and counterclaim, a party is labeled as such, e.g., "Plaintiff (Defendant in the Counterclaim)" or "Defendant (Plaintiff in the Counterclaim)."

749. Where a party sued or was sued based on third-party standing, the relationship between the party and the third party is set forth, e.g., "Plaintiff (Appointed Party)," or "Plaintiff (Bankruptcy Trustee B for the Debtor A)."

750. If a party has a statutory agent, his/her name is entered. The representative of a legal person or organization without legal personality, and the attorney of record are also specified. When the attorney of record is a law firm, its name and the attorney in charge of the case are set forth.

(e) Date of close of the hearing for oral arguments and date of rendition of the judgment

751. These dates are entered because the date the hearing for oral arguments closes serves as the standard time for preclusive effects, and the judgment takes effect at the time it is rendered (§205 CPA).

(f) The operative provisions

752. The operative provisions of a judgment are the conclusions as well as the decision on the claim or an appeal. The court dismisses a lawsuit without prejudice when it lacks a procedural prerequisite. The operative provisions of a judgment on the merits use different sentence types and formats depending on the type of the judgment: performance judgment, declaratory judgment or formative judgment.

753. Under the principle of party-disposition, the operative provisions of a judgment may not quantitatively or qualitatively exceed the prayer for relief asserted in the complaint. When granting less than the relief prayed for, the court must dismiss the rest of the claims. The judicial decision on the burden of litigation costs and declaration of eligibility for provisional enforcement are included in the operative provisions. The following is an example of the operative provisions of a judgment.

1. This Court dismisses Plaintiff's action without prejudice against Defendant A.
2. Defendant B shall pay KRW 10,000,000 to Plaintiff at the same time as Defendant B takes delivery of the machine specified on the attached list from Plaintiff.
3. This Court dismisses, with prejudice, Plaintiff's remaining claims against Defendant B.
4. Plaintiff shall bear the litigation costs incurred by Plaintiff and Defendant A. Defendant B shall bear four fifths of the litigation costs incurred by Plaintiff and Defendant B, and Plaintiff shall bear the remaining litigation costs.
5. Plaintiff may provisionally enforce Article 2 of this judgment.

(g) Prayer for relief

754. The prayer for relief is the conclusion of the complaint and corresponds to the operative provisions of a judgment. Should the plaintiff win the case entirely, the operative provisions of the judgment are identical to the prayer for relief. Comparing the latter with the former, we can see precisely what the court granted and what the court dismissed with or without prejudice.

(h) Reasons

755. The statement of reasons for a judgment logically explains the process in reaching the court's decision. When dismissing all or part of a case without prejudice, the court concisely summarizes the claims asserted by the plaintiff, and then points out the procedural defects leading to their dismissal. When the defendant raised a procedural defense which is denied, the content of the defense and the reason why the defense lacked merit are set forth.

756. After dealing with procedural issues, the grounds for a judgment on the merits follow. When granting all or part of the claims, the court sets out the facts, the evidence supporting the facts, and the statutes and legal theories which were applied. If affirmative defenses were raised, they are examined in logical order. When denying all or part of the claims or affirmative defenses, the reasons why the court does not agree with the factual or legal allegations made by the relevant party are explained. If the court disregards any evidence, the reasons for that are also provided in the judgment.

757. Lastly, a summary of the reasons for the judgment is provided and the decision on the burden of litigation costs and the eligibility for provisional enforcement of the operative provisions are explained briefly.

(i) Signature and seal of the participating judges

758. The judges who heard the last oral argument and participated in the decision conference must sign and stamp the seal on the judgment document. Should a judge on a judicial panel who participated in the decision conference be unable to sign the judgment document due to unavoidable circumstances, e.g., official trip abroad or transfer to a different court, another judge on the panel writes the circumstances on the judgment document, and signs and stamps his/her seal under the absent judge's name. Should a single judge be in the same situation, the hearing for the case must be held anew.

E. Rendition of Judgment and Service

759. According to the Civil Procedure Act, a court of first instance should render a judgment within five months after a lawsuit is filed. The Supreme Court and a court of second instance should do so in the same period after the record of proceedings of the lower court is received (§199 CPA). Also, a judgment should be pronounced within two weeks after close of the hearing for oral argument unless there are unavoidable circumstances (§207(1) CPA). These statutory time frames are not mandatory. However, in practice the two weeks' time frame after close of the hearing is relatively well observed.

760. A date for issuing a judgment is set in advance. A judgment on the merits as well as one on the procedural grounds must be rendered on that date.[168] In handing down a judgment, the presiding judge briefly explains the grounds on which the judgment is based and pronounces the operative provisions in the courtroom (§206 CPA). The parties do not need to be present at the hearing for rendition of the judgment. A judgment takes effect at the time it is rendered (§205 CPA).

761. A judgment document should be promptly delivered to the court clerk after it is rendered (§209 CPA). This means that the judgment document is completed beforehand. The court clerk sends a copy of the judgment document to the parties within two weeks after its receipt from the presiding judge (§210 CPA).

F. *Effects of a Judgment*

1. Intraprocedural Binding Force

762. A judgment binds the court which rendered it. Thus, a court may not change or revoke its judgment even though it is found to be wrong. An interlocutory judgment has the same binding force so that the final judgment must not be contrary to an interlocutory judgment.

763. If an appellate court reverses the judgment of the original court and remands the case, the court is bound by the appellate judgment. The Supreme Court does not review questions of fact determined by a lower court. This means that the findings of fact made in the lower court binds the court of final appeal.

764. Should the court find typographical errors, computational errors and other obvious inaccuracies in a judgment, it may issue a decision mandating corrections of the judgment (§211(1) CPA). A correction of a judgment that modifies the content or rectifies an omission in a judgment runs afoul of the binding effect of a judgment and is not allowed.

765. A decision ordering the correction of a judgment is issued by the court upon petition by a party or *sua sponte*. After the case records have been received by an appellate court due to filing of an appeal, that court is in charge of correcting the judgment. In general, correction of a judgment is made by a separate court decision. However, when dismissing an appeal, an appellate court may correct minor errors and include the corrections in the operative provision of the judgment.

168. Supreme Court Decision 96Nu2699 decided on May 28, 1996.

2. Final and Binding Effect

766. The binding effect of a judgment means that once a judgment is final and unappealable, the parties may not dispute the subject-matter of the suit. The enforceability, preclusive effects and formative effects of a judgment exist on the premise that the judgment is final and binding.

767. An appealable judgment becomes final and binding when the time limit for filing an appeal has expired, when the aggrieved party waives the right to appeal, or when the appellant withdraws an appeal after the time limit for filing an appeal. A judgment that is not subject to appeal is final and binding at the time it is rendered. Examples are a judgment rendered by the Supreme Court or a judgment which the parties agreed not to appeal.

768. When a party appeals part of a judgment which partially granted and partially dismissed the claims, all the claims adjudicated by the judgment become pending before the appellate court but only the appealed part is reviewed. Scholars are divided over the time when the rest of the judgment the party did not appeal becomes final and binding and thus enforceable. The Supreme Court has held that the remaining part of the judgment is final and binding when the appellate court renders a judgment on the appealed part of the judgment.[169]

3. Claim Preclusion

a. Definition and Meaning

769. The operative provisions of a judgment define the relationship between the parties with respect to the subject-matter of a lawsuit. Therefore, the parties may not reassert factual or legal allegations and a court may not render a judgment contrary to a prior judgment between the same parties. This binding force of a judgment is referred to as claim preclusion.[170]

770. There have been debates about the essential nature of claim preclusion. The prohibition of contradiction theory posits that a court must not rule differently than a previous judgment on the same subject-matter or cause of action. Under this theory, if a plaintiff loses a case and then files another lawsuit based on the same subject-matter, the suit must be dismissed with prejudice for being contradictory to the preclusive effect of the prior judgment. If a plaintiff won a prior case and files the same lawsuit again, it should be dismissed without prejudice as lacking a legitimate interest to sue.[171]

---

169. Supreme Court Decision 2011Da18864 decided on July 11, 2013.
170. Si-yoon Lee, *supra* n. 8, at 616.
171. Supreme Court Decision 87DaKa2478 decided on June 27, 1989; Supreme Court Decision 2015Da73753 decided on December 22, 2017.

771. On the other hand, the prohibition of repetition theory explains that the claim preclusion is the same as the principle of *non bis in idem*, which is a legal doctrine that no lawsuit may be brought twice for the same cause of action. According to this theory, nonexistence of a preclusive effect is a procedural prerequisite for a lawsuit. Accordingly, if a person files a lawsuit again based on the same claim on which a preclusive effect exists, the court must dismiss the case without prejudice.[172]

b. Judicial Decision with Preclusive Effect

772. A judgment on the merits as well as a procedural judgment has a preclusive effect. A court decision or court order does not, in general, have such an effect. However, court decisions may have such an effect where it finally determines a substantive legal relationship. For instance, a decision to fix the amount of litigation costs (§110(1) CPA), a decision ordering the debtor to pay the creditor a certain amount of money in an indirect compulsory enforcement (§261(1) CEA), a decision setting forth the terms of a settlement (§231 CPA) and a decision in lieu of mediation (§29 JCCDA) are all preclusive.

773. A foreign judgment which is final and binding has the same preclusive effect as a judgment rendered by a domestic court provided it satisfies following requirements: (a) The country where the foreign court is located has international jurisdiction over the subject-matter according to Korean law; (b) The defendant was properly served with notice of the proceedings, and in such time to allow him/her to defend the suit, or the defendant responded to the lawsuit even though not served; (c) The judgment is not contrary to Korean public policy; and (d) There exists a reciprocal guarantee, or the requirements for recognition of a foreign judgment in the foreign jurisdiction and those in Korea are well balanced and not substantially different (§217 CPA).

774. A court may refuse to recognize all or part of an award for money damages by a foreign judgment (§217-2 CPA). Therefore, when the standard or method of calculating money damages in a foreign court is so different from those allowed in Korea that the judgment amount is excessively large compared with the amount a Korean court would have granted (e.g., punitive damages), the judgment is likely not to be recognized in whole or in part.[173]

775. In some particular cases, the record of the hearing has the same effect as a final and binding judgment (§220 CPA). When the plaintiff waives the claim for relief before the court, it is entered in the record of the hearing. This transcript has the same effect as a final judgment dismissing the plaintiff's claim with prejudice. Likewise, an acknowledgement entered in the record of the hearing is equivalent to a final judgment granting the claim for relief. A record of the hearing that evidences a settlement or mediation (§29 JCCDA) is the same.

172. Si-yoon Lee, *supra* n. 8, at 618; Dong-yoon Chung et al., *supra* n. 7, at 763-764.
173. Supreme Court Decision 2015Da207747 decided on January 28, 2016.

776. The Debtor Rehabilitation and Bankruptcy Act stipulates that, in business rehabilitation procedures and bankruptcy procedures, final and binding tables of unsecured creditors, secured creditors and shareholders have the same effect as a final and binding judgment with respect to each unsecured claim, secured claim and equity interest (§§168,255,460 DRBA). However, the Supreme Court's interpretation of these provisions limits the final and binding effects to status of rights set out in the tables and participants may not further dispute the confirmed rights in the insolvency proceedings. But the tables do not preclude further claims based on the status of creditors set out in the tables as a judgment might. Accordingly, a rehabilitation trustee may file a lawsuit seeking affirmation of the nonexistence of a claim entered in a final and binding table of unsecured creditors for the reason that the claim was assigned to a third party before the table of unsecured creditors became final and binding.[174]

c. The Function of Preclusive Effect

777. According to case law and the prohibition of contradiction theory, claim preclusion is triggered only when a party asserts claims or affirmative defenses contrary to a decision on the claim in a prior final and binding judgment.

778. Even when the subject-matter of a pending lawsuit is different from a previous lawsuit in which a final judgment was rendered, the court must adjudicate the case based on the legal relationship covered by preclusive effect of a previous judgment. For example, if a plaintiff files a lawsuit seeking interest as damages for repayment of a loan that was the subject-matter of a previous lawsuit in which a court dismissed the claim on the merits, the second suit must be dismissed with prejudice because the existence of the loan principal is a precondition for interest as damages.[175]

779. Likewise, if a subsequent lawsuit is logically incompatible with a judgment on the merits in a previous lawsuit, the claim must be dismissed with prejudice due to the claim preclusive effect. For example, if the ownership transfer of real property was registered in accordance with a prior final and binding judgment favoring the plaintiff, the defendant in that case is precluded from filing a subsequent lawsuit against the plaintiff, seeking cancellation of ownership transfer registration for the same property.[176]

d. Scope of Preclusive Effect

(1) Time span covered by the preclusive effect

780. Since parties may present allegations and evidence until close of the hearing for oral argument, the preclusive effect takes place as of the time the hearing is

174. Supreme Court Decision 91Da4096 decided on December 10, 1991.
175. Supreme Court Decision 76Da1488 decided on December 14, 1976.
176. Supreme Court Decision 94Da61649 decided on February 9, 1996.

closed. Accordingly, the parties may not allege a claim or cause of action based on matters that existed before close of the hearing in the previous litigation. However, legal or factual matters that take place after close of the hearing are not precluded even if they are based on the legal relationship established in a prior lawsuit.

781. Case law also holds that, after the close of the hearing for oral argument, a party may not seek to alter a legal relationship that could have been addressed before the close of oral arguments. For example, the plaintiff-purchaser enforced a prior final and binding judgment ordering ownership transfer registration on a real property. In the prior suit, the plaintiff's claim was based on a contract for sale and the defendant-seller could have revoked the contract because the plaintiff failed to pay the purchase price. However, the defendant did not do so until after close of the oral hearing in the prior suit. Now, the seller is precluded from filing a subsequent lawsuit asking for cancellation of the ownership transfer even though the seller revoked the contract for sale after close of the hearing for oral argument. It is because the grounds for revoking the contract already existed before the close of the hearing in the previous lawsuit.[177]

782. However, the right to a setoff is an exception. Even when the claims of each party to a setoff become appropriate before close of the oral hearing, the defendant may set off the plaintiff's claim thereafter and have the final judgment for the plaintiff vacated by filing a lawsuit objecting to the enforcement of the plaintiff's claim (§44(2) CEA).[178]

(2) With respect to the claim

783. A procedural judgment has a preclusive effect on the fact that the case lacks a certain procedural prerequisite upon which the judgment was rendered. But, a new lawsuit on the same subject-matter is lawful if the procedural defect is corrected.

784. The preclusive effect of a judgment on the merits is limited to the subject-matter of the lawsuit. According to the substantive law approach and case law in defining the subject-matter, if the claim and cause of action prescribed by substantive law in the second lawsuit is not the same, the subject-matter is different and the preclusive effect does not affect the second lawsuit. For example, a claim under a tort and a claim for a money damage award based on a breach of a contract arising from the same incident, each cause of contested divorce listed in the Civil Act, and a claim for surrender of a property based on the terms of the lease agreement expired and that based on its ownership are separate subject-matters of a lawsuit, so that the exclusive effect of a judgment on a claim in the first lawsuit does not reach the other claim in the second lawsuit.

785. However, according to case law, in a lawsuit seeking the return of unjust enrichment, a void underlying contract, the avoidance of a declaration of intent and

177. Supreme Court Decision 80Da2751 decided on July 7, 1981.
178. Supreme Court Decision 2005Da41443 decided on November 10, 2005.

the revocation of the contract are all causes of action that give rise to a claim of unjust enrichment. Thus, insofar as a claim for the return of unjust enrichment is the same in these respects, a second lawsuit, though denominated by a different cause of action is still precluded.[179] The same is true regarding a lawsuit seeking cancellation of ownership transfer registration on the grounds that the underlying contract was void, revoked, or otherwise invalid.[180]

786. In a case where only a part of a dispute was decided, it has been debated whether filing the second lawsuit for the remaining part of the claim is precluded. The Supreme Court held that, if the complaint in the first lawsuit was clear that the plaintiff was seeking a partial remedy, the preclusive effect does not reach the rest of the claim and the plaintiff may file a subsequent lawsuit. If that is not the case, the rest of the claim is barred by the judgment in the first lawsuit.[181]

(3) With respect to the parties and their proxies

787. A final judgment binds the parties as well as their proxies. This includes a party by virtue of third-party standing and the person possessing the object of a claim in dispute.

788. This also includes those who become successors after the oral hearing or after rendition of a judgment absent an oral hearing (§218(1) CPA). A successor can be a general successor or a specific successor. A general successor could be an heir or a surviving company or a new company in a merger or a division of a company. A specific successor refers to the person who succeeds to a claim, obligation or legal status, for instance, an assignee of a claim, the transferee of a debt or the person who acquires ownership of property in a quiet title lawsuit.

789. Jurists are divided over whether the preclusive effect reaches a person who acquires ownership or possession of property which was the object of a prior lawsuit. The Supreme Court has held that when the subject-matter is an obligatory claim such as a contractual claim, such a person is not bound by the judgment rendered in the first lawsuit. But when the subject-matter is a claim based on a real right, the person is a successor regarding the preclusive effect.[182] For example, a final judgment ordering delivery of a specific car based on a contract for sale does not bind a person who bought the same car from the defendant after close of the oral hearing and is in possession of the car. However, if, in the above lawsuit, the claim was based on ownership of the car, the preclusive effect would reach the new buyer.

790. "The person possessing the object of the claim" includes such entities as a warehouse owner (§155 ComA), a carrier (§125 ComA), or a borrower of property

179. Supreme Court Decision 2007Da49960 decided on February 29, 2008.
180. Supreme Court Decision 93Da11050 decided on June 29, 1993.
181. Supreme Court Decision 92Da33008 decided on June 25, 1993.
182. Supreme Court Decision 2000Da24856 decided on March 28, 2003.

(§609 CA). By contrast, it does not include persons having their own right to the object; for example, a lessee or a holder of a right of retention.

791. An appointed party (§53 CPA), a rehabilitation trustee (§78 DRBA) and a bankruptcy trustee (§359 DRBA) are parties to a lawsuit based on third-party standing and the persons they stand in for as a plaintiff or defendant or debtor are respectively subject to the preclusive effects of a judgment.

792. When a creditor sued a third-party debtor based on his/her subrogation right to exercise the right belonging to the debtor in order to preserve his/her own claim against the debtor (§404 CA), the judgment binds the debtor if he/she was aware of the litigation while the case was pending.[183]

§2. Provisional Proceedings

I. Provisional Orders Prior to Rulings

793. When a case is pending before a family court, the court may issue provisional orders. Provisional orders prior to a ruling on the primary case are recognized only in the Family Litigation Act, not in other statutes governing civil procedure. The orders can be issued by the court, the court's mediation committee or the mediation judge on their own motion or on motion by a party (§62(1) FLA).

794. What a provisional order issued by a family court and a preservative measure under the Civil Execution Act have in common is that both are temporary measures. However, the provisional orders are distinguished from the preservative measures in that they have nothing to do with eventual enforcement of court rulings on the merits. In addition, family court provisional orders may be issued only when a case is pending while a preservative measure may be ordered prior to filing of a lawsuit. When a party fails to comply with the order, the court imposes an administrative fine but compulsory enforcement of the order is not allowed. That is because a provisional order is not based on a specific claim of a party.

795. For example, a family court may issue a provisional order prohibiting sale of properties when a petition for division of property between divorced spouses or among heirs is pending. A provisional order might also direct the person who is going to be an adult guardian to have the ward get mental health treatment. In a divorce case, the court might allow, limit or prohibit visitation between a parent and a child, or order payment of child support or alimony. However, such orders are not issued to preserve a specific claim or secure enforcement of it.

183. Supreme Court Decision 93Da52808 decided on August 12, 1994.

II. Preservative Measures under the Civil Execution Act

796. When a debtor does not voluntarily perform a duty, a creditor may sue or take other measures to obtain an enforceable title and enforce it. However, should the debtor dispose of his/her assets prior to the enforcement of a monetary claim, an enforceable title becomes useless. It is the same when the subject-matter of a dispute is the delivery or transfer of specific property based on a contract and the debtor disposes of the property.

797. There are three types of preservative measures depending on the right to be preserved: pre-judgment seizure, injunction regarding the object of the litigation and injunction serving to provide a temporary status.

798. A more detailed explanation of these measures is provided in "Part IX. Preservative measure and enforcement of judgment."

§3. DEFAULT PROCEEDINGS

I. Nonappearance of a Party

A. Constructive Statement

799. When a party fails to appear at a hearing for oral argument or a pretrial hearing after he/she submits the complaint, answer or a preparatory brief, the court may deem that the absent party has stated the particulars contained in the submitted documents and give the present party an opportunity to make statements (§148(1) CPA). There is no difference between a constructive statement and oral statement of facts in their effects. Provided, however, in such a case, the court may, in its own discretion, postpone the hearing date after barring the present party from making an oral argument.

800. The effect of the nonappearance of a party takes place only when notice of the hearing date has been served on the parties by means of other than service by publication. An appearance in this context means that the party responds when the case is called by the presiding judge and they approach the podium for oral statements in the courtroom. If the court issued a decision prohibiting a party from speaking before the court, his/her appearance in the courtroom does not have any effect. Also, should a party fail to make any statement on the merits or just alleges that the case must be dismissed, it amounts to a nonappearance.

801. If an absent party submitted an answer or preparatory brief waiving or acknowledging a claim and such documents were notarized, the waiver or acknowledgment of the claim is deemed to have been effected (§148(2) CPA). If terms of a settlement were offered in notarized documents and the present party accepts them, the settlement before the court is deemed to have been effected (§148(3) CPA).

B. Constructive Admission

802. Should a party fail to appear at an oral hearing without submitting the answer or a preparatory brief, he/she is deemed to have admitted the facts alleged by the other present party (§150(3) CPA). However, such a constructive admission is limited to the matters asserted in the present party's brief (CPA §276).

803. When a defendant fails to submit the answer within thirty days after being served a copy of the complaint, the court may render a judgment without holding any trial by deeming that the defendant has admitted the allegation of facts in the complaint (§257(1) CPA).

II. Nonappearance of Both Parties

804. When both parties fail to appear at the oral hearing or do not make any statement on the merits, the presiding judge must designate another date for a hearing (§268(1) CPA). Should both parties not appear or make statements on the new date or other subsequent date once again, the lawsuit is deemed to have been withdrawn unless either party files a petition for the designation of a hearing date within one month (§268(2) CPA). Should both parties fail to appear on the new date after a petition by a party or on other subsequent date, the lawsuit is deemed to have been conclusively withdrawn (§268(3) CPA).

805. In counting the number of nonappearances, they need not be consecutive. However, nonappearances must take place in the same type of proceedings in the same court. Thus, nonappearances at the pretrial hearing and hearing for oral argument may not be summed up. Nonappearances at the hearings in the first instance and the second instance courts, or those in the second instance prior to the final appeal and those in the same instance after the case is remanded by the Supreme Court also may not be added together.[184]

§4. Ex Parte Proceedings

I. Preservative Measures

806. The court may decide a petition for prejudgment seizure or an injunction regarding the object of the litigation based on only a prima facie showing made by the petitioner without participation of the debtor. The court may hold an in-person hearing or hearing for oral argument or opt not to do so at its discretion (§§280(1),301 CEA). However, in practice, adjudication of cases for preservative measures are usually done by examining documents submitted by the petitioner without holding a hearing, considering the need for secrecy and quickness.

184. *Supra* n. 144.

807. The enforcement of the court decisions ordering prejudgment seizure or a temporary injunction is also carried out without notifying the debtor. This is because the debtor might evade the enforcement of the court decision ordering preservative measures by disposing of, concealing, damaging or fictitiously transferring the properties subject to the enforcement.

808. On the other hand, an injunction serving to provide a temporary status gives the creditor the benefit for a limited period of time as if a judgment favoring him/her was enforced. At the same time, a debtor might sustain irreparable damage once such an injunction is issued even though it is revoked later. In this context, the court must hold an in-person hearing or hearing for oral argument at which the debtor may be present. However, this does not apply when there exist any circumstances in which the objectives of the petition are likely not to be achieved by holding a hearing (§304 CEA).

II. Summary Proceedings for a Payment Order

809. The court may issue a payment order upon petition of a creditor that the debtor pay a specific amount of money or other fungibles, provided it is possible to serve a copy of the order in Korea by a means other than service by publication (§462 CPA). In practice, this procedure is used to obtain an enforceable title for monetary claims. In the petition, the creditor must set forth, in the prayer for relief, the amount of money or the number of securities sought and the grounds on which the claim is based. The court issues an order based on the petition of the creditor without holding a hearing at which the debtor may be present (§467 CPA).

810. Should the debtor lodge an objection to the payment order within two weeks after he/she is served a copy of the order, the order does not have any effect and a lawsuit is deemed to have been brought by the creditor at the time the petition was filed (§472(2) CPA). If not, the payment order becomes final (§470(1) CPA). A final and binding payment order is enforceable but does not have any claim preclusive effect.[185]

811. When it is not possible to serve a copy of the payment order upon a debtor by a means other than service by publication, the court must order the creditor to correct the debtor's place of service. Upon receipt of such order from the court, the creditor may file a request for instituting a lawsuit (§466(1) CPA). Also, when it is impossible to serve a copy of the payment order upon the debtor without resorting to service by publication, or when the place of service is located in a foreign country, the court may, on its own motion, refer the case for litigation procedures (§466(2) CPA). In these cases, the effect of filing a lawsuit is retroactive to the time when the petition for a payment order was filed.

---

185. Supreme Court Decision 2006Da73966 decided on July 9, 2009.

III. Judicial Public Notice and Judgment of Exclusion

A. *Definition and Meaning*

812. A judicial public notice is the public announcement made by the court concerning a specific claim or right. It notifies creditors or right holders that they must file a report on their rights with the court by a certain date and if they fail to do so, they risk a legal penalty or forfeiture. If a creditor or right holder fails to report, he/she does not automatically lose his/her right. The forfeiture of the rights related to the public notice is accomplished by a judgment of exclusion.

813. A judicial public notice is undertaken only in cases provided for by statutes (§475 CPA). The Civil Procedure Act regulates public notices as to declarations of invalidity of legal instruments (§492 CPA) and as to cancellation of registration of property rights (§56 RREA).

814. When a party's right is infringed upon by an adverse party but the identification of the party to be sued is unknown, the aggrieved party may resort to a judicial public notice and judgment of exclusion. For example, if promissory notes are lost or stolen, the owner may file a petition for a public notice and judgment of exclusion to invalidate the notes held by an unknown person. On the other hand, if a mortgage debt no longer exists but the whereabouts of the mortgagee is unknown, the owner of the real property may file a petition for a public notice to cancel registration of the mortgage right in the registration record of the real property.

B. *Proceedings*

1. Judicial Public Notice

815. A petition for a public notice to cancel registration of real rights must contain a prima facie showing that the rights registered are nonexistent, that the registered right holder is missing and the petitioner's intention to ask for a judgment of exclusion. In a petition for public notice to invalidate a legal instrument, the petitioning party must set forth prima facie evidence that the instrument was lost, stolen or destroyed and his/her intention to seek a judgment of exclusion.

816. The court rules on the petition for a public notice by issuing a decision (CPA §478(1)). The court may hold an in-person hearing at its discretion prior to ruling on the petition (CPA §478(2)). If the court permits the public notice, it is implemented by the court clerk. The public notice is effected by placing a notification on the court's bulletin board or advertising it in an official gazette, official report, newspaper or court website (r.142 RCP). It must contain such particulars as the identification of the petitioning party, a request that a report on the relevant claim or right be filed within a specific period, a warning that the claim or right may be forfeited unless a report is filed timely, and the date for a hearing to be held after the deadline (§479(2) CPA). The time span between the implementation of the public notice and the deadline for filing of a report on the rights must be at least three months (§481 CPA).

2. Judgment of Exclusion

817. The petitioning party must appear at the hearing held after the deadline and present statements regarding the grounds upon which the petition for a judgment of exclusion is based and the rights reported by the creditors or right holders (§486 CPA). The court denies a petition for a judgment of exclusion in the form of a decision when the petition is groundless. But the court renders the judgment when the petition is granted. With a judgment of exclusion, the petitioning party is deemed to be a rightful possessor of the legal instruments and he/she is able to exercise related legal rights. Also, he/she can cancel the registration of the right in the relevant registration record.

Chapter 2. Review Proceedings

§1. Appeal

I. Introduction

A. *Definition and Meaning*

818. An appeal is a process of challenging the judgment rendered by a court and asking for a competent higher court to reverse or modify it. There are two types of appeals: an appeal from the court of first instance and the final appeal to the Supreme Court. An appeal is distinguished from a retrial in that the latter is a new lawsuit initiated against a judgment that is final and not appealable.

819. There are two different paths to take for appeals from the court of first instance. A judgment rendered by a single judge is subject to appellate review by a judicial panel (appellate panel) in the same District Court. A judgment rendered by a judicial panel in the District Court or the Branch Court is appealed to a High Court. The final appeal from a High Court, the Patent Court, and an appellate panel in the District Court is to the Supreme Court.

B. *Prerequisites for an Appeal*

820. An appeal must be filed within two weeks after a copy of the judgment document is served (§§396(1),425 CPA). In general, if a party fails to observe a deadline due to circumstances outside of his/her control, he/she may subsequently complete the procedural act within two weeks after those circumstances cease to exist (§173 CPA). This rule also applies to the time frame for filing appeals.

821. A notice of appeal should be filed in the court that rendered the judgment (§397(1) CPA). If an appellant erroneously submits the notice to the appellate court and that court sends it to the appropriate lower court, the deadline for filing the appeal is determined when the lower court received the notice.[186]

822. An appeal lodged by a party who does not have a legitimate interest to appeal is unlawful. A legitimate interest to appeal is determined by comparing the prayer for relief and the operative provisions of the judgment. If the former is the same as the latter, it means that the plaintiff won the case entirely and only the defendant may appeal the judgment. If the court dismisses the complaint entirely, only the plaintiff may appeal. If the complaint was partially dismissed and partially granted, both parties have a legitimate interest to appeal.

186. *Supra* n. 85.

823. When the court dismisses the case without prejudice, either of the parties has a legitimate interest to appeal because a dismissal with prejudice is more advantageous to the defendant than the dismissal without prejudice.

824. There are some exceptions regarding a legitimate interest to appeal. If a complaint does not reveal that the suit is for only a part of a claim, the preclusive effect of a judgment reaches the remaining parts of the claim and a new lawsuit is therefore not allowed. However, according to court decisions, a plaintiff who wins the partial case entirely in the court of first instance has a legitimate interest to appeal in order to enlarge the claim for relief by encompassing the remaining parts of the claim in the intermediate appellate court.[187] Also, even when the plaintiff's claim is dismissed with prejudice, the defendant has a legitimate interest to appeal provided the dismissal is due to the defendant's affirmative defense of a setoff and the defendant's other defenses was denied.[188] This is because the defendant's claim against the plaintiff has been extinguished by the setoff although the defendant prevailed.

C. *Waiver of the Right to Appeal*

825. The waiver of the right to appeal is a procedural and unilateral act that extinguishes the right to appeal. In a necessary joinder of parties, joinder of parties in the alternative and joinder of a primary party and contingent party, the waiver of the right to appeal is valid provided all the co-parties waive the right (§§67,70 CPA). In a case where a third party intervened as an independent party, the waiver is valid only when all loosing parties waive the right (§§79(2),67 CPA).

826. According to the prevailing opinion, a party cannot waive the right to appeal in advance of a final judgment because an appeal is premised on a final judgment.[189] A waiver of the right to appeal must be filed in the court which rendered the judgment prior to filing of an appeal, and thereafter, in the appellate court (§§395(1),425 CPA). If an appellant waives the right to appeal, it has the additional effect of withdrawing an appeal (§§395(3),425 CPA).

D. *Agreement Not to Appeal*

827. An agreement not to appeal a judgment is a procedural contract, which precludes the right of appeal. Parties may reach an agreement not to appeal even before a dispute between them takes place. If there is an agreement not to appeal from the court of first instance, the judgment becomes final at the time it is rendered. If the

187. Supreme Court Decision 96Da12276 decided on October 24, 1997.
188. Supreme Court Decision 2002Da34666 decided on September 6, 2002.
189. Si-yoon Lee, supra n. 8, at 831.

parties agree not to appeal a judgment of an intermediate appellate court, the judgment of the court of first instance is appealable but the judgment rendered by the intermediate appellate court is final.

E. Effects of an Appeal

828. Once an appeal of the original court judgment is filed timely, the finality of the entire judgment is held in abeyance even when the appellant's claim was partially granted and that part of the judgment is not appealed. The subject-matter of the action adjudicated by the lower court is transferred to the appellate court and examined there. If the lower court failed to rule on an independent claim among claims joined in a judgment, the undecided claim remains pending before the lower court and it must render a supplementary judgment.

829. As the effect of an appeal reaches all the claims, the appellant can expand the extent to which the judgment is being contested and the respondent can lodge a cross-appeal after the initial time frame for filing appeals has passed. For example, a plaintiff filed a lawsuit seeking payment of KRW 20 million based on two claims: a loan claim of KRW 10 million and a claim for the purchase price of KRW 10 million. The trial court rendered a judgment awarding KRW 6 million based on the claim for the purchase price and dismissed the rest of the purchase price claim and the entire loan claim. In this case, if the defendant appealed the judgment granting a part of the claim for the purchase price, both the purchase price claim and the loan claim become pending before the appellate court. However, only the claim for the purchase price (KRW 6 million) is reviewed.

830. If a waiver of the right to appeal was effected or an agreement not to appeal was entered into regarding a certain claim among joined claims, the judgment becomes partially final with respect to that claim. Also, in the joinder of independent parties, the effect of an appeal is confined to the appellant and the respondent, and the rest of the parties are not affected by the appeal.

II. Appeal from the Court of First Instance

A. Filing of the Notice of Appeal

831. A party may appeal the judgment of the court of first instance by submitting a notice of appeal to the same court within two weeks after a copy of the judgment document has been served (§396(1) CPA).

832. The single judge or the presiding judge of the judicial panel that rendered the judgment inspects the formality of the notice of appeal and the procedural prerequisites, including indispensable particulars of the notice, observance of the time frame, and judicial stamps. Should the judge find any procedural defect, he/she issues an order to correct it. If the defect is uncorrectable or the appellant fails to comply with the order, the judge dismisses the notice of appeal in the form of an order (§§399(1),(2) CPA). The appellant may lodge an immediate appeal against this order (§399(3) CPA). If the notice of appeal passes the examination by the presiding judge, the litigation records of the case are sent to the appellate court. The presiding judge of the appellate court also examines the notice of appeal in the same manner as the judge in court below (§402 CPA).

B. Cross-Appeal

833. The respondent may file a cross-appeal by submitting a notice of cross-appeal to the court of appeals, taking advantage of the appellate procedure initiated by the appellant. The cross-appeal is a means of defense for the respondent corresponding to the fact that the appellant may expand the extent to which the judgment of the court below is contested. The respondent may file a cross-appeal even after his/her right of appeal was waived or extinguished by the lapse of the time for filing appeals (§403 CPA). Where only the defendant filed an appeal, the plaintiff may expand the claim for relief by means of the cross-appeal.

834. The cross-appeal must be filed prior to the close of the hearing for oral argument in the appellate court (§403 CPA). The cross-appeal is deemed to have been withdrawn if the principal appeal is withdrawn or dismissed on procedural grounds. However, if the respondent lodged an appeal within the time frame for filing appeals, it is deemed an independent appeal and not affected by the principal appeal (§404 CPA).

C. Procedure in the Intermediate Appellate Court

835. An intermediate appellate court is a trial court in Korea. The adjudication of the case at the intermediate court of appeals is based on the litigation records of the court below. However, submitting new evidence is allowed. It is the same as a resumption of the hearing for oral argument.

836. The procedural acts including various motions, oral statements, admission of facts, affirmative defenses and examination of evidence made in the court below have the same effects as if they were done in the intermediate appellate court. However, the scope of adjudication is limited to the extent the appellant contests the judgment below. Accordingly, if only the defendant appeals a judgment dismissing the main claim and granting a contingent claim, the effects of the appeal reach both the claims but the appellate court may only review the judgment regarding the contingent claim.

837. An alteration of action and filing of a counterclaim is allowed in the intermediate appellate court. In this case, the scope of review by the court above may go beyond the extent the appellant contested the judgment below.

D. Final Judgment in the Intermediate Appellate Court

838. If an appellate court reaches the same conclusion as the operative provisions of the judgment below on the merits, it must dismiss the appeal with prejudice even though the grounds of the judgment below were incorrect.

839. However, there are some exceptions. If a court below accepted a defendant's affirmative defense of a setoff and dismissed the plaintiff's claim with prejudice and the defendant appeals and the appellate court finds another affirmative defense also has good grounds, the appellate court accepts that defense rather than the setoff. It would then reverse the judgment below and dismiss the plaintiff's claim with prejudice instead of dismissing the appeal. The same applies when lower court grants a claim among joined claims in the alternative but the appellate court grants a different claim.

840. When the intermediate appellate court reaches the different conclusion from that of the judgment below, in principle, the appellate court reverses the part of the judgment that was contested and renders a judgment on the merits. However, when the appellate court reverses a judgment which dismissed a lawsuit without prejudice based on procedural grounds, the appellate court remands the case to the lower court. The appellate court could also render a judgment on the merits when additional hearings are not necessary (§418 CPA). In addition, the intermediate appellate court reverses a judgment of first instance and transfers the case to the competent court when the court below lacked the exclusive jurisdiction to adjudicate the case (§419 CPA).

841. The intermediate appellate court may not render a judgment which is more disadvantageous to the appellant than the judgment in the first instance. This is called the prohibition of disadvantageous modification. This principle is invoked frequently by legal professionals but it comes naturally from Section 415 of the Civil Procedure Act stipulating that the scope of review by the appellate court is confined to the extent the appellant contested the judgment below (§415 CPA).

842. The prohibition of disadvantageous modification applies when one of the parties file an appeal. When both the parties appeal, it does not apply. Where a third party intervened as an independent party, or a primary party and contingent party were joined, disadvantageous alteration to the appellant may be resulted in the appellate court due to the necessity of unified conclusion as to the claims of each party.

843. This principle, by its nature, also does not apply to lawsuits seeking a formative judgment based on perfunctory causes, such as an action for partition of jointly owned properties (§268 CA) and an action for settling land boundary lines.

III. The Final Appeal

A. Definition and Meaning

844. A final appeal is an appeal to the Supreme Court from a judgment by High Courts, the Patent Court and appellate panels of District Courts. High Courts and appellate panels of District Courts are intermediate appellate courts.

845. Where both parties agree to appeal the final judgment of a first instance court directly to the Supreme Court (skipping an intermediate appellate court), the Supreme Court has the appellate jurisdiction over the case (§§422(2),390 CPA). This is called a "jump-up appeal" but seldom used in practice.

846. The Supreme Court is the court of last resort and hears appeals on points of law. The main function of the Supreme Court lies in the pursuit of a unified interpretation of the law and correction of errors in the rulings made by the lower courts.

847. The Constitutional Court has held that the right to a fair trial enshrined in the Constitution does not include the right to appeal any case to the Supreme Court.[190] However, the public has traditionally had a firm belief that the losing party should have the opportunity to bring a case to a second instance court and then to the highest court of the land. As a result, cases are flooding the Supreme Court. In 2018, the number of cases filed with the Court reached 65,944.

848. In 2014, the Supreme Court exerted all its efforts to create a new appellate court, namely the National Court of Appeals, situated between High Courts and the Supreme Court to alleviate the workload of the Justices. If the National Court of Appeals had been created, the Supreme Court would have selected the cases of legal and social importance to review in its sole discretion whereas the rest of the cases would have been automatically transferred to the new appellate court. However, the Ministry of Justice and the Korean Bar Association adamantly opposed this judicial reform. Therefore, in the National Assembly the bill to create the new appellate court did not come to a vote because it did not come up for deliberation before the term of the National Assembly expired in 2016.

B. Grounds for the Final Appeal

849. A party may appeal the ruling by an intermediate appellate court or the Patent Court to the Supreme Court only on the grounds that it is inconsistent with the Constitution, a statute, enforcement decree, regulation or rule, and that such an error affected the conclusion of the lower court ruling (§423 CPA). An erroneous interpretation or application of law in the judgment is not enough. The appellant

190. Constitutional Court Decision 99HunBa1 decided on January 20, 1995.

must establish that the error resulted in a judgment that is prejudicial to the appellant. The violation of law in this context includes procedural errors and the term "law" encompasses the evaluation of the facts with respect to such issues as negligence, public policy, unavoidable reasons and good faith.

850. When the violation of law is grave enough to fall into any of the categories listed below, a party may appeal to the Supreme Court even though it did not affect the conclusion (the operative provisions) of the judgment. These cases are set out in the Civil Procedure Act as absolute grounds for a final appeal. They are: when the court that ruled on the case was not constituted in compliance with the relevant statutes; when a judge who is prohibited from participating in the decision did so; when the provisions as to exclusive jurisdiction have been violated; when an attorney of record or statutory agent performed procedural acts beyond his/her authority as an agent; when the open court principle was violated; and when the grounds for the judgment are not set forth clearly or are contradictory (§424(1) CPA).

851. A retrial is a procedure to rescind a final judgment and adjudicate the case anew if there was one of the serious procedural defects listed in Section 451 of the Civil Procedure Act. When comparing the grounds for the retrial with the absolute grounds for final appeal, some of the former are not included in the latter even though more serious violations of law are supposed to result in the retrial. For example, "documents or any other objects on which the judgment was based had been forged or altered" is one of the reasons for retrial but it is not stipulated as one of the absolute grounds for a final appeal. However, the Supreme Court has held that each of the grounds for retrial constitutes an absolute ground for a final appeal.[191]

C. Procedure in the Supreme Court

852. The provisions of the Civil Procedure Act concerning the presiding judge's examination of the notice of appeal and procedural prerequisites for appeal from the first instance court apply to a final appeal (§§425,399,402 CPA). The court clerk of the Supreme Court should, upon receipt of the litigation records from the court below, promptly notify the parties that the records were received (§426 CPA).

853. The appellant must submit a statement of the grounds for a final appeal to the Supreme Court within twenty days after he/she receives the notification that the litigation records of the court below were received by the Supreme Court (§427 CPA). Should the appellant fail to do so, the Supreme Court must dismiss the appeal with prejudice unless there exists a matter to be examined *sua sponte* (§429 CPA).

854. The Supreme Court reviews the prior lower court judgment to the extent it is contested in the notice of appeal based on the statement of the grounds for a final appeal (§431 CPA). As the Supreme Court is the court of review and adjudicates

191. Supreme Court Decision 2014Da11376 decided on June 12, 2014.

the appeal on points of law, the facts established by the lower court are binding upon it (§433 CPA). Thus, the parties are not allowed to assert new allegations on the merits or present new evidence. Nor is an alteration of action permitted.

D. Final Judgment in the Supreme Court

855. Should a final appeal be unlawful on procedural grounds, the Supreme Court dismisses the appeal without prejudice. If the final appeal is procedurally lawful but the violation of law in the judgment is not established, the appeal is dismissed with prejudice.

856. The Act on Special Cases Concerning Procedure for Trial by The Supreme Court was enacted in 1994 to alleviate the workload of the Justices. If the statement of the grounds for a final appeal does not assert one of the reasons prescribed in that Act, the Supreme Court may close the proceedings at any time and render a judgment dismissing the appeal with prejudice. The grounds listed in the Act include an assertion that the lower court judgment violated the Constitution, a statute, enforcement decree, regulation or rule; or that its interpretation was improper; or that it is contrary to the precedents of the Supreme Court (§4 ASPTS).

857. When the final appeal is well-founded, the Supreme Court reverses the prior judgment and remands the case to the lower court (§436(1) CPA). However, where the case is ready for a judicial decision without further oral arguments, the Court renders a judgment on the merits (§437(1) CPA). Where the lower court did not have exclusive jurisdiction or it overlooked the fact that the first instance court had lacked exclusive jurisdiction, the Supreme Court reverses the relevant judgments below and transfers the case to the competent court to hear the case (§436(1) CPA).

858. The lower court to which the Supreme Court remands or transfers a case must resume the hearing and adjudicate the case anew in compliance with the reasons stated by the Supreme Court (§436(2) CPA).

IV. Appeal Against Decision and Order

859. A party may appeal a decision or order issued in the court of first instance to an intermediate appellate court and appeal those rulings issued in the court of second instance and the Patent Court to the Supreme Court. Not all decisions and orders are subject to appeal. Only those which denied a motion on procedural matters and which are subject to appeal by statute are appealable (§439 CPA). In some cases, a party who is dissatisfied with an order must lodge an objection on which the court rules in the form of a decision and this decision is appealable. There are some decisions and orders that statutory provisions prohibit the parties from appealing or by interpretation are unappealable.

860. An immediate appeal of a decision or order is allowed when it is permitted by statute. The time frame for an immediate appeal is one week after the appellant has notice of it (§444 CPA). Once an appeal is lodged, enforcement of a decision or an order is stayed automatically (§447 CPA). A special appeal against a decision or order may be filed with the Supreme Court even if the ruling is unappealable, when it is, nevertheless, in violation of the Constitution or the lower court's opinion on the constitutionality or legality of an enforcement decree, regulation or rule is erroneous and affected the result of the ruling (§449 CPA).

861. When the original court decides that an appeal against its decision or order is lawful and well-founded, the court which issued the ruling may alter or correct its decision or order *sua sponte* (§446 CPA). The provisions concerning litigation proceedings in the intermediate appellate court and the Supreme Court apply to those for an appeal and immediate appeal against a decision or an order in the respective courts (§443 CPA).

§2. Retrial

I. Definition and Meaning

862. When there is a serious procedural defect with respect to a final judgment, the aggrieved party may file a complaint seeking rescission of the judgment and a new trial. Theoretically, the procedure for a retrial has two steps. The first one is an examination of whether the grounds for retrial alleged by the plaintiff exist or not. The second one is an adjudication of the case when there are grounds for a retrial.[192] A lawsuit for a retrial is an action for a procedurally formative judgment. It is different from an appeal in that it is raised against a final and binding judgment and must be filed with the court which rendered the judgment. In addition, the original judgment remains in effect while the lawsuit for retrial is pending.

863. An action for a retrial may also be filed in a case where there existed a ground for retrial in the proceedings for a settlement before the court, a settlement prior to filing of a lawsuit, mediation, waiver of a claim and acknowledgement of a claim. Also, a party may bring a lawsuit for retrial against a decision and order which are subject to an immediate appeal (§461 CPA). This type of actions for a new trial is called a quasi-retrial.

II. Grounds for Retrial

864. The grounds for a retrial are: ① where the court that ruled on the case was not constituted in compliance with the relevant statutes; ② where a judge who was prohibited from participating in the decision did so; ③ where an attorney of record or statutory agent performed procedural acts beyond his/her authority as an agent;

192. Supreme Court Decision 92Da22473, 92Da22480 decided on December 27, 1994.

④ where a judge who participated in the decision committed a crime in connection with his/her duties in the case; ⑤ where a party was forced to admit a fact or prevented from presenting allegations or evidence due to another person's criminal conduct and this affected the judgment; ⑥ where documents or any other evidence on which the judgment was based were forged or altered; ⑦ where false sworn statements by a witness, expert examiner, or interpreter, or by a party or statutory agent were used as evidence in the judgment; ⑧ where the civil or criminal judgment or other judicial decision, or the administrative disposition, on which the judgment was based has been modified by a subsequent judicial decision or administrative disposition; ⑨ where the reasoning for the judgment was omitted on important matters that might have affected the judgment; ⑩ where the judgment is precluded by a prior final and binding judgment of the same claim; or where a party who was aware of the other party's address or residence instituted a lawsuit with a statement that he/she did not know the other party's whereabouts or set forth an incorrect address or residence (§451(1) CPA).

865. A party may not file a lawsuit for a retrial when the party has appealed the judgment on the same grounds as those for retrial or knowingly did not allege them in an appeal (§451(1) CPA).

III. Procedure

866. A retrial case falls under exclusive jurisdiction of the court which rendered the judgment (§453(1) CPA). The plaintiff must file a complaint for retrial with that court (§455 CPA). The complaint must set forth the judgment against which the action for retrial is directed and a prayer for relief and the grounds on which the complaint is based (§458 CPA). While there are debates over whether the plaintiff may join claims in the lawsuit for retrial, courts have held that joinder of claims is not allowed in retrial proceedings.[193] That is because the judgment remains final and binding while the lawsuit for retrial is pending.

IV. Final Judgment

867. If an action for a retrial lacks a procedural prerequisite or a requirement for retrial, the court renders a judgment dismissing the case without prejudice (§455 CPA). If the grounds for retrial have not been established in the proceedings, the court renders a judgment dismissing the case with prejudice.

868. Where the grounds for retrial are established, the court adjudicates the case anew by resuming the hearing for the previously concluded case. If the court reaches a different conclusion in the retrial proceedings, it renders a judgment rescinding the previous judgment and ruling on the merits. If the conclusion of the judgment is the same as the court's previous judgment, the court dismiss the case with prejudice (§460 CPA).

193. Supreme Court Decision 96Da41649 decided on May 28, 1997.

Part V. Incidents

Chapter 1. Interruption and Suspension of the Proceedings

§1. Concept

869. The Civil Procedure Act and other statutes specify circumstances that require courts to halt proceedings until the reason for the stoppage is resolved. This type of stoppage is distinguished from an adjournment of proceedings while the court waits for the response of a fact inquiry or results of an expert examination.

870. The Civil Procedure Act distinguishes between an interruption and a suspension. The proceedings are interrupted when a party's capacity or status to participate in a lawsuit changes due to such things as the loss of standing, death or a change in corporate status. The proceedings are suspended temporarily by a statute or court decision when the court or a party are faced with an obstacle such as a natural disaster or a party is incapacitated for some other reason.

§2. Interruption of the Proceedings

I. Causes of Interruption

A. Death of a Party

871. A lawsuit is pending before the court when a copy of the complaint is served upon the defendant. If a party dies once a lawsuit is pending, the proceedings are interrupted (§233 CPA). Should a party die before a copy of the complaint is served, the lawsuit is simply invalid, it is not pending and no interruption occurs. In this case, if the plaintiff amends the complaint and names a successor, the lawsuit is deemed to have been properly filed as of the time the complaint was filed initially.

872. When a party dies during the pendency of a lawsuit based on an inalienable right of the deceased party, the proceedings are terminated, rather than interrupted, for example, when a party dies during pendency of the lawsuit seeking a divorce and division of property.[194]

B. Merger or Division of a Company

873. Proceedings are interrupted when a company that is a party ceases to exist due to a merger or division and a newly incorporated company or surviving company succeeds to the rights and obligations of the nonsurviving company.

C. Loss of Litigation Capacity

874. Proceedings are interrupted if a party loses litigation capacity, or when, for instance, his/her statutory agent dies or loses agency authority (§235 CPA). Because the termination of an agent's authority takes effect upon notification to the other party (§63(1) CPA), the proceedings are interrupted at the time of the notification. The provisions regarding a statutory agent also apply to the representative of a legal person (§64 CPA).

D. Loss of Standing

875. Proceedings are interrupted when the duties of a trustee terminate during the pendency of a lawsuit related to property held in trust (§236 CPA); when a bankruptcy court issues a decision ordering commencement of business rehabilitation or bankruptcy procedures (§59(1) DRBA, §239 CPA); or when a person who is a party based on third-party standing dies or loses standing as a party. This includes a business rehabilitation trustee, a bankruptcy trustee and an appointed party (§237(1) CPA).

II. Exceptions to Interruption

876. When a party is represented by an attorney, proceedings are not interrupted even though a circumstance stated in the Civil Procedure Act occurs (§238 CPA). In this case, the case moves forward. But once the judgment document is served on each of the parties, litigation is interrupted unless the attorney is authorized to appeal.[195] In addition, the time to appeal does not run during this interruption of the proceedings.

---

194. Supreme Court Decision 94Meu246,94Meu253 decided on October 28, 1994.
195. Supreme Court Decision 2014Da210449 decided on April 2, 2016.

877. However, when business rehabilitation procedures or bankruptcy procedures are ordered by a court, litigation is interrupted even though the relevant party is represented by an attorney because Section 238 of the Civil Procedure Act does not apply to such a case.

III. Resumption of the Proceedings

878. Interrupted proceedings are resumed by a court decision granting the petition of a successor or other party (§241 CPA). The successors include an heir, an administrator of inherited property and an executor of a will; a newly incorporated company or surviving company where a company is merged or divided; a statutory agent after a party loses litigation capacity; the principal or new statutory agent where a statutory agent dies or is unable to proceed; and a rehabilitation trustee or bankruptcy trustee.

879. When there is an interruption in a case with multiple heirs, each heir resumes the proceedings according to his/her share of the inheritance. If some of the heirs petition for succession in title and the remaining heirs do not, the proceedings are resumed only as to the petitioners' share. Litigation as to the nonpetitioning heirs continue to be interrupted.[196]

880. When litigation is interrupted and parties do not take steps to resume proceedings, the court may, *sua sponte,* order the parties to do so (§244 CPA). The interruption is terminated by this decision. Thereafter, the court may designate a date for a hearing or examination of evidence.

§3. Suspension of the Proceedings

I. Automatic Suspension

881. Where the court is unable to function due to a natural disaster or other circumstances, proceedings are automatically suspended until the situation is remedied (§245 CPA). Should a party file a motion to challenge or disqualify a judge, proceedings are suspended until a final decision on the motion (§48 CPA). Where the trial court, including first and second instance courts, refers a case to mediation, the proceedings are suspended until the mediation procedure is concluded (r,4(2) RCM). If a court refers a case to the Constitutional Court, proceedings are suspended until the Constitutional Court delivers a decision on the constitutionality of the relevant statute (42(1) CCA).

196. Supreme Court Decision 93Da31993 decided on November 4, 1994.

II. Suspension by a Decision

882. Where a party is unable to participate in a case for an indefinite period due to unavoidable circumstances, e.g., natural disaster or illness, the court may issue a decision ordering suspension of proceedings. Also, where a petition is filed for rehabilitation procedures, the court may, if deemed necessary, issue a decision ordering suspension of the proceedings until the court issues a decision on the rehabilitation petition (§44(1) DRBA).

§4. Effects of Interruption or Suspension of Proceedings

883. While the proceedings are interrupted or suspended, the court may not take procedural measures and the parties may not conduct procedural acts. However, if the proceedings are interrupted or suspended after the hearing for oral argument is closed, the court may render a judgment (§247(1) CPA). During an interruption or suspension, any deadlines or schedules are also suspended. Once the case resumes, deadlines are reset anew starting from the date the case resumes (§247(2) CPA).

Chapter 2. Termination of an Action

§1. Declaratory Judgment Affirming the Termination

I. Concept

884. When a lawsuit is terminated by means other than a final judgment, such as withdrawal, settlement, mediation, or waiver or acknowledgement of a claim, there can be a dispute on whether the lawsuit ended or not. In this circumstance, the court renders a declaratory judgment *sua sponte,* affirming the termination of a case.

II. Causes

A. Motion for Designation of Hearing Date

885. Where a party asserts that a case is still pending even after an action to terminate the case has occurred, the court holds a hearing for oral argument to determine whether the lawsuit has ended or not (r.67(2) RCP). Such disputes usually arise when there was a miscommunication between the court and the parties in the process of mediation or settlement, or when a party alleges that a legal document submitted to the court to terminate a case was invalid.

886. If the court finds that the case is pending because there were defects in the procedural acts to terminate it, the court must continue the proceedings and set forth the reasons in an interlocutory judgment or a final judgment. However, should the court find that the case is not pending anymore, it issues a declaration affirming the termination of the lawsuit (r.67(3) RCP).

887. In a case where the lawsuit is withdrawn after the court rendered a judgment which was appealed by both parties and a party disputes the validity of the withdrawal, the appellate court determines whether the lawsuit has been terminated. If only one party has appealed, the court that rendered the judgment determines the finality of the case. If the court finds that the withdrawal is invalid, it renders a declaratory judgment to that effect. If the withdrawal was valid, the court renders a declaratory judgment affirming termination of the lawsuit (r.67(4) RCP).

888. If a party asserts the pendency of a case that was terminated by a settlement or mediation, the court holds a hearing to determine whether the case was concluded or not and render a judgment to that effect.[197]

---

197. Supreme Court Decision 99Da67703 decided on March 10, 2000; Supreme Court Decision 2000Da58668 decided on March 9, 2001.

B. When the Court of Prior Instance Overlooked the Termination of an Action

889. If a court of prior instance overlooks the termination of an action and renders a judgment, the appellate court reverses that judgment and renders a judgment affirming the termination of the lawsuit.[198] This happens more often than not because courts make mistakes in counting the number of nonappearances by a plaintiff in determining a constructive withdrawal or the court fails to note the alteration of an action. This is especially true where there is replacement of claims.

§2. Causes for the Termination of an Action

I. Withdrawal of a Lawsuit

A. Concept

890. The plaintiff may withdraw the lawsuit by an oral statement at a pretrial hearing or the hearing for oral argument, or by filing a document evidencing his/her intent to withdraw the case (§266(3) CPA).

891. If the parties execute an agreement among themselves for the plaintiff to withdraw a lawsuit, the lawsuit is not withdrawn because it is not a procedural act before the court. However, in this case, if the plaintiff does not withdraw the lawsuit in violation of the agreement, the court dismisses the case without prejudice on the grounds that the plaintiff does not have a legitimate interest to pursue the case.[199]

B. Requirements

892. A lawsuit may be withdrawn even after the judgment is rendered and until it becomes final and binding. Thus, the plaintiff may withdraw a lawsuit in the appellate court (§266(1) CPA). However, if the defendant has already submitted an answer or brief on the merits, or made statements on the merits at a hearing, the withdrawal does not take effect without the consent of the defendant (§266(2) CPA).

893. When a lawsuit is withdrawn, the court serves the document of withdrawal or the record of the hearing containing the plaintiff's statement of withdrawal on the defendant. Should the defendant not raise an objection within two weeks after the service of the documents, he/she is deemed to have consented to the withdrawal (§266(6) CPA).

---

198. Supreme Court Decision 90Nu5153 decided on September 10, 1991.
199. Supreme Court Decision 2013Da19571 decided on July 12, 2013.

C. *Effects*

894. When a lawsuit is withdrawn, the effects of procedural acts concerning the lawsuit are extinguished retroactively as if the case had not been filed. The interruption of the statute of limitations period based on the filing a lawsuit is also removed retroactively. However, the statute is again tolled if, within six months, the plaintiff takes any measure to interrupt the limitations period (§170(2) CA).

895. A plaintiff may file a new lawsuit for the same claim if he/she withdrew a lawsuit before a judgment on the merits is rendered. If he/she does so after rendition of a judgment, a new lawsuit for the same claim is considered a repetitive action and unlawful (§267(2) CPA). However, where the plaintiff withdraws a lawsuit after a judgment according to an agreement with the defendant and the defendant fails to perform an obligation that is a precondition for the withdrawal, the Supreme Court has held that a new lawsuit on the same subject-matter may be filed.[200]

II. Waiver or Acknowledgement of a Claim

896. The waiver of a claim is the plaintiff's unilateral affirmation before the court that his/her claim is without merit. The acknowledgement of a claim is the defendant's unilateral affirmation before the court the plaintiff's claim is well-founded. When the waiver of a claim is entered in the record of the hearing, it has the same effect as a final and binding judgment dismissing the plaintiff's claim with prejudice. Likewise, the record of the hearing containing the acknowledgement of a claim has the same effect as a final and binding judgment granting the plaintiff's claim (§220 CPA).

III. Settlement Before the Court

A. *Concept*

897. A settlement before the court is an agreement between parties to resolve the pending case by making mutual concessions at a hearing. It is distinguished from a waiver or acknowledgement of a claim in that the plaintiff partially waives his/her claim and the defendant, in return, partially acknowledges the plaintiff's claim. It is different from an out-of-court settlement in that the former is a procedural act conducted before the court while the latter is a contract outside the court proceedings and regulated by substantive law.

200. Supreme Court Decision 93Da22074 decided on August 24, 1993.

B. Requirements

898. There should be mutual concessions between the parties in settling a case before the court. The concessions may be made on legal relationships other than the subject-matter of the lawsuit. A third party may be included as a party to the settlement.

899. If the terms of a settlement agreement violate a statutory prohibition or contradicts a public policy, the settlement is invalid. However, the motivation of the settlement agreement or the circumstances in which the agreement was reached dos not affect its binding force.[201] When the parties orally state the terms of the settlement agreement at a pretrial hearing or hearing for oral arguments and these statements are entered in the record of the hearing, the settlement takes effect (§220 CPA). In addition, where a party does not appear at a pretrial hearing or hearing for oral argument but submits a preparatory brief containing an offer of settlement and the brief is notarized, a settlement is concluded if the party who does appear accepts the terms of settlement before the court (§148(3) CPA).

C. Effects

900. The record of the hearing in which a settlement agreement is entered has the same effect as a final judgment (§220 CPA). This means that the terms of the settlement agreement have the same binding force as the operative provisions of a final judgment which have formal conclusive effects, enforceability and claim preclusion. Absent serious errors that render a judgment void, the settlement is effective insofar as it is not rescinded by a quasi-retrial.[202]

901. The settlement before the court has the same effect as an out-of-court settlement creating legal relationships under substantive law. Therefore, the claims and obligations created by a settlement supersede those based on previous relationships.[203]

IV. Court Decision Setting Forth the Terms of a Settlement

902. The court, a delegated member of a judicial panel or a commissioned judge may issue a decision *sua sponte* setting forth the terms of a settlement to resolve a pending case that is within the scope of the prayer for relief asserted in the complaint §225(1) CPA). This means that the terms of a settlement agreement are determined by the court. In this case, the court clerk serves a copy of the decision document or the record of the hearing in which the decision is entered upon the parties (§225(2) CPA).

201. Supreme Court Decision 2002Da44014 decided on December 6, 2002.
202. *Supra* n. 201.
203. Supreme Court Decision 2009Da90856 decided on July 28, 2011.

903. Either of the parties may raise an objection to the decision within two weeks after he/she is served the document (§226(1) CPA). With the objection, the case remains pending and not affected by the settlement decision. Absent a timely objection, the decision takes the same effect as a settlement before the court (§231 CPA).

V. Mediation

904. The court hearing a case may, if deemed necessary, refer it to mediation procedures. The possibility of meditation exists until a judgment is rendered in the intermediate appellate court (§6 JCCDA). The court may preside over the mediation proceedings or send it to the judge in charge of mediation (§§7(1),(3) JCCDA). Mediation is effected when the parties reach an agreement and the terms are entered in the mediation record (§28 JCCDA). The mediation agreement entered in the record of the hearing has the same effect as a settlement before the court (§29 JCCDA).

Part VI. Legal Aid and Legal Costs

Chapter 1. Legal Aid

§1. Legal Aid under the Civil Procedure Act

I. Definition and Meaning

905. Legal aid is provided under the Civil Procedure Act to ensure that people who cannot otherwise afford the costs of litigation, have access to the court system, can defend themselves in the court and can be represented by an attorney. This system protects the right to a fair trial and the right to counsel guaranteed by the Constitution.

906. The court may issue a decision granting legal aid *sua sponte* or on petition by a party. This aid takes the form of exempting fees and costs or giving a grace period for the payment of court costs (§129(1) CPA).

907. The local bar association designates attorneys who are willing to provide legal services to legal aid beneficiaries (r.8 GMLA). Where the demand for legal aid is high, the local bar association submits a list of the attorneys to the court and the court selects an attorney. The legal aid lawyers are compensated by the State as prescribed by the Supreme Court Guidelines on Management of Legal Aid (r.9 GMLA).

II. Requirements

908. The requirements for legal aid are as follows.

(1) When it is obvious that the legal position of a party who is financially eligible for legal aid is untenable, the court may not grant such aid (§128(1) CPA). The petition for legal aid is considered by the court hearing the case or retaining the court records (§128(3) CPA).
(2) The petitioner must present prima facie evidence showing that he/she is financially unable to pay the costs and expenses. The court decides the petition based on the materials submitted. However, the following persons are deemed

to meet the financial requirements: (a) recipients under the National Basic Living Security Act, (b) persons eligible for support under the Single-Parent Family Support Act, (c) recipients of a basic pension under the Basic Pension Act, (d) recipients under the Persons with Disabilities Act, and (e) persons eligible for protection under the North Korean Refugees Protection and Settlement Support Act (r.3-2 GMLA).

III. Effects of Decision on Legal Aid

A. Scope of Legal Aid

909. Legal aid covers the expenses and costs incurred in the court which granted the aid. Legal aid includes: (a) deferment of payment of court costs, (b) deferment of payment of compensation for a lawyer and an enforcement officer, (c) exemption of the security deposit for the litigation costs, and (d) deferment or exemption of other expenses prescribed by Supreme Court Regulations (§129(1) CPA).

910. Court fees, costs for service of documents and other litigation costs are paid by the State as requested by the court clerk (r.25(1) RCP). The fees for an enforcement officer and a lawyer are paid at the request of them after the proceedings are terminated (r.26(1) RCP).

B. Collection of Expenses and Costs

911. If at a later date it is determined that a legal aid beneficiary was ineligible for legal aid or he/she becomes able to pay the litigation costs, the court must issue a decision, on petition by an interested party or *sua sponte*, revoking the decision for legal aid and ordering payment of the expenses previously granted (r.17(1) GMLA).

912. On the other hand, when a court renders a judgment ordering the opposing party to bear all or part of the expenses and costs, the attorney or the enforcement officer may file a petition to fix the amount of the litigation costs and enforce that decision (§132(2) CPA).

§2. The Korea Legal Aid Corporation

I. Organization

913. The Korea Legal Aid Corporation (KLAC) is a public interest organization founded in 1987 in order to advance legal aid based on the Legal Aid Act. KLAC provides legal services to people who are in poverty or specified in the Legal Aid Act, including victims of crimes (§21-2 LAA).

914. The president, directors, and the auditor of KLAC are appointed by the Minister of Justice (§13(2) LAA). The nonprofit revenue for KLAC comes from contributions and subsidies by the Government, proceeds generated from activities of KLAC, and cash and other properties donated by individuals and organizations other than the Government (§24 LAA). KLAC employs attorneys full time for legal aid. As of the end of the year 2019, the number of such attorneys exceeds eighty.

II. Requirements for Legal Aid and Beneficiaries

915. The requirements for legal aid, the scope of the assistance and the procedures for providing the aid are determined by the internal rules of KLAC and must be approved by the Minister of Justice (§22 LAA). Presently, the beneficiaries are Korean citizens as well as foreign nationals residing in Korea. They are divided into two groups depending on their income level compared with the national median income. The same income group is further divided according to an individual's profession, background, and circumstances. Some groups are provided legal aid at no charge and other groups must pay for certain expenses and court costs in whole or in part.

Chapter 2. Litigation Costs

§1. Scope

I. Court Costs

916. Court costs are paid to the court by the parties when filing a lawsuit, petition or motion. They include the costs and fees of the court itself and also deposits from which fees for a witness, expert examiner, enforcement officer and other expenses are paid by the court.

917. In general, the judicial stamp accounts for the largest portion of court costs. The judicial stamp is issued by the State. Parties buy and attach these stamps to documents submitted to the court, including a complaint, brief, notice of appeal or petition form. If a stamp is more than KRW 10,000, a payment is made to the bank account designated by the court instead of attaching stamp (rr.27(1),28 RSACL).

918. Except for a complaint and notice of appeal, the amount of stamp is fixed depending on the petition or motion (§9 ASACL). The amount of stamp to be attached to a complaint or notice of appeal increases in proportion to the amount in controversy (§2(1) ASACL).

919. Court costs other than judicial stamp include costs for service of documents; costs for public notice by means of an official gazette, official reports, newspapers, etc.; expenses of witnesses and interpreters including an attendance fee and travel and subsistence costs; compensation for an expert examiner; and travel expenses and lodging for a judge and court clerk in the case of an on-site examination of evidence.

II. Expenses of the Parties

920. Expenses of the parties are the costs that the parties incurred in order to prepare and proceed with the lawsuit. They include reasonable compensation for postage, long-distance calls, photocopying, travel, daily wages and services rendered by paralegals and attorneys.

III. Attorney's Fee

921. The compensation for services rendered by attorneys is included in litigation costs pursuant to the criteria as prescribed by the Supreme Court Regulations (§109(1) CPA). The Regulation on Inclusion of Attorney's Fee into Litigation Cost (RAF) sets forth the method to calculate the amount of attorney's fee to be included in litigation costs. This increases in proportion to the amount in controversy. In addition, the court, in its discretion, may reduce or increase the amount to be included in the litigation costs, taking into account the complexity of the case, the necessity of hiring attorneys and other circumstances (rr.3,6 RAF).

922. If a party has paid attorney's fee exceeding theamount determined by the court in accordance with the Supreme Court Regulation, the remaining amount is excluded from the litigation costs and has to be borne by the party. However, where the defendant, the plaintiff's former agent, had paid unduly large amount of agency fee to a sub-agent in a foreign country in violation of his fiduciary duty and so the plaintiff had to sue the sub-agent in the foreign country to have the agency fee returned, the Supreme Court held that the defendant was liable to compensate for the attorney's fee the plaintiff paid to sue the sub-agent insofar as the amount of the attorney's fee is reasonable.[204]

§2. Allocation of Litigation Costs

I. The Parties

923. Usually litigation costs are borne by the losing party (§98 CPA). However, the court may require the prevailing party to bear all or part of litigation costs that were unnecessary for the expansion or defense of his/her rights, or that were due to the prevailing party's delay of the proceedings (§§99,100 CPA). In the case of a partial loss, the allocation of litigation costs for each party is determined by the court in its discretion (§101 CPA).

II. A Third Party

924. Should a person acting as a statutory agent or attorney fail to prove his/her authority to do so or fail to have the act ratified, the court may order the agent or attorney to bear the litigation costs incurred due to the unauthorized act (§107(2) CPA). If a lawsuit is dismissed without prejudice on the grounds that it was filed by an unauthorized person, that person should bear the litigation costs (§108 CPA).

925. Where a statutory agent, attorney, court clerk or enforcement officer, intentionally or by gross negligence, causes a party to pay unnecessary costs, the court may order that person to reimburse the amount of such costs (§107(1) CPA).

§3. Procedure for the Assessment of Costs

926. The court decides *sua sponte* on the allocation of litigation costs incurred between parties in the final judgment (§104 CPA). Where the appellate court renders a final judgment altering the lower court judgment, or where the court to which a case has been remanded or transferred renders a final judgment, the court decides

---

204. Supreme Court Decision 2010Da81315 decided on January 27, 2012.

on the allocation of litigation costs including those incurred in the proceedings of other courts (§105 CPA). A final judgment includes a decision on the imposition of costs in the operative provisions, which sets forth a certain proportion of the costs to be borne by each party. While the court may assess litigation costs in a final judgment, in practice, the amount is fixed later after the judgment becomes final and not appealable.

927. The petition for assessing costs is filed with the court of first instance which keeps the litigation records including those of the appellate courts. The petitioning party must submit the computation of the costs and supporting documents and a copy of them to be served on the opposing party (§110(2) CPA). The opposing party may submit a statement regarding costs, the computation of the costs incurred and supporting documents (§111(1) CPA). The court determines the total amount of litigation costs and the amount to be borne by each party based on the materials submitted and the litigation records. The amount assessed against each party is deemed to be set off by the amount assessed against the other party (§112 CPA). Thus, the court issues a decision ordering a party to pay a certain amount to the other party. The judicial assistant officials in the District Court are in charge of the procedure for assessment of litigation costs (§54(2) COA).

928. When there is a settlement before the court and the proportion of costs to be borne by each party is specified in the terms of the settlement agreement, the court determines the amount to be reimbursed in the same way as if a final judgment was rendered (§113 CPA). When a case is terminated by other than a final judgment, the court determines the amount to be reimbursed on petition by a party and issues a decision (§114(1) CPA).

Part VII. Evidence

Chapter 1. Facts and Burden of Proof

§1. Definition and Meaning

929. The facts constituting a cause of action or the elements of an affirmative defense are those that give rise to, alter or extinguish a legal right. These facts are referred to as material or essential facts and must be proved to achieve the desired legal effects.

930. In certain fact situations, fact A is inferred from fact B as a matter of common sense, intelligence or reasoning. That is, if fact B is established, then there is a rebuttable presumption that fact A is true. Fact B is a basic fact and fact A is a presumed fact. If fact A is a material fact and the evidence supporting fact A itself is not sufficient, the party with the legal responsibility to prove fact A may present proof of fact B and attempt to persuade the court of the existence of fact A. The building blocks that establish the existence of a material fact are referred as subsidiary facts. Parties also need to present facts to persuade the court on issues related to the admissibility or credibility of evidence. These are referred to as evidentiary facts. Subsidiary facts and evidentiary facts are merely tools to prove the existence of material facts. The ultimate facts that must be proved are the material facts.

931. If a party fails to persuade the court of the existence of the material facts alleged in the pleadings, the court cannot apply the law to these facts and the legal effects sought by a party do not take place. The responsibility of a party to establish material facts is referred to as the "burden of proof."

932. If an opposing party admits the existence of material facts, the burden of proof is satisfied and the court is bound by that admission. Therefore, the burden of proof rule applies when the opposing party denies material facts and the burdened party fails to prove them.

§2. Standard of Proof

933. A court finds facts based on the examination of evidence and rules on the case by applying the law to the established facts. In the Civil Procedure Act, there are different standards of proof depending on the degree of conviction necessary for the court to apply the law to the alleged facts. The degree of conviction ranges from a prima facie showing to higher standards of proof like "beyond a reasonable doubt" (discussed below). A prima facie case is established when a party presents evidence that, absent rebuttal evidence, is sufficient for the court to draw a legal conclusion. Under the Civil Procedure Act, courts can issue evidentiary and procedural decisions or orders based on a prima facie showing. However, a judgment on the merits of a case requires a higher standard of proof.

934. For example, the authority of a statutory agent (§59 CPA), the authority of an attorney (§89 CPA), and facts underlying a judgment on the merits (§§274(2),280,288) must be proved; and grounds to challenge a judge or those of motion for recusal of a judge (§44(2) CPA), grounds of petition for appointment of a special agent (§62 CPA), grounds for the application for litigation intervention (§73 CPA), and causes for legal aid (§128(2) CPA) are to be established by prima facie evidence.

935. To prove facts related to the merits of a civil case, a higher degree of proof than a prima facie showing is necessary, but less strict than the "beyond a reasonable doubt" standard. Commentators are divided over whether facts must be proved by a "preponderance of the evidence" or by "clear and convincing evidence." According to the minority opinion, adopting the "preponderance of evidence" standard, a fact is true if the evidence shows it is more likely than not to be true.[205] The majority "clear and convincing" standard requires a higher degree of probability so that a reasonable person, based on his/her everyday life experiences would believe, with more than 80% certainty, that the factual allegations are true.[206] This "clear and convincing evidence" standard has been adopted by the courts.[207]

§3. Distribution of Burden of Proof

I. General Principles

936. From the perspective of legal impact, material facts are divided into four groups: facts that give rise to a legal right, those that keep a legal right from arising, those that extinguish a legal right and those that impede the exercise of a legal right. The plaintiff who alleges a legal right as a cause of action has the burden to prove the material facts that give rise to that right. The defendant who asserts an affirmative defense has the burden to prove that the right did not arise because of other facts or it was extinguished or there are limits on the exercise of the right. In response, the plaintiff might raise factual allegations that invalidates the defendant's defense. The facts corresponding to such affirmative defenses must be proved by the party that asserts them.

205. Dong-yoon Chung et al., *supra* n. 7, at 545-546.
206. Si-yoon Lee, *supra* n. 8, at 526.
207. Supreme Court Decision 2009Da56603,56610 decided on December 10, 2009.

937. For example, where the plaintiff sues for payment of the purchase price, he/she must prove the fact that a contract for sale was executed (facts giving rise to a legal right). If the defendant raises an affirmative defense based on the statute of limitations, the defendant has the burden of proving that the statutory period has passed. The plaintiff then has the burden to counter that defense by, e.g., proving facts that show the statute of limitations was suspended.

938. In general, the plaintiff bears the burden of proving the facts giving rise to a legal right. However, there are some exceptions. In a lawsuit seeking a declaratory judgment affirming the nonexistence of an obligation, the burden of proof is on the defendant. In addition, in principle, the burden of pleading accompanies the burden to prove the alleged facts. However, where a party to a transaction sues the agent of the other party seeking performance of the contractual obligation on the grounds that the defendant lacked authority as an agent, the plaintiff bears the burden of pleading the cause of action. The defendant bears the burden to prove his/her authority as an agent in order to avoid the plaintiff's claim (§135 CA).

II. Shifting of Burden

A. Shifting by Legislation

939. Where an employee intentionally or negligently injures a third party in the course of his/her employment, the employer is jointly and severally liable unless the employer proves that he/she exercised reasonable care in selecting and supervising the employee (§765 CA). This provision shifts the burden of proof. The employer must raise an affirmative defense asserting that he/she exercised due care as an employer. Absent this provision, the plaintiff seeking tort damages against the employer would have to prove that the employer intentionally or negligently contributed to the employee's tortious act.

940. There are other examples of statutory provisions that shift the burden of proof. The person who takes care of an animal is liable to compensate for the damage caused by the animal unless he/she proves that he/she managed the animal with reasonable care according to the kind and nature of the animal (§759 CA). In a personal injury or wrongful death lawsuit involving an automobile, if the victim was other than a passenger, the operator of the vehicle including the owner is liable for damages unless he/she proves that the driver exercised his/her duty of care, the victim or a third party negligently or intentionally caused the accident and the motor vehicle was not defective at the time of the accident. If the victim was a passenger, the operator is liable unless he/she proves that the accident occurred due to the victim's intentional or suicidal act (§3 GAACA). In a product liability claim, the statute requires the plaintiff to prove that he/she was injured or suffered a loss due to a product, the product was defective, the defect caused the damage and he/she was using the product as intended by the defendant-manufacturer. To avoid liability, the manufacturer has the burden to prove that the defect could not be identified considering the scientific and technical knowledge at the time he/she supplied the product, and that the standards prescribed by the law were followed (§4(1) PLA).

B. Statutory Presumption

941. By statute, certain facts are presumed to be true if a factual predicate is proven. This is referred to as a statutory presumption. Thus, if fact A set out in a statute is proved, the judge is required to deduce the existence of fact B. For example, the possessor of a property is presumed to hold it with the intention to own it openly, peacefully and in good faith (§197(1) CA); and if someone has possessed a property at two different points in time, it is presumed that the possession continued during the interval (§198 CA). In a multi-unit building, the part designated for common use is presumed to be jointly owned by the owners of the units (§215(1) CA); each co-owner of a property is presumed to have an equal share (§262(2) CA); the penalty amount stipulated in a contract to be paid in case of breach is presumed to be the liquidated damages that the parties agreed upon at the time of signing the contract (§398(4) CA); and, in a partnership, the operating partner is presumed to have the authority as an agent for other partners (§709 CA).

942. With a statutory presumption, a party who bears the burden of proof may opt to prove a basic fact which is relatively easy to prove, so that the material fact is, by statute, presumed true. At the same time, statutory presumption is rebuttable. An opposing party may prove facts that are contrary to a presumed fact. For example, the acquisitive prescription of ownership for immovable property requires the possessor to possess the property owned by another for twenty years peacefully and openly with an intention to own (§245(1) CA). In a lawsuit seeking ownership transfer registration on these grounds, the plaintiff may opt to prove the basic facts that he/she possessed the property at a certain time and at another time after twenty years and rely on the statutory presumption that there was continuous possession for the requisite twenty years. In this case, the burden of proof shifts to the defendant (the owner of the property) to rebut the presumption of continuous possession that meet the requirements of the statute. Thus, the defendant must raise an affirmative defense and prove that the plaintiff's possession was interrupted during the period of time.

Chapter 2. Admissibility of Evidence

§1. Definition and Meaning

943. The admissibility of evidence is the question of whether an item of evidence is allowed to be presented to the court. When a party offers evidence, the court decides whether to receive it and must exclude evidence which is inadmissible.

944. The Criminal Procedure Act has detailed provisions regarding the admissibility of evidence, e.g., confession of the defendant (§§309,310, CrPA), hearsay evidence (§310-2 CrPA), etc. However, the Civil Procedure Act is silent on the admissibility of evidence. Given this silence and the principle of free evaluation of evidence, a majority of commentators take the view that any evidence is admissible in civil cases.[208] There are several court precedents that adopt this opinion.[209]

945. On the other hand, the Supreme Court has held that if the court has grossly violated the rules and procedure prescribed by statute in examining an item of evidence, that evidence must be excluded. Thus, the report of an expert examiner is inadmissible if the examiner did not swear to give a truthful report before a judge when appointed.[210] In addition, a photocopy of a document is inadmissible unless the existence of the original and its authenticity is proven.[211]

946. According to the Protection of Communication Secrets Act, it is prohibited to censor mail, wiretap telecommunications, provide communication data to a third party, record a conversation without consent or eavesdrop unless authorized by this Act (§3(1) PCSA). Any evidence obtained in violation of this Act is inadmissible in court (§4 PCSA). But note that the Supreme Court has held that the audiotape of a conversation recorded by one of the parties to the conversation without consent was admissible because the Protection of Communication Secrets Act bans a recording by a third party.[212]

§2. Admission and Exclusion of Evidence

I. Offer of Evidence

947. When asserting facts, a party has to set forth the evidence that proves or disproves the asserted facts as well as the type of evidence (witness, documentary evidence, inspection, expert examination, party witness, etc.) (§289(1) CPA; r.74 RCP). In the interest of a speedy trial, all evidence should be offered prior to the

208. Si-yoon Lee, *supra* n. 8, at 449.
209. *Supra* n. 5.
210. *Supra* n. 6.
211. Supreme Court Decision 95Da12125 decided on May 26, 1995.
212. Supreme Court Decision 2009Da37138,37145 decided on September 10, 2009.

trial date. The offer of witnesses and party witnesses should especially be made at once absent special circumstances (r.75 RCP).

948. Either party may make an evidentiary objection to the evidence offered by the other party (§274 CPA). This can be done in a preparatory brief or at a hearing. The basis for the objection could be such grounds as relevancy to the case, trustworthiness, procedural legitimacy or necessity of the evidence.

II. Court's Decision of Admission and Exclusion

949. The court admits and considers only the evidence which is admissible and submitted in due time. The court may exclude any evidence that it considers unnecessary unless it is the sole evidence to prove a material fact (§290 CPA).

950. The exclusion of the sole evidence would mean that the party bearing the burden of proving a material fact would lose the case without any opportunity for his/her evidence being considered. This provision is based on the view that not allowing examination of the sole evidence, in the discretion of the court, is likely to infringe upon a party's right to due process of law. Of course, even the sole evidence must be excluded if it is otherwise inadmissible or in violation of procedural rules. This might occur if the offered evidence unduly delays the trial (§149(1) CPA), the offer comes after the court-designated time frame for submission of evidence (§147(2) CPA), the evidence is submitted after the pretrial hearing (§285(1) CPA) or it is not possible to examine the offered evidence (§291 CPA).

951. The court issues decisions of admission or exclusion on each item of evidence. Once admitted, the evidence is allowed to be presented before the court. The Supreme Court held that if the lower court neither issued any decision on an item of evidence nor examined it, the evidence is deemed to have been excluded by decision.[213]

213. Supreme Court Decision 92Nu5096 decided on September 25, 1992.

Chapter 3. Administration of Evidence

§1. Forced Production of Documents

I. Order to Produce a Document

A. Documents to Be Produced

952. The court may issue an order to anyone to produce a document in their possession; if it was cited by a party in litigation; if the requesting party has a right to inspect it or to request delivery of it; or if it was made in the interest of, or with regard to, the legal relationship with the requesting party. However, the person in possession of a document may refuse to do so if the document contains matters on which he/she is excused from testifying (§344(1) CPA), or if the document was made for the exclusive personal use of the individual in possession and the disclosure is likely to result in irrevocable damage.[214]

B. Procedure

953. The judicial decision ordering production of a document is issued on a motion of a party. The moving party must set forth the indications of the document, its nature and purport, the person in possession and the document's relevance to the litigation (§345 CPA). Where the moving party does not know the full particulars of documents held by the opposing party or a third party, the court may issue an order directing the person in possession to submit a list of the documents he/she holds and a description of each document (§346 CPA). The court may order production of a part of a document if the rest is unnecessary or contains matters that can be legitimately withheld (§§347(1),(2) CPA).

C. Effects

954. When a party ordered to produce a document refuses to comply, destroys the document or makes it unusable, the court may conclude that the allegation of the other party seeking production of the document is true with respect to the document (§§349,350 CPA). Here, what is deemed to be true is limited to the authenticity of the document and its content, not the facts to be proved by the document.[215] If a third party does not comply with an order to produce a document without justifiable reasons, the court may impose an administrative fine (§351 CPA).

214. Supreme Court Decision 2015Ma4147 decided on December 21, 2015.
215. Supreme Court Decision 93Da41938 decided on November 23, 1993.

II. Order to Send the Document to the Court

955. On a motion by a party, the court may order a person or organization in possession of documents to send them to the court (§352 CPA). This method is used where the documents are in the possession of a government agency or public organization, the volume of the files is very large, or it is difficult to specify the relevant documents until the moving party inspects all the records.

956. Absent special circumstances, the agency or organization must comply with the court order (r.114 RCP). In practice, agencies usually permit the moving party access to the records and then send a copy of the documents designated by the moving party to the court.

III. On-Site Examination of Documentary Evidence

957. Where sending a document to the court is inappropriate or difficult, the court may examine the documents on-site. In this case, the documents are offered and admitted as evidence by the judge and are also examined on-site. This method is usually used when the documents are not open to the public.

§2. Examination of Witnesses

I. Privilege and Exemption of Duty to Swear under Oath

958. A witness may refuse to testify if the evidence is likely to incriminate or disgrace the witness or a person who is (or was) his/her relatives, guardian or ward (§314 CPA). In addition, persons who are prohibited by law from divulging confidential information learned in the course of their professional activities may refuse to give testimony on matters related to such information. These professionals include a current or former attorney, patent attorney, notary public, certified public accountant, certified tax consultant, medical service provider, pharmacist, and a member of the clergy. A witness may do the same when examined with regard to a technical or business secret (§315 CPA).

959. A witness may refuse to testify under oath when examined on the matters in which the witness or his/her current or former relatives, or current or former guardian or ward under guardianship have a significant interest at stake (§324 CPA). The court may exempt a witness from swearing under oath when he/she voluntarily gives testimony even though the witness is entitled to claim a privilege based on kinship or guardianship (§323 CPA). In this case, the witness testifies without taking an oath and is exempted from criminal charges even if he/she provides false testimony.

II. Appearance of Witness

960. When a witness fails to appear at a hearing without legitimate reasons after a summons was served, the court issues a decision ordering him/her to bear litigation costs incurred by the failure to appear and an administrative fine not exceeding KRW 5 million (§311(1) CPA). Should the witness again fail to appear, the court may issue a decision sentencing him/her to administrative detention for not more than seven days (§311(2) CPA). Such administrative fine and detention may be imposed repeatedly until the witness makes an appearance.

961. In addition, the court may issue a subpoena requiring the witness to appear before the court when he/she fails to appear without a legitimate reason (§312 CPA). The subpoena is enforced by a police officer or court clerk under the direction of a prosecutor (§81 CrPA), or by an enforcement officer (§6 EOA). In this case, the witness is forcibly escorted to the court.

III. Methods of Witness Examination

A. Testimony at Hearing

1. List of Questions for Witness Examination

962. After the court admits a witness to testify and designates a hearing date to examine the witness, the party offering the witness must submit a document and necessary copies setting forth the matters upon which the witness will be questioned, within the time frame set by the court (r.80(1) RCP). The court clerk serves a copy on the opposing party (r.80(2) RCP), who prepares for cross-examination based on these questions. At the hearing for examination of the witness, the party who called the witness asks questions in direct examination based on the items set forth in the document.

2. Procedure of Witness Examination

a. Taking an Oath

963. A witness takes an oath standing in the witness box by reading a written statement that he/she solemnly affirms, under the penalty of perjury, that his/her testimony will be the truth. When examining a person under 16 years of age or person who is unable to understand the purpose of swearing under oath as a witness, the court may not have the witness take an oath (§322 CPA).

b. Progress of Witness Examination

964. Direct examination or examination-in-chief is the first stage of witness examination which is conducted by the party who called the witness. Direct examination is usually performed to prove material facts corresponding to the cause of action or the party's affirmative defense. Cross-examination is performed by the opposing party following direct examination. The opposing party usually attempts to elicit helpful testimony or challenges the witness' credibility by bringing out contradictions and improbabilities in their testimony. Following cross-examination, the party who called the witness may examine the witness on testimony given in cross-examination. The presiding judge may also examine the witness at any time regardless of who called the witness.

965. In the witness examination, a party must keep questions simple and clear. Parties are prohibited from asking two questions at a time, asking broad and vague questions, or asking complex or confusing questions. A witness may not give an opinion unless he/she is an expert witness (r.95 RCP). Leading questions are not allowed in direct examination. Exceptionally, leading questions are permitted when the witness is hostile toward the examining party or when the witness gives testimony contradicting his/her previous testimony. Leading questions are also allowed to establish preliminary, foundational or undisputed matters (r.91(2) RCP).

966. In cross-examination, questions are limited to the matters covered by the testimony in direct examination (r.92(1) RCP). Parties may ask leading questions in cross-examination but the presiding judge may restrict use of such questions (r.92(3) RCP). In redirect examination, parties may ask questions only about the matters raised at cross-examination and matters related thereto (r.93(1) RCP). The same rules on direct examination apply to redirect examination (r.93(2) RCP).

B. Witness' Written Statement

967. A witness' written statement is used to enhance the efficiency of witness examination. When deemed necessary, the court may order the party requesting witness examination to submit a written statement prepared by the witness (r.79(1) RCP). The witness sets forth what he/she experienced in chronological order and signs the form (r.79(2) RCP). When this statement is submitted, the court clerk serves a copy on the opposing party so that the party can prepare for cross-examination based on this statement (r.79(4) RCP).

968. The court admits the written statement as documentary evidence and cross-examination is conducted based on the statement without direct examination. If the witness fails to appear after the written statement is submitted, and the opposing party waives the right to cross-examination and does not dispute the authenticity of the statement, the statement may be admitted as documentary evidence.

C. Witness Examination Through an Audio and Video Transmission System

969. The court may examine a witness by contemporaneous video transmission if the witness has difficulty in appearing before the court because he/she resides in a remote area or due to other circumstances. Video testimony is also allowed if a witness is likely to become significantly disturbed in confronting an interested party in the courtroom. In this case, the court considers the witness' age, physical or mental state, relation with the party and other circumstances (§327-2 CPA).

970. If the court allows video testimony, the court orders the witness to appear at a location other than the courtroom where an audio and visual transmission system is installed. The witness testifies in facilities where the witness and the other participants in the courtroom can communicate and are aware of one another's presence (r.95-2(1) RCP).

D. *Written Testimony*

971. If deemed reasonable considering the witness and the nature of the testimony, the court may have a witness submit a letter of testimony in lieu of giving testimony in person (§310(1) CPA). In this case, the court orders the party requesting the witness examination to submit a written list of questions. The opposing party may also be permitted to submit a list of questions (r.84(1) RCP). The court then orders the witness to provide written testimony in response to the questions.

972. The court may also order a witness who submits written testimony to appear in court and testify in person when the other party raises an objection or when it is deemed necessary to do so (§310(2) CPA). The written testimony is distinguished from a witness' written statement in that the latter is documentary evidence whereas the former is the same as testimony given in person before the court.

§3. Examination of Party Witnesses

973. If a party is also a witness, they are placed under oath. If a party witness is found to have lied, instead of being charged with the crime of perjury, he/she is subject to an administrative fine, not exceeding KRW 5 million (§370(1) CPA).

974. If a party to be examined fails to appear, or refuses to take an oath or to testify without justifiable reasons, he/she is deemed to have testified giving positive answers to the questions prepared by the other party but is not subject to an administrative fine (§369 CPA).

§4. Expert Examination and Expert Witness

975. The court may appoint an expert to examine evidence related to an issue in a pending case and file a report about his/her opinion or assessment. Examples of when a court might use an expert examiner are an independent medical examination in a workers' compensation case or a personal injury lawsuit (tort claim); the examination of patient records in a medical malpractice case; an appraisal of property value in a property damage case; a survey of land boundaries to settle property lines; and the appraisal of repair costs in construction defects cases. There are three ways to obtain expert evidence: appointment of an expert examiner, commissioning an institute to perform an expert examination, and testimony of an expert witness.

976. An expert examiner is designated by the court or a delegated member of the judicial panel (§335 CPA). A person who is privileged to refuse to give testimony or to refuse to swear under oath is disqualified from becoming an expert examiner. A party may challenge the qualifications of an expert examiner to perform a fair examination (§336 CPA). After examining a prospective expert examiner on his/her expertise and professional experience (§338 CPA), the court has him/her swear under oath to perform his/her duties truthfully and fairly. The expert examiner must submit a report to the court (§339 CPA), and this report is admitted as evidence.

977. A public institution, university or a foreign organization equipped with laboratories, facilities and expertise may be commissioned by the court to conduct an expert examination. In this case, the court issues a document authorizing the organization to do so. The court does not examine any particular person or place anyone under oath. In general, an organization having a good reputation and public trust is selected to conduct the examination. When the commissioned organization completes its task, it submits a report to the court, which is admitted as evidence.

978. An expert witness is a witness who testifies or otherwise provides evidence based on specialized information, knowledge and experience (§340 CPA). Unlike a lay person witness, an expert witness may give testimony based on his/her opinion regarding facts or evidence in a case.

§5. Inspection

979. An inspection is a judge's personal examination of physical evidence. This might include an examination of the shapes, features and functions of an object. A judge may visit the place where an object is located or where an accident occurred and investigate for himself/herself. If a party destroys an object to be inspected or makes it unusable in order to obstruct it from being used as evidence, the court may decide that the allegations of the opposing party as to the object are true (§§366(1),350 CPA). The court may also order a third party who is holding an object to submit it to the court. If the holder fails to comply with the order, the court may impose an administrative fine (§366(2) CPA).

980. The examination of digital evidence such as audio files, video recordings, and digital images is conducted by means of an inspection while such evidence is played in court (r.121(2) RCP). The party who tenders digital evidence must submit a transcript of the recording or any other documents explaining the contents of such evidence if ordered by the court or at the request of the opposing party (r.121(3) RCP).

Part VIII. Particular Proceedings

Chapter 1. Procedure for Small Claims Court

§1. Scope of Small Claims

981. Small claims cases are civil cases where the amount in controversy does not exceed KRW 30 million and the plaintiff's claim is for payment of a specific amount of money, fungibles or securities (§2 TSCA; r.1-2 RTSC). The Trial of Small Claims Act regulates the proceedings for such cases. A single judge, as opposed to a judicial panel, at a court of first instance has exclusive jurisdiction over small claims cases. The proceedings for a small claims case are exceptionally simple, speedy and informal in the first instance court. However, once a party appeals the judgment, the procedural rules in the appellate court uniformly apply to all the cases pending there.

982. Where the amount in controversy in a lawsuit initially filed as a small claims case, later exceeds the threshold of KRW 30 million, the procedural rules for a small claims case do not apply. The amount in controversy might grow due to an expansion of the claims for relief, intervention of an independent party, joinder of independent claims, or the filing of a counterclaim.

§2. Special Procedural Provisions for Small Claims Cases

983. In most cases, only an attorney can serve as a litigation representative for a party (§87 CPA). In the proceedings for a case which is subject to jurisdiction of a single judge and in which the amount in controversy does not exceed KRW 100 million, a party's spouse, relatives within the fourth degree, or employee who takes care of the ordinary business related to the case may serve as a litigation representative with permission of the court (r.15 RCP). However, in the proceedings for a small claims case, a party's spouse, blood relatives in the direct line of descent or brother and sister may become a litigation representative for the party without permission of the court (§8 TSCA).

984. When it is evident that a plaintiff's claim is without merit based on the allegations in the complaint and briefs, the court may render a judgment dismissing the case with prejudice without holding a hearing (§9(1) TSCA). In addition, the court may, *sua sponte,* examine evidence not offered by a party. The judge, rather than the parties, conducts the questioning of witnesses (§10 TSCA). In ordinary civil cases, the court clerk must make the record of the hearing immediately after a hearing is held. However, it is not necessary in a small claims case if the court permits and the parties do not object (§11 TSCA).

985. The small claims court may render a judgment immediately after the close of the hearing for oral argument (§11-2(1) TSCA), whereas, in ordinary civil cases, the court must designate the date for rendition of a judgment and deliver it on that date. Also, the reasons of the judgment may be omitted in the judgment document in a small claims case (§11-2(3) TSCA).

§3. Recommendation of Performance by Decision

986. In a small claims case, the court may issue a decision recommending the defendant pay the amount set forth in the prayer for relief (§5-3(1) TSCA). Unless the defendant objects to the decision in writing within two weeks after receiving a copy thereof (§5-4(1) TSCA), the decision becomes final and binding. This has the same effect as a final and binding judgment (§5-7(1) TSCA). However, the Supreme Court interprets "the same effect as a final and binding judgment" as limited to enforceability, and does not include the claim preclusive effect of a judgment.[216] This interpretation is inferred from the provision of the Trial of Small Claims Act that the defendant may file a lawsuit raising an objection to the claim being enforced on the grounds that existed prior to the issuance of the decision recommending the performance as well as thereafter (§5-8(3) TSCA). Should this decision have a claim preclusive effect, a lawsuit raising an objection to the claim being enforced would be allowed based only on the grounds that took place after the issuance of the decision.

987. If the defendant files a timely objection to the decision, the court immediately designates a date for trial (§5-4(3) TSCA). The defendant may withdraw the objection until a judgment of the first instance court is rendered (§5-4(4) TSCA). When the court renders a judgment, the decision for recommendation of performance loses validity (§5-7(3) TSCA).

§4. Restriction on the Final Appeal

988. Since small claims cases are under the subject-matter jurisdiction of a single judge based on the amount in controversy, an appeal from that court lies with the appellate panel of a District Court. A party to a small claims case may appeal the judgment of the appellate panel of a District Court to the Supreme Court only if the court below erred on the constitutionality of the statutes or legality of the subordinate laws; or if the judgment is contrary to the precedents of the Supreme Court (§3 TSCA).

216. Supreme Court Decision 2006Da34190 decided on May 14, 2009.

Chapter 2. Summary Proceedings for a Payment Order

§1. Petition for Payment Order

989. A creditor may resort to summary proceedings for a payment order when a debtor is obliged to pay a specific amount of money, fungibles or securities. The summary proceedings are preferred by financial institutions in order to obtain an enforceable decision when the debtor does not dispute the creditor's claim but is unable to pay back the debt. The proceedings for a payment order are distinguished from litigation proceedings in that a hearing is not held and the case is concluded by a decision, not by a judgment.

990. A petition for a payment order would be allowed only when the creditor's claim is mature and unconditional.[217] A lawsuit for future performance may be filed if it is deemed necessary (§251 CPA). However, it would be inappropriate for the court to address the necessity of filing a petition for payment order where the due date has not arrived. Insofar as the petitioner seeks payment of money, fungibles or securities, the amount of the debt or its nature does not matter.

991. The payment order is issued where it is possible to serve a copy of the decision upon the debtor in Korea, without resorting to service by publication (§462 CPA). When the copy of the decision cannot be served on the debtor at the place of service, the court orders the petitioner to correct the place of service. At that time, the petitioner may bring a motion to institute a lawsuit (§466(1) CPA). If service by publication is the only possible means of service or the place of service is located in a foreign country, the court may, *sua sponte,* issue a decision referring the case to litigation procedures (§466(2) CPA).

§2. Proceedings

992. A judicial assistant official in the District Court or the Branch Court rules on a petition for a payment order (§54(2) COA) The petition cannot be filed in a City Court or a Town Court because these courts do not have judicial assistant officials (§34(1) COA). The court issues the payment order in the form of a decision based on the documents submitted by the petitioner, without holding a hearing or participation of the debtor (§467 CPA).

993. The petition for a payment order is dismissed without prejudice if the petition is filed in a court that lacks jurisdiction or if the petition has a procedural defect. When the petition is clearly groundless, the court dismisses the petition without prejudice (§465(1) CPA). The decision dismissing the petition cannot be appealed (§465(2) CPA), and it does not have a preclusive effect.

217. Si-yoon Lee, *supra* n. 8, at 950.

994. The court issues a payment order unless the petition has a procedural defect or it is groundless on its face. The order is served on the petitioner and the debtor (§469(1) CPA). A final and binding payment order is enforceable but does not have a preclusive effect.

§3. Objection to the Order

995. The debtor may raise an objection to a payment order within two weeks after service of the order. If an objection is filed, the decision ordering payment loses validity (§470(1) CPA). In this case, a lawsuit is deemed to have been brought by the creditor at the time the petition for a payment order was filed (§472(2) CPA). This is the same as where the petitioner files a motion to institute a lawsuit, or where the court issues a decision referring the case for litigation (§472(1) CPA).

Part IX. Preservative Measures and Enforcement of Judgment

Chapter 1. Preservative Measures

§1. Proceedings

I. Petition for Preservative Measure

996. Preservative measures to secure enforcement of judgment include a prejudgment seizure and an injunction regarding the object of dispute. An injunction providing a temporary status is also a preservative measure. However, it is distinguished from other preservative measures in that its aim lies in avoiding any substantial detriment or imminent danger that would occur to the creditor with regard to the relationship of rights in dispute (§300(2) CEA).

997. A decision for prejudgment seizure may be issued upon petition by the creditor when it is likely that the enforcement of a monetary claim might be impossible or significantly difficult unless a part or whole of the debtor's properties is frozen immediately (§276(1) CEA). The claim to be preserved includes nonmonetary claims convertible to money, and monetary claims that are conditional or has not yet become due (§276(2) CEA).

998. In theory, the creditor does not have to specify the property to be seized at the time of petitioning for a prejudgment seizure because it is effected against general assets of the debtor, and the creditor may apply for its enforcement against a specific property. However, in practice, the creditor designates a specific property when he/she files a petition for a prejudgment seizure to the effect that he/she seeks both the decision for a prejudgment seizure and its enforcement at the same time. Thus, the property against which the decision is to be enforced is set forth in the decision.

999. An injunction regarding the object of dispute is a preservative measure to secure the enforcement of a claim for specific performance regarding the specified things, which includes an obligatory claim and a claim based on real rights, e.g., a claim for delivery of a movable, a claim for transfer of a property right, a claim for setting-up of a mortgage, etc.

1000. The petition for a preservative measure must be made in writing. In the petition, the claim to be preserved, the prayer for relief, and the reasons on which the petition is based must be set forth (§279(1) CEA). In addition, the amount in dispute must be specified in the petition for a prejudgment seizure.

II. Discretionary Hearings

1001. The court rules on the petition for a prejudgment seizure or for an injunction regarding the object of dispute after holding a hearing for oral argument, or without holding a hearing at its discretion (§§280(1),301 CEA). In practice, the court decides based only on the documents submitted by the creditor without holding a hearing.

1002. The petitioner must submit documents including evidence supporting the reasons, especially the existence of the claim to be preserved and the necessity for the preservative measure, or a danger that the property sought to be seized would be concealed, substantially impaired in value, or otherwise made unavailable to levy, if issuance of the decision was to be delayed until the judgment on the merits.

1003. The petitioner needs to present only a prima facie case, rather than to prove reasons. The court considers items of evidence that can be immediately examined (§299(1) CPA). The court may have the petitioner make a deposit of money in court or swear under oath in lieu of establishing a prima facie case (§299(2) CPA). When a deposit of money is made in lieu of a prima facie showing, and then the petitioner ends up losing the case by a final judgment on the merits, the court confiscates the deposited money in the form of a decision (§300 CPA). However, in practice, money deposit in court or swearing is seldom used. Instead, if the petitioner fails to present prima facie evidence, the court dismisses the petition generally.

III. Adjudication

A. Provision of Security

1004. The court dismisses petitions with procedural defects, in the form of a decision. Even when the prima facie showing of the claim to be preserved, or the necessity for the preservative measure is insufficient, the court may issue a decision ordering a prejudgment seizure or an injunction after having the petitioner provide a security in court to compensate for the damage the debtor would sustain due to the preservative measure in case the claim is groundless (§280(2) CEA). However, in practice, if the petitioner fails to present prima facie evidence, the court dismisses the petition. In addition, the court orders the provision of security prior to issuing the decision ordering the preservative measure even when the petitioner established a prima facie case (§280(3) CEA).

1005. Therefore, a court orders provision of security only when the prima facie showing of the claim to be preserved as well as the necessity for the preservative measure is sufficient. The provision of security must be made by way of making a deposit of money or securities in court, or submitting a payment guarantee letter issued by a financial institution approved by the court, within a time frame specified by the court (§122 CPA; r.22 RCP). If the petitioner fails to provide a security in compliance with the court order, the petition for a preservative measure is dismissed.

1006. Where the lawsuit, based on the claim preserved by the preservative measure, was dismissed by a judgment on the merits and the respondent sustains damage due to the preservative measure, the respondent may exercise its security interest as a pledge holder against the petitioner's right to the deposited property.[218] If, after the conclusion of litigation, the respondent fails to exercise the right to the security within a certain time frame determined by the court, then the court will issue a decision releasing the security. When the creditor prevails in the lawsuit based on the claim preserved by the preservative measure, the court will also do so.

B. Decision for Preservative Measure

1. Prejudgment Seizure

1007. In the operative provision of the court's decision, the statement ordering the prejudgment seizure and the property to be seized are set forth. Where the property to be seized is the debtor's claim, the order prohibiting the third-party debtor from paying the debt is included (§296(3) CEA). In addition, the amount of money (money for release from a prejudgment seizure) must be specified, which the debtor must deposit in order to stay the enforcement of the prejudgment seizure, or in order to have the enforcement already carried out repealed. Following the operative provision, the monetary claim to be preserved and its amount are specified. If the petitioner has provided a security in advance in compliance with the court order, the security and its amount are stated.

1008. If the debtor deposits the amount of money for release from a prejudgment seizure, the enforcement of the prejudgment seizure is effected against the debtor's claim to the deposited money, and the seized property is released.

2. Injunction Regarding the Object of Dispute

1009. Decisions ordering an injunction regarding the object of dispute may be issued when there is a likelihood that the petitioner's exercise of his/her right will be impossible or extremely difficult due to any changes to the existing state of the

218. Supreme Court Decision 2014Da34126 decided on September 10, 2015.

property in dispute. The operative provision of the injunction prohibits the debtor from transferring, encumbering, or concealing the property to preserve the creditor's right thereto.

1010. The statutory provisions regarding prejudgment seizure are applied to injunctions regarding the object of dispute, unless they are inconsistent with the nature of the latter. In the decision ordering an injunction, the claim to be preserved must be set forth, but the amount of money need not be specified. The scope of the injunction regarding the object of dispute is limited to the claim for relief that may be sought in a lawsuit filed by the creditor. Because the injunction regarding the object of dispute is to preserve a specific claim, the court may not set the amount of money for release from the injunction.[219]

C. Effects of Preservative Measure

1. Prejudgment Seizure

1011. Prejudgment seizure or injunction regarding the object of dispute takes effect only when it is enforced. An enforcement officer effectuates the prejudgment seizure of movables by taking possession of them. If the movables subject to the prejudgment seizure are likely to considerably decline in price, or if retaining them requires an inappropriate amount of costs, the enforcement officer must sell them and make a deposit of the proceeds in court (§296(5) CEA). The prejudgment seizure of an immovable is enforced by way of entry thereof in the registration record of the property (§293(1) CEA). An injunction regarding the object of dispute is enforced in the same manner.

1012. The debtor is free to use, transfer, and encumber the immoveable even after a prejudgment seizure has been enforced. However, when the creditor files a lawsuit based on the claim to be preserved and prevails in whole or in part, he/she may enforce the judgment on the property against which the prejudgment seizure was carried out even after its ownership has been transferred to a third party.

1013. Prejudgment seizure does not provide the creditor with any security interest in the property seized. If another creditor enforces a seizure or prejudgment seizure on the same property, or a third party acquires a security interest therein after the prejudgment seizure has been implemented, the proceeds of the judicial sale of the property are distributed to the former and latter creditors on an equal basis. Property rights for use, including superficies and servitude, which were obtained after the prejudgment seizure, are terminated by the judicial sale.

---

219. Supreme Court Decision 2000Ma282 decided on September 25, 2002.

2. Injunction Regarding the Object of Dispute

1014. An injunction prohibiting disposition of a property takes effect when it is enforced in the same manner as a prejudgment seizure. If a third party acquires a real right in the property after the injunction is executed, the third party is a legitimate holder of the right insofar as the creditor does not realize his/her right preserved by the injunction. For example, if the title transfer of the immovable is effected by entry thereof in the registration record in violation of the injunction, and thereafter the creditor enforces the judgment granting the preserved right, the registration of the title transfer is cancelled at the request of the creditor, and then he/she is registered as the owner.

§2. Judicial Review

I. Objection to Preservative Measure

A. Filing an Objection

1015. The debtor or his/her successor may raise an objection with the court which issued the judicial decision for the preservative measure (§§282,301 CEA). It is not an appeal in that the court that rendered the initial decision holds a hearing for oral argument or an in-person hearing and rules anew on the petition for the preservative measure.

1016. Grounds for objection include the nonexistence of the right to be preserved or necessity to preserve it at the time when the decision was issued. However, the respondent may file an objection on the grounds that the right or the necessity to preserve no longer exists due to change in circumstances.

B. Hearing

1017. Upon filing of an objection, the court reassesses the petition for the preservative measure, where the creditor remains as a petitioner, and the debtor is still a respondent. A hearing for oral argument or in-person hearing to be attended by both parties must be held (§286(1) CEA). The petitioner seeks approval of the decision, and the respondent asks for revocation thereof along with dismissal of the petition. For this reason, the petitioner is burdened to make a prima facie showing that there exists the claim to be preserved and the necessity of preservation.

C. Adjudication

1018. After hearing the parties, the court approves the judicial decision for the preservative measure if the decision is well-grounded. If the petitioner fails to make a prima facie showing of the right and the necessity to preserve it, the court revokes the decision and dismisses the petition. Should the right to be preserved be separable, and a prima facie showing be made in respect of part of it, the court approves the decision in part and revokes the rest of it.

II. Revocation of Preservative Measure

A. Definition and Meaning

1019. Revoking a judicial decision for a preservative measure is based on the causes that take place after the decision was issued. In this procedure, the debtor is the petitioner, and the creditor is the respondent. The debtor is burdened to make a prima facie showing of the grounds on which the decision for the preservative measure should be set aside. The debtor, his/her successor, and a third party who acquired rights to the object which the decision for preservative measure was enforced against, have a standing to petition for the revocation.[220]

B. Revocation for Failure to File a Lawsuit on the Merits

1020. The creditor petitions for a preservative measure on the premise that he/she is going to file a lawsuit based on the right to be preserved. However, the creditor may neglect to file a lawsuit after the judicial decision for such preservative measure has been issued. In this case, the debtor sustains a significant disadvantage in disposing of the property against which the decision was enforced. The debtor can compel the creditor to file a lawsuit on the merits by moving the court to issue a decision ordering the creditor to do so.

1021. Upon the debtor's petition, the court that issued the decision of the preservative measure orders the creditor to file a lawsuit on the merits within a time frame of two weeks or longer to be decided by the court, in the form of a decision. Should the creditor fail to submit a document certifying such filing, the court revokes the decision for the preservative measure upon the debtor's petition (§§287(2)③ CEA).

C. Revocation due to Change in Circumstances

1. Definition and Meaning

1022. Where the right or the necessity to preserve it has ceased to exist, or circumstances have changed after the decision for preservative measure was rendered,

220. Supreme Court Decision 66Da842 decided on January 31, 1968.

the court revokes the decision upon petition by the debtor (§288(1) CEA). In revoking the decision, the court does not take into account the fact that it approved the decision as the debtor lodged an objection thereto.

2. Change in Circumstances

a. Concerning Cause of Preservative Measure

1023. Changes in circumstances include the extinction of the right to be preserved due to revocation of contract or performance of obligation. In addition, the necessity to preserve the right no longer exists when the creditor neglects to enforce the judgment for a long time (§288(1) CEA).

1024. According to case law, the fact that the judgment on the merits dismissing the lawsuit brought by the creditor becomes final and binding constitutes a change in circumstances; however, a dismissal without prejudice does not.[221]

b. Provision of Security

1025. The prejudgment seizure aims to secure the enforcement of a money judgment. Thus, the creditor need not keep the prejudgment seizure effective if the debtor provides a proper security. The debtor may petition the court to stay or revoke the enforcement of the prejudgment seizure after he/she deposits money for release therefrom in court. Further, the debtor may petition the court to revoke the prejudgment seizure decision after he/she deposits the amount decided by the court (§288(1) CEA).

1026. It is interpreted that a revocation of the decision for prejudgment seizure by reason of providing security does not apply to injunctions regarding the object of dispute or injunctions providing a temporary status.

c. Failure to File a Lawsuit Within Three Years

1027. The court, upon petition by the debtor or an interested third party, revokes the preservative measure decision when the creditor fails to file a lawsuit based on the preserved right within three years after its enforcement (§288(1) CEA).

d. Revocation of Injunction due to Special Circumstances

1028. Special circumstances in this context include the following: where the loss of the right to be preserved by the injunction may eventually be compensated by a monetary award, and where the debtor would sustain an extraordinarily significant loss by the injunction compared with the right to be preserved.[222]

221. Supreme Court Decision 2017Ma5829 decided on February 9, 2018.
222. Supreme Court Decision 96Da21188 decided on March 14, 1997.

1029. When there are such special circumstances, the court orders the debtor to provide a security and then issues a decision revoking the injunction after the debtor deposits the security in court (§307(1) CEA).

Chapter 2. Enforcement of Judgment

§1. Proceedings

I. Enforcement Authorities

A. Types

1030. The Civil Execution Act divides enforcement authorities into three types including the enforcement officer, the court of enforcement, and the trial court of first instance. Enforcements requiring physical force and relatively simple procedures are subject to jurisdiction of the enforcement officer. The court of enforcement deals with the tasks that are completed by issuing decisions and those which involve complicated legal and factual issues. The trial court of first instance has jurisdiction over enforcement cases which need judicial discretion in enforcing judgments.

B. Enforcement Officer

1031. An enforcement officer is an independent office in charge of the tasks designated by statutes, including enforcement of judgment, service of court documents, etc. (§44(2) COA, §2 EOA). In principle, an enforcement officer is authorized to undertake such tasks only in the venue where the District Court or the Branch Court which he/she is associated with is located. An enforcement officer's tasks include those he/she deals with as an independent authority and those he/she does as a supporting staff for the court of enforcement.

1032. The enforcement officer exercises an independent authority in enforcing a monetary claim against tangible movables (§189 CEA), delivery of movables (§257 CEA), delivery or surrender of real property including vessels (§258 CEA), prejudgment seizure against movables (§296 CEA). He/she also administers a judicial sale of tangible movables for execution of security interests (§§272,274(1) CEA).

1033. An enforcement officer performs his/her duty as a supporting staff for the court of enforcement in taking a claim deed for a seizure against a claim (§234(2) CEA), selling a claim or property right at the transfer order (§§241(1),251(1) CEA), investigating the shape, possession status, and any other current conditions of immovables for a judicial sale and compulsory administration (§§85,163,268 CEA), and enforcement of a delivery order in a judicial sale of an immovable (§136(6) CEA).

C. Court of Enforcement

1034. In principle, a court of enforcement is the District Court in the district where the enforcement is being or must be sought (§3(1) CEA), and its tasks are performed by a single judge (§7(4) COA). However, the enforcement of a judicial decision ordering a preservative measure is administered by the court which rendered the decision because such a decision need to be enforced immediately.

1035. This court implements enforcement of a monetary claim against immovables, ships, automobiles, airplanes, etc., the ownership transfer of which is effectuated by entry in the register (§§78,172 CEA). In addition, the enforcement of a money judgment against a claim or other property rights (§223 CEA) and distribution of the proceeds after a judicial sale of movables (§252 CEA) are under the authority of this court. It supports or regulates the enforcement officer in performing his/her duty by permitting enforcement on a holiday or at night (§8 CEA), making a request to a public agency for assistance (§20 CEA), rendering a decision on the scope of seizure-prohibited movables (§196 CEA), and ruling on the objection to the measure regarding enforcement or the manner of proceeding to be observed (§16 CEA). The court of enforcement performs its duty by way of issuing decisions regarding enforcement.

1036. The amended Court Organization Act which took effect on July 1, 2015 created the position of a judicial assistant official. Significant portions of the enforcement tasks that were previously performed by single judges in the court of enforcement were assigned to judicial assistant officials.

1037. Such tasks include issuing orders for issuance of the court certificate of enforceability, judicial sale of immovables, implementing property disclosure procedures and issuing orders for the creditor to file a lawsuit, who has the preservative measure enforced. However, a single judge still is in charge of the tasks that require judicial discretion, such as ruling on the objection to the commencement order for a compulsory judicial sale (§86 CEA), issuing a decision ordering the debtor to deliver the immovable to the purchaser in the judicial sale (§136 CEA), and modifying the scope of seizure-prohibited claims (§§246(3)(4) CEA).

D. Trial Court of First Instance

1038. This is the court which adjudicated the claim to be enforced and granted the enforcement title. This court is authorized to issue a decision permitting the enforcement by substitute (§260 CEA) and to implement an indirect compulsory enforcement by ordering the debtor to pay to the creditor a certain amount of money for securing performance of the obligation (§261 CEA).

II. Prerequisites for Compulsory Enforcement

A. Enforcement Title

1039. The enforcement title is an official document acknowledging the existence and scope of enforceable claims of the creditor. They include final and binding judgments for performance, provisionally enforceable judgments (§24 CEA), foreign court judgments for which enforcement judgments have become final and binding (§26 CEA), settlement agreements before the court, acknowledgments before the court, payment orders (§56 CEA), and enforcement deeds (§56 CEA). An enforcement deed refers to a notarized document with regard to a claim for payment of a certain amount of money or securities, which contain a statement that the debtor will immediately accept a compulsory enforcement.

B. Enforcement Clause

1040. An enforcement clause is a court certificate of enforceability that is attached to the authentic copy of the enforcement title. It is an official statement entered at the end of the enforcement title by the court clerk at the request of the creditor, which sets out the judgment creditor, judgment debtor, purports of granting the enforcement clause, date, and the name of the clerk (§28(2) CEA). When the enforcement title is a deed, the notary public who notarized it enters the enforcement clause.

1041. The reason why an enforcement clause is required for the creditor to commence enforcement proceedings is that not all of the judgments for performance are eligible for compulsory enforcement. Thus, the authority stipulated in the statutes determines whether the enforcement title is enforceable; whether the unspecified due date has arrived, or the conditions attached to the performance of the obligation have been met in the judgment for future performance; and who the judgment creditor and the judgment debtor are when discrepancies between the parties set forth in the enforcement title and the parties in the enforcement proceedings occurred due to inheritance, assignment of the claim, or assumption of the obligation. It is inappropriate for the enforcement authority to examine the said requirements.

1042. In principle, the creditor can initiate an enforcement procedure only after an enforcement clause is granted for the enforcement title. However, the decision of a preservative measure (§§292,301 CEA), the payment order which is final and binding (§58(1) CEA), and the judgment ordering the obligor to manifest his/her intention are enforced without an enforcement clause.

1043. Where the performance of an obligation is conditional, or where the judgment creditor or the judgment debtor has been replaced due to inheritance, assignment of the claim, assumption of the obligation, etc., after the enforcement title was effected, the enforcement clause is required without an exception, and the court clerk may grant it only when a judge or a judicial assistant official orders him/her to do so (§§32(1),31 CEA).

C. Prerequisites for Commencement of Enforcement Proceedings

1044. In principle, the creditor may immediately initiate enforcement proceedings once an enforcement clause is granted regarding a specific enforcement title. As an exception, there are cases where certain requirements must be met further. Where the enforcement title is a judgment for future performance, the arrival of the specified due date is required in order to commence enforcement proceedings. In such a case, the enforcement authority can determine whether the specified due date has arrived or not because it is evident in itself.

1045. Where an enforcement title orders the debtor to perform his/her obligation in exchange for the creditor's performance of the obligation, the performance of the obligation or tender thereof by the judgment creditor is necessary for commencement of enforcement proceedings. In such a case, the creditor's performance or tender thereof is not a necessity for granting an enforcement clause. If so, the judgment creditor would be forced to perform his/her obligation prior to the performance of the obligation by the debtor.

III. Compulsory Enforcement Procedure

A. Introduction

1046. Compulsory enforcements are divided into enforcement of a monetary claim and enforcement of a nonmonetary claim. The former is based on the enforcement title that orders the debtor to pay a specified amount of money to the judgment creditor, with which he/she may force the sale or administration of the debtor's property until it is paid off with the proceeds thereof. The latter is a method the judgment creditor uses to force the debtor to perform nonmonetary obligations.

1047. Compulsory enforcements of monetary claims include enforcement against immovables; enforcement against ships; enforcement against automobiles, construction machinery, and small ships; enforcement against airplanes; enforcement against tangible movables; and enforcement against claims and other property rights.

1048. An enforcement of a monetary claim has three stages: seizure, judicial sale, and distribution of the proceeds. When the enforcement authority seizes the debtor's property, it is authorized to dispose of the property for the purpose of paying the debt, and the debtor is banned from exercising his/her right to the property insofar as it intervenes the compulsory enforcement proceedings. The seizure process is carried out by the enforcement officer when the property to be seized is a movable, and in other cases it is done by the court of enforcement.

1049. Methods of implementing seizure vary depending on the types of the properties to be seized. As for immovables, ships, automobiles, construction machinery, small ships, and airplanes, the court of enforcement issues a commencement order for a compulsory judicial sale thereof. The court clerk requests the registrar for registration of the seizure pertaining to such commencement order. When the registrar enters the order in the register of the property, the seizure takes effect. On the other hand, in order to seize tangible movables, the enforcement officer physically takes the possession of them. A compulsory enforcement against a claim for payment of money or delivery of a vessel or movable is commenced as the court of enforcement issues an order of seizure. The seizure becomes effective when a copy of the order is served on the third-party debtor.

1050. The judicial sale and compulsory administration are the means by which the enforcement authority turns the seized immovables, tangible movables, and property rights into money. When a monetary claim is seized, the court of enforcement may issue an order assigning the seized claim to the creditor, an order authorizing the creditor for debt collection, among others.

1051. The proceeds of a judicial sale or compulsory administration of the seized property are paid to the creditors according to the distribution plan in which the order of payment is determined by relevant statutes.

B. Compulsory Enforcement of Monetary Claims

1. Proceedings for Disclosure of Property

a. Definition and Meaning

1052. Proceedings for disclosure of property are used by the creditor in order to get information on the debtor's assets or pressure him/her to voluntarily pay off the debt when it is difficult to locate any property to be seized and the debtor refuses to give information thereon. The proceedings include property declaration, entry in the defaulters list, and court inquiry into properties.

b. Declaration of Property

1053. For the purpose of enforcing a monetary claim, the court of enforcement issues an order to the debtor upon petition by the creditor, to submit a statement containing information on his/her properties potentially subject to the compulsory enforcement (§62(1) CEA).

1054. To file such a petition with the court, the creditor must have an enforcement title based on the monetary claim, which is final and binding (§61(1) CEA).

Thus, the creditor cannot initiate proceedings for disclosure of property with a provisionally enforceable judgment. In addition, the enforcement clause is required to have been granted, and all other prerequisites for commencement of compulsory enforcement must be met. Furthermore, it must be deemed that the properties of the debtor are difficult to locate (§62(2) CEA).

1055. The debtor may file an objection to the court order within a week after a copy of the order has been served on him/her (§63(1) CEA). When the order becomes final and binding, the court designates the date for property disclosure and summons the debtor (§64(1) CEA). Under oath at the hearing, the debtor must submit a written statement containing information on his/her properties potentially subject to the compulsory enforcement and the dispositions thereof with monetary consideration made within the past year and those without monetary consideration made within the past two years from the date the order has been served (§§64(2),65(1) CEA).

1056. Where the debtor refuses to make an appearance at the hearing to submit the written statement or to take an oath, the court may issue a decision ordering him/her to be placed under coercive detention for no more than twenty days (§68(1) CEA). If the debtor has submitted a false statement, he/she is subject to imprisonment of no more than three years or a fine not exceeding KRW 5 million (§68(9) CEA).

c. Defaulters List

1057. When six months have passed since an enforcement title has become final and binding, or the debtor fails to comply with the court order for property declaration or submits a false statement at the hearing, the court of enforcement may issue a decision ordering the debtor be entered in the defaulters list upon petition by the creditor (§§70(1),71(1) CEA). The defaulters list is kept in the court which has issued the decision for the entry (§72(1) CEA). The court must forward a copy of the defaulters list to the municipality in the district where the domicile of the debtor is situated (§72(3) CEA). The defaulters list is open to the public (§72(4) CEA).

d. Court Inquiry into the Debtor's Assets

1058. The court of enforcement may request public agencies, financial institutions, and other organizations that maintain financial information on individuals to provide information on the debtor's properties in the following circumstances; (a) when the process server is unable to serve the order for property declaration upon the debtor, or (b) when the properties listed in the statement of the debtor are not sufficient to pay the debt, or (c) when the debtor fails to comply with the court order for declaration of property or submits a false statement at the hearing (§74(1) CEA).

1059. Public agencies, financial institutions, and other organizations may not refuse to answer such inquiry without good cause (§74(4) CEA).

2. Compulsory Enforcement Against Immovables

a. Compulsory Judicial Sale

(1) Seizure

1060. In order to initiate a forced sale, the creditor must file a petition with the court of enforcement, setting forth the parties, the real property to be sold, the judgment claim, and its amount (§80 CEA). The authenticated copy of the enforcement title with the enforcement clause and other documents verifying that the requirements for commencement of compulsory enforcement are met must be attached to the petition (§81(1) CEA).

1061. Upon petition by the creditor, the court of enforcement issues the decision ordering the commencement of a compulsory judicial sale and seizure of the real property (§83(1) CEA). Immediately afterward, the court clerk requests the registrar to register the commencement thereof in the registration record (§94 CEA). The registrar must, when having made registration of the commencement, send a certificate of the registered matters to the court (§95 CEA). The seizure takes effect when a copy of the decision ordering the commencement of compulsory judicial sale is served on the debtor and the registration thereof is entered (§83(4) CEA). As a result of the seizure, the court of enforcement is authorized to sell the seized property.

1062. Even if the debtor transfers the real property to a third party, creates security interest in the property, or grants usufruct over it, the person who acquires ownership or other rights pertaining to the real estate may not challenge the legal status of the judgment creditor.

1063. The effect of a seizure restricting disposition by the debtor is relative in that such disposition remains valid until the successful bidder of the judicial sale pays the purchase price acquiring ownership of the property. Upon the payment of the purchase price by the bidder, the real rights created in the property after the seizure has taken effect terminates. If the petition for commencement of a compulsory judicial sale is withdrawn or dismissed, the said property rights remain unaffected by the seizure.

1064. The debtor may manage and make use of the seized property as usual (§83(2) CEA). However, where the debtor or the possessor thereof commits or is likely to commit an act that reduces the value of the seized property, the court of enforcement may, upon petition by the creditor, issue a temporary restraining order prohibiting him/her from committing such an act or ordering him/her to release the property from his/her possession and deliver it to the enforcement officer. Where the debtor needs to take an appropriate measure to preserve the value of the property, the court may also order the debtor to do so (§83(3) CEA).

(2) Proceedings for compulsory judicial sale

(a) Deadline for a demand for distribution and its public notice

1065. When the seizure following the court decision on commencement of a compulsory judicial sale has become effective, the court of enforcement fixes the time limit for the demand for distribution of the proceeds as being prior to the first sale date, taking into account the period required for the proceedings. The court gives public notice of the commencement order and the deadline for the demand for distribution and notifies the creditors known to the court, who are entitled to receive distributions (§§84(1),(2) CEA).

(b) Preparation for sale

1066. Immediately after issuing the decision ordering the judicial sale of the seized property, the court orders an enforcement officer to investigate the shape, possession status, and other current conditions thereof (§85(1) CEA). The enforcement officer may enter the real estate for investigation and ask questions to the debtor or a third party occupying it or request him/her to present documents concerning his/her legal relationship thereto (§§85,82 CEA). Also, the court appoints an appraiser and orders him/her to appraise the price of the property. The court determines the reserve price by taking the appraised value into account (§97(1) CEA).

1067. Based on the enforcement officer's report on the current conditions of the property and the appraiser's written appraisal, the court makes a description of the property which contains detailed information about the legal relationships over the property (§105(1) CEA). The court must keep these documents and make them available for public inspection (§105(2) CEA).

(c) Terms of sale

1068. The court determines the reserve price of the seized property considering the appraised value (§97(1) CEA). A purchase offer price must be equal to or higher than the reserve price (§110(1) CEA).

1069. When the court finds that there remains no surplus if all priority claims that take preference over the claim of the judgment creditor and estimated procedural expenses are paid off with the reserve price, the court notifies him/her to the effect (§102(1) CEA). In such a case, if the judgment creditor offers to purchase the seized property at a price that exceeds the aggregate amount of the priority claims and procedural expenses in case there is no bidder who offers the same or higher price and provides a guaranty whose value equals the amount of the gap between the reserve price and the offered price, the court continues the proceedings for the sale. If not, the court rescinds the proceedings for the judicial sale (§102(2) CEA).

1070. The terms of sale include whether security rights or the usufruct would be extinguished by the sale. All the security rights over the seized immovable are to be extinguished (§91(2) CEA). However, in principle, the right of retention remains unaffected by the judicial sale (§91(5) CEA).

1071. Easements, servitudes, leases which are real rights, and registered leases are to be extinguished if such rights were created after a mortgage, a prejudgment seizure, or a seizure takes effect (§91(4) CEA). Otherwise, they survive the judicial sale. However, where the lease which is a real right is not affected by the sale, the lessee may opt to demand for the distribution of the proceeds. In such a case, the lease is terminated, and the proceeds of the sale are distributed to the lessee as a security interest holder (§91(4) CEA).

(d) Types of judicial sales

1072. There are three types of judicial sales for immovables: a date bidding conducted on the date of the sale, a term bidding tendered within the bidding period and to be opened on the date of the sale, and an auction (§103(2) CEA). In practice, date biddings are generally used.

(e) Proceedings for date bidding

1073. There is a courtroom for judicial sales in the District Court (§107 CEA), where there are bidding slips, bidding envelops, and facilities in which bidders can enter their bidding prices without being noticed by others.

1074. The bidding proceedings are presided over by an enforcement officer who is acting as a supporting staff of the court of enforcement (§2 CEA). The date bidding begins when the enforcement officer announces the bidding closure time and the time for opening of the bidding slips and demands bidders to submit their bidding slips. Bidders insert the bidding slips containing the purchase offer price into the bidding box. Bidders must provide a guaranty in the amount specified by the court of enforcement at the time when they submit the bidding slip, which is usually one tenth of the reserve price (r.63 RCE).

1075. The enforcement officer must close bidding at the bidding closure time and immediately open the bidding slips. After opening all the bidding slips, the enforcement officer determines the successful bidder who made a purchase offer at the highest price and provided a proper guaranty. Immediately afterward, the guaranty money submitted by other bidders is returned.

1076. When there is no bidder who offered a purchase price that is equal to or higher than the reserve price, the court reasonably lowers the minimum sale price and designates a new bidding date (§119 CEA). In practice, the reserve price for the new bidding date is usually 20% less than that at the previous date.

(f) Permission of sale

1077. After a successful bidder has been determined, the court of enforcement holds a hearing where persons who have a legitimate interest in permission or non-permission of sale of the real property may state their opinions. At the same time, the court investigates *sua sponte* whether there exists any cause for nonpermission of the sale and renders a decision for permission or nonpermission thereof in the courtroom (§126(1) CEA).

1078. The causes for nonpermission of the sale include where the judicial sale lacks prerequisites therefor, where the highest purchase offeror is unable or unqualified to buy the property, or where there exists a serious procedural error in the proceedings (§121 CEA).

1079. When the court renders a decision for permission of the sale, it gives a public notice thereof (§128(2) CEA). Anyone who has a legitimate interest in the permission of the sale may lodge an opposition to the decision therefor, but he/she must provide a guaranty in cash or securities, equivalent to one tenth of the purchase price offered by the successful bidder (§130(3) CEA).

1080. When the decision for permission of the sale becomes final and binding, the successful bidder obtains the status of a purchaser. The court may, upon petition by the purchaser or the judgment creditor, order a court-appointed administrator to manage the property until it is delivered to the purchaser upon payment of the purchase price (§136(2) CEA).

(g) Payment of purchase price

1081. After the highest purchase offeror becomes the purchaser by the court decision permitting the sale, the purchaser must pay off the purchase price within the time limit fixed by the court (§§142(1),(2) CEA). The money provided by the purchaser as a purchase offer guaranty is allotted to the payment of the price. If the purchaser has provided a guaranty other than money, the court of enforcement realizes it and allots the amount to the payment (§§142(3),(4) CEA).

1082. The purchaser acquires the ownership of the seized property at the time of payment of the price (§135 CEA). The transfer of a real right is effectuated by the agreement between the transferee and the transferor, and the registration thereof in the record of registration of the real property, except insofar as otherwise stipulated by statutes. In this context, the ownership transfer in a judicial sale is not by an agreement, but by statutory provisions.

1083. Upon the payment of the purchase price, the court clerk must request the registrar to register the ownership transfer to the purchaser, to cancel registrations of the security interests, usufructs, registered lease, etc., which are extinguished by the sale and registration of the court decision ordering the judicial sale (§141(1) CEA).

1084. Should the purchaser fail to pay the purchase price, the court of enforcement orders *sua sponte* a resale of the real property (§138(1) CEA). The reserve price and other terms of sale at the previous one must be applied to the proceedings for the resale (§138(2) CEA). In this case, the guaranty provided by the purchaser is allotted to the amount to be distributed to the creditors, and the purchaser may not claim a return thereof (§147(1) CEA).

(h) Delivery order

1085. Because the debtor may possess and use the seized real property, the Civil Execution Act provides for a device by which the purchaser can easily secure delivery of the property. In case where the debtor or the possessor refuses to deliver the property, the court of enforcement may, upon petition by the purchaser who has paid the price, order him/her to do so. The petition for delivery must be filed within six months after payment of the price. However, the delivery order does not apply to the possessor who has a real right over the property, which has not been extinguished by the sale (§136(1) CEA).

1086. The delivery order is an enforcement title which requires an enforcement clause to be executed.

(3) Distribution proceedings

(a) Proceeds of the sale

1087. The proceeds of the sale to be distributed include the price paid by the purchaser of the seized property, which is the largest part of the amount to be distributed. Also included are the guaranty provided by the former purchaser who is prohibited from claiming a return thereof and a portion of the guaranty provided by those whose appeal to the decision for permission of sale has been dismissed (§147(1) CEA). Because procedural expenses are paid at a highest priority, the remaining amount is to be distributed to the creditors in the order of priority.

(b) Order of creditors for distribution

1088. When the proceeds of a sale are insufficient to satisfy all the creditors taking part in the distribution, the court of enforcement makes a distribution in the order of priority prescribed by the Civil Act, the Commercial Act, and other relevant statutes (§145(2) CEA).

1089. Where a house or a building is sold at a judicial sale, part or whole of which has been leased for residence with a security deposit not exceeding a certain amount, the lessee's claim for return of the deposit is paid in the highest priority over any security rights or tax claims. The extent of the security deposit in amount that is eligible for the most preferential treatment varies depending on the area where the seized real property is located and is regulated by the Enforcement Decree of the President (§§8(1) HLPA, 35(1) FANT, 71(1) LTA). The lessee's claim for return of the deposit, when it exceeds the said amount, is considered a secured claim provided that the lessee has possessed the house; has filed a move-in report with the municipality in the area where the house is located under the Resident Registration Act; and has obtained the fixed date on the lease contract document (§3-2(2) HLPA).

1090. The claims for wages for a period of the last three months and those for retirement allowances for a period of the last three years prior to the retirement are also paid in the same highest priority to that of the said security deposit in distribution (§38(2) LSA);12(2) AGER).

1091. According to general principles of the Civil Act, a mortgage and a lease right which is a real right are equally treated in distribution, and the order of their priorities are determined by the chronological order of registration. Where the holder of a security right based on provisional registration of ownership transfer has demanded for distribution, he/she is treated like a lien holder (§13 PRSA).

1092. The remnants of the proceeds after they have been paid for priority claims and secured claims are distributed to the rest of the unsecured creditors on an equal basis. The creditors who have executed a prejudgment seizure or a seizure prior to the time limit for a demand for distribution, or who has demanded for distribution based on an enforcement title are treated equal, irrespective of the chronological order of their filing or registration. Here, the equal treatment means a *pro rata* distribution according to the amount of each claim.

1093. In case where a lien, a lease right which is a real right, and other security rights have been created over the seized property after a prejudgment seizure was implemented, the secured claims and the claim preserved thereby are equal. However, among the secured claims, the order of priority is determined as if it had not been for the prejudgment seizure.

1094. For example, after A enforced a prejudgment seizure against a real property, B had a security interest registered and then C did on the same property. A's unsecured claim is KRW 10 million; B's secured claim, KRW 20 million; and C's secured claim, KRW 30 million. The proceeds from the judicial sale, which can be distributed to these creditors, are KRW 30 million. In this case, at first KRW 5 million, KRW 10 million and KRW 15 million are distributed to A, B and C respectively on an equal basis. However, B must be satisfied prior to C. As a result, A, B and C receive KRW 5 million, KRW 20 million (10 million + 10 million) and KRW 5 million (15 million – 10 million) respectively.

(c) Demand for distribution

1095. The demand for distribution filed by a creditor is a request to the court of enforcement to pay his/her claim with the proceeds of the sale. Some creditors need not file a demand for distribution to receive it, but others must do so.

1096. The former includes creditors who seized the property anew, after the prior seizure took effect, no later than the time limit for a demand for distribution; creditors who effected a prejudgment seizure before the commencement of a judicial sale was registered; and creditors secured by a lien, lease right which is a real right and other security interests that were registered prior to the registration of commencement of judicial sale and that are to be extinguished thereby (§148 CEA).

1097. As mentioned above, after making registration of a seizure at the request of the court clerk, the registrar must send a certificate of the registered matters to the court of enforcement. Because the certificate of the registered matters contains information on the rights over the seized property, the holders of such rights may receive distributions without making a demand therefor. These creditors must submit a calculation of their respective claims in terms of principal, interest, and costs no later than the time limit for a demand for distribution (§84(4) CEA). When the creditors fail to file the calculation, the court of enforcement determines the amount to be distributed based on the case records including a certificate of registered matters (§84(5) CEA).

1098. Creditors who have an enforcement title with an enforcement clause, creditors who effected a prejudgment seizure upon the seized property after the commencement of judicial sale was registered, and priority creditors prescribed in statutes must make a demand for distribution no later than the time limit therefor (§88(2) CEA). This is because the information on the claims of such creditors are not contained in the certificate of registered matters.

1099. As for a lease right which is a real right and which is not affected by the sale because it was registered earlier than other rights to be extinguished thereby, the lessee may opt to make a demand for distribution. If not, the lease right survives the judicial sale (§91(4) CEA).

(d) Distribution hearing

1100. The court of enforcement must make a distribution plan at least three days prior to the distribution hearing and keep it in the court, open to the debtor and creditors (§149(1) CEA). The distribution plan contains a statement regarding the amount of the proceeds of the sale; each amount of the principal of the claims, interest, and any other incidental claims; the amount of procedural expenses; and the order and amount of distribution to the respective creditors (§150(1) CEA).

1101. A creditor, present at the hearing, may raise an opposition to the distribution plan alleging that any error in the plan harms his/her interest, benefiting other specific creditors (§151(3) CEA). The creditors involved must make a statement thereon at the hearing (§152(1) CEA). If the respondent acknowledges the opposition of the dissatisfied creditor or reaches an agreement with him/her, the distribution plan is corrected pursuant thereto (§152(2) CEA). If a creditor is not present at the hearing, he/she is deemed to have agreed on the distribution plan (§153(1) CEA).

1102. The debtor, present at the hearing, may lodge an opposition to the distribution plan in the best interest of all the creditors and himself/herself. He/she may, not appearing at the hearing, do so in writing no later than the close of the hearing (§§151 (1),(2) CEA).

1103. If the objection is not resolved by either acknowledgement of the respondent or mutual agreement, the creditor who lodged an opposition must file a lawsuit against the respondent, seeking correction of the distribution plan (§154(1) CEA). However, if the debtor raised an opposition and the claim of the creditor involved is based on an enforcement title, he/she must file a lawsuit raising an objection to the claim being enforced (§154(2) CEA).

(e) Lawsuit brought in support of an opposition

1104. The lawsuit to oppose the distribution plan is an action for formation seeking correction thereof. The creditor or debtor who raised an opposition which was not resolved becomes the plaintiff, and the creditor involved therein becomes the defendant. This lawsuit is subject to jurisdiction of the trial court, not the court of enforcement. The court renders a judgment ordering revision of the distribution plan if the opposition is well-grounded. The judgment granting whole or part of the opposition binds only the parties of the lawsuit when the plaintiff is a creditor, whereas it binds the debtor and all the creditors in the plan when the debtor brings the lawsuit.

1105. Even if the court finds, in the lawsuit in support of an opposition by a creditor, that the defendant does not have any right to receive distribution, the revision of the plan is limited to the extent that the plaintiff receives the full payment of his/her claim. Thus, the rest of the amount, if any, is still to be distributed to the defendant.

(f) Implementation of distribution

1106. If there is no opposition to the distribution plan, the order and amount of each claim are fixed as set forth therein. When an opposition is raised by a creditor against another creditor, the distribution plan for the rest of the creditors is not affected. Between the dissatisfied creditor and the respondent, the distribution plan regarding the amount of their claims is to be determined pursuant to the resolution of the opposition.

1107. When the distribution plan regarding the order and amount of a claim becomes final and binding, the court of enforcement directs the disbursement of the proceeds for the specific creditor. However, for a claim which is subject to a condition precedent or one with an unspecified due date; which has been preserved by a prejudgment seizure on the sold property; or which is held by the creditor whom a lawsuit in support of an opposition to the distribution plan has been filed against; the court of enforcement makes a deposit of the proceeds to be distributed to the corresponding creditors in court.

b. Compulsory Administration

1108. A compulsory administration is a method of compulsory enforcement for a monetary claim. The judgment creditor is satisfied by the earnings from the seized immovable property instead of the proceeds of a judicial sale thereof.

1109. Upon petition by the judgment creditor, the court of enforcement issues a commencement order for a compulsory administration, declaring that the real property is seized for the creditor and prohibiting the debtor from disposing of earnings therefrom (§§163,83(1),164(1) CEA). The earnings include natural fruits and civil ones (§164(2) CEA). At the same time, the court appoints an administrator, who is authorized to collect earnings and conduct a realization with regard to the seized real property (§166 CEA).

1110. The administrator must pay the tax or public charges imposed on the real property, the remuneration for himself/herself and any other necessary expenses from the earnings or the realization price (§169(1) CEA). The remaining amount is allotted to distributions to the creditors. If an agreement upon the order and amount of the claims is reached among the creditors, the distribution is carried out by the administrator (§169(2) CEA). If not, the court of enforcement makes a distribution plan and implements the distribution proceedings (§169(4) CEA).

3. Compulsory Enforcement Against Ships, Automobiles, Construction Machinery and Airplanes

1111. Ships, automobiles, construction machinery, and airplanes are movables under the Civil Act. However, the real rights on these properties are registered in the registration record thereof, and there are many similarities between them and real properties. In this context, generally, provisions regulating enforcement of a monetary claim against an immovable apply to enforcements against these properties, except as otherwise provided for by the provisions of the Civil Execution Act.

4. Compulsory Enforcement Against Tangible Movables

a. Seizure

(1) Objects and scope

1112. Trees and stones are fixtures that are permanently attached to land. A fixture is part of a real property, but it becomes a tangible movable once separated physically therefrom. A specific garden tree, garden rock, etc., may be treated as a movable while they are fixed to land under the Civil Execution Act. Natural fruits prior to being separated from land, which are to be harvested within one month for certain are treated in the same manner. Securities other than those forbidden to be endorsed are also considered as movable properties under the Civil Execution Act (§189(2) CEA).

1113. The enforcement officer is prohibited from seizing movables if the amount of proceeds therefrom is not expected to exceed the amount of the procedural expenses (§188(3) CEA). After the seizure of movables, the enforcement officer must retract the enforcement proceedings if the amount of proceeds from the seized property is not expected to reach the total amount of the procedural expenses, and the amount of any claims that take precedence over the claim of the judgment creditor (r.140(2) RCE).

1114. The enforcement officer must carry out the seizure of movables only within the limit required to pay the judgment claim and procedural expenses (§188(2) CEA). This means that an unnecessary and excessive seizure is banned when the enforcement of a monetary claim is implemented against multiple movables.

1115. Personal, family, and household items necessary for living of the debtor and his/her family; tools of the debtor's trade, business, or profession; health aids, etc., are exempted from seizures. Examples include the following: clothes, beds, furniture, kitchen utensils, and other fittings that are indispensable for living; food and fuel necessary for two months' living; money in the amount specified by the Enforcement Decree of the President taking into account the household's necessary living expenses for one month; equipment, fertilizers, work animals, and their feeds that are indispensable for agriculture as well as seeds and any other similar agricultural products; fish nets and any other fishing equipment; a family tree, ancestral memorial table, or other similar objects; a medal or any other object representing honor; artificial limbs, glasses, and other aids (§195 CEA).

1116. The court of enforcement may, upon petition by a party, order a rescission of all or part of a seizure or permit a seizure of the items exempted therefrom, considering all the circumstances (§196(1) CEA). The court is expected to exercise its discretion to limit or expand the scope of the items subject to seizures, taking into account the living conditions of the persons involved.

(2) Proceedings

1117. The enforcement officer is the enforcement agency in enforcement of judgments against movables. The judgment creditor may delegate the enforcement to any enforcement officer associated with the District Court or the Branch Court seated in the area where the property to be seized is located. The enforcement officer may not refuse to accept the delegation made by a judgment creditor.

1118. The proceedings for an enforcement against a movable are commenced by a seizure thereof. The seizure is implemented by way of an enforcement officer taking possession of the movable. When the movable is difficult to transport, or upon the creditor's consent, the enforcement officer may leave the seized property in the custody and control of the judgment debtor. In this case, the seizure takes effect when the seized movable is visibly and clearly indicated through sealing or any other methods (§189(1) CEA).

b. Judicial Sale of Movables

1119. The enforcement officer sells the seized movables on the designated date for the judicial sale. There must be an interval of time that is longer than one week between the date of seizure and that for judicial sale (§202 CEA). The judicial sale is carried out in the office of the municipality in the area where the seized property is located. If the debtor and creditor agree upon another place for the judicial sale, the judicial sale may take place at that location (§203 CEA).

1120. The enforcement officer makes a sale of the seized property by bidding or an auction (§199 CEA). He/she permits the sale after announcing the name of the highest bidder and the price offered by him/her (§205(1) CEA). The sold property is delivered to the purchaser in exchange for the payment of the purchase price (§205(2) CEA).

1121. Seized cash must be delivered to the creditor for the purpose of paying his/her claim at the place of seizure (§201(1) CEA). When the enforcement officer has seized securities which have an exchange price or market price, he/she must sell them at the then current price in an appropriate manner. Where they do not have such a price, they are to be sold in accordance with the provisions regulating judicial sale of tangible movables (§210 CEA).

c. Demand for Distribution

1122. The holders of priority claims under the Civil Act, the Commercial Act, and other statutes may make a demand for distribution of the proceeds of the sale (§217 CEA). They include a pledgee of the seized property (§329 CA) and a creditor who has claims for wages (§38 LSA). Unsecured creditors, except priority creditors, are not qualified to make a demand for distribution even though they have an enforcement title with an enforcement clause. These creditors may receive distributions only when they have executed an overlapping seizure against the seized property.

d. Distribution Proceedings

1123. The enforcement officer deducts procedural expenses from the seized cash and proceeds of the sale and then delivers remaining amounts to the judgment creditor and other creditors who made a demand for distributions (r.155(1) RCE). If there is any remaining amount after satisfying the creditors' claims, it must be delivered to the debtor.

1124. If there are multiple creditors and the proceeds of the sale are not enough to satisfy all the claims, the enforcement officer must designate a date for a distribution hearing (r.155(2) RCE). Should the participating creditors reach an agreement with regard to distribution of the proceeds, the enforcement officer implements distributions accordingly (r.155(3) RCE).

1125. Should the creditors fail to reach an agreement, the enforcement officer must deposit the seized cash and proceeds of the sale in court (§222(1) CEA). In this case, the court of enforcement implements distribution proceedings.

5. Enforcement Against Claims and Other Property Rights

a. Objects and Scope

1126. The claims include a monetary claim and clams for delivery of a real property, a tangible movable, a ship, an automobile, construction machinery, and an airplane. Claims for transfer of rights over these properties are also included (§§242,243,244 CEA). Examples of the property rights include co-ownership share of a tangible movable; intellectual property rights including a patent right and a copyright; a trademark right; rights of a partner in a partnership company; a membership of an association; and rights of a shareholder prior to issuance of shares.

1127. The right to receive benefits under the Public Officials Pension Act (§32 POPA), the claim for accident compensation under the Labor Standards Act (§86 LSA), and the right to receive retirement benefits (§7 AGER) are monetary claims. However, these claims are not subject to seizure because the assignment thereof is prohibited by the above statutes.

1128. The creditor and debtor may execute a contract containing a nonassignment clause, which prohibits the assignment of the contractual claims. However, these claims are subject to seizure.[223]

223. Supreme Court Decision 76Da1623 decided on October 29, 1976.

1129. Also, there are claims, a portion of which is exempted from seizure for the reason of public interest and social policy. In a case of a claim pertaining to continuous payments that the debtor receives for the purpose of maintaining his/her living; a claim pertaining to a compensation, wage, salary, retirement pension, bonus, etc.; a claim pertaining to a retirement allowance or any remuneration similar in nature; one half of the amount of the aforementioned claims is not subject to seizure. If the seizure-prohibited amount is below the minimum cost of living, the amount equivalent to the latter is free from seizure (§246(1) CEA).

b. Enforcement Against a Monetary Claim

(1) Seizure

(a) Proceedings

1130. The enforcement proceedings commence when the court of enforcement issues a decision ordering a seizure of the monetary claim. The judgment creditor must submit an enforcement title with an enforcement clause in filing a petition for the seizure. The court renders a decision based on written documents without holding a hearing. The decision containing a declaration of a seizure prohibits the third-party debtor from making any payment to the judgment debtor and the judgment debtor from collecting or disposing of the claim (§227(1) CEA).

1131. The court of enforcement serves *sua sponte* a copy of the seizure order upon the judgment debtor and the third-party debtor. The seizure takes effect when the seizure order is served upon the third-party debtor (§227(2) CEA). If the seized claim is a secured one, the effect of the seizure reaches the collateral.

1132. The court of enforcement may order, upon petition by the creditor, the third-party debtor to submit a written statement declaring whether and to what extent he/she acknowledges the claim as being justified and is prepared to make payment, and whether the claim has already been seized by other creditors (§237 CEA).

(b) Effects

1133. Even if the debtor disposes of the seized claim or receives payment from the third-party debtor, the debtor may not assert the effect thereof to the judgment creditor. However, the debtor may file a lawsuit seeking payment of the debt against the third-party debtor based on the seized claim and obtain a judgment in his/her favor.[224] It is sometimes necessary for the debtor to file such a lawsuit to stop the statute of limitations from running. However, in this case, the debtor may not enforce the judgment.

---

224. Supreme Court Decision 2001Da59033 decided on April 26, 2002.

1134. The third-party debtor is prohibited from paying the debt. Should he/she do so, he/she may not assert to the judgment creditor that the seized claim does not exist anymore. However, the third-party debtor may raise any ground as a defense against the judgment creditor, which might have been raised against the debtor at the time the seizure took effect.[225]

1135. In case where there were grounds at the time of the seizure, on which the third-party debtor might revoke or rescind the contract having created the claim, he/she may extinguish the seized claim by doing so. In addition, where the debtor had a monetary counterclaim against the creditor and the due dates of both the seized original claim and counterclaim have reached when the seizure order was served on the third-party debtor, or where the due date of the counterclaim was to come not later than that of the seized claim, the third-party debtor may plead for the setoff.[226]

1136. The effects of the seizure extend to the entirety of the claim unless the judgment creditor specified the amount thereof in the petition for the seizure. In cases where a part of a claim has been seized or has been subjected to a prejudgment seizure, and another seizure order is issued beyond the remaining portion of the relevant claim, the effects of each seizure or prejudgment seizure reach the entirety thereof (§235 CEA).

(2) Realization of the seized claim

(a) Collection order

1137. The court of enforcement may issue a decision authorizing the judgment creditor to collect the seized claim on behalf of the debtor. In principle, the creditor must collect the entire amount of the seized claim beyond the amount of his/hers. However, the court may, on motion of the debtor, limit the amount to that of the judgment debt (§232(1) CEA). The judgment creditor may collect the amount that exceeds that of his/her claim because other creditors may make a demand for distribution of the collected money.

1138. Should the third-party debtor fail to pay the debt, the judgment creditor has a standing to sue him/her (§238 CEA). When the creditor has collected the seized claim, he/she must immediately notify the court of enforcement to that effect and then satisfy his/her claim. The remainder is to be delivered to the judgment debtor (§236(1) CEA).

1139. When there has been another seizure or prejudgment seizure against the seized claim, or a demand for distribution prior to the notification of collection to

225. Supreme Court Decision 92Da55794 decided on September 28, 1993.
226. Supreme Court Decision 2011Da45521 decided on February 16, 2012.

the court, the creditor must promptly deposit the collected amount in court (§236(2) CEA). In such a case, the court of enforcement implements the distribution proceedings (§252 CEA).

(b) Assignment order

1140. The court of enforcement may, upon petition by the judgment creditor, issue an order (in the form of a decision) to assign the seized monetary claim to him/her at the face value in lieu of payment. When the assignment order becomes final and binding, the seized claim is transferred to the judgment creditor, and the creditor's claim is deemed to have been satisfied in respect of the same amount (§231 CEA). Because the seized claim is transferred to the judgment creditor in lieu of payment of the creditor's claim, the assignment order does not take effect if an overlapping seizure or prejudgment seizure has been carried out on the seized claim, or if a demand for distribution has been made, by the time the assignment order is served upon a third-party debtor (§229(5) CEA).

1141. Anyone who has a legitimate interest may raise an immediate appeal against the decision ordering assignment of the seized claim (§229(6) CEA). The assignment order takes effect when it becomes final and binding. The effects of the order are retroactive to the time when the decision was served on the third-party debtor. Therefore, unless there were overlapping seizures or a demand for distribution at the time of service of the decision, the assignment order is effective (§229(5) CEA).

1142. As the seized claim is assigned to the judgment creditor by the assignment order, the judgment creditor as an assignee may file a lawsuit seeking payment of the claim. Where the claim to be seized did not exist or was assigned to a third party in part or as a whole as of the time the assignment order was served upon the third-party debtor, the assignment order is invalid in respect of the amount (§231 CEA).

(c) Other methods of realization

1143. It is difficult to collect the seized claim when it is subject to a condition, the payment due date has not arrived, or it relates to counter-performance. In such cases, the court of enforcement may, upon petition by the judgment creditor, issue an order to transfer the seized claim to the creditor at the price specified by the court in lieu of payment. Otherwise, the court may order an enforcement officer to sell the claim by the method specified by the court in lieu of collection (§241(1) CEA).

c. Enforcement Against Claims for Delivery of Tangibles and Claims for Transfer of Real Right

(1) Claims concerning movables

1144. The debtor's claim for delivery of a tangible movable against the third-party debtor is a property right and subject to enforcement of a monetary claim. The claim to be seized may be based on a contract or real rights.

1145. The seizure order prohibits the judgment debtor from disposing of the claim or receiving performance and prohibits the third-party debtor from performing his/her obligation in respect of the seized claim. At the same time, it orders the third-party debtor to deliver the movable to the enforcement officer who was designated by the judgment creditor (§243(1) CEA).

1146. Since the judgment creditor is not a party to the proceedings for the delivery order, he/she may not enforce it even if the third-party debtor refuses to comply with the order. In this case, the court of enforcement may, upon petition by the creditor, issue an order demanding the third-party debtor to deliver the movable to the enforcement officer designated by the creditor (§243(2) CEA). This order is enforceable.

1147. Once the movable is delivered to the enforcement officer, the seizure thereof takes effect. The enforcement officer sells the seized movable by the method of a compulsory judicial sale and delivers the proceeds to the court of enforcement. The court implements the distribution proceedings (§243(3) CEA).

(2) Claims concerning real properties

1148. With respect to a seizure of a claim for delivery of a real property, the court appoints a custodian and orders the third-party debtor to deliver the property to the custodian, upon petition by the creditor or the third-party debtor (§244(1) CEA). In proceedings for a seizure of the claim for transfer of a real right, the court also appoints a custodian and orders the third-party debtor to file for a registration for transfer of the real right in the name of the judgment debtor (§244(2) CEA). In this case, the custodian becomes a statutory agent of the debtor (§244(3) CEA).

1149. In a case where the third-party debtor refuses to deliver the real property to the custodian or to file for a registration for transfer of the real right, the court may, upon petition by the creditor, issue a decision ordering the third-party debtor to do so (§244(4) CEA). The creditor may file a lawsuit based on this decision, seeking delivery or registration therefor.

1150. When the real property is delivered to the custodian or the registration is implemented for the debtor in these ways, a compulsory judicial sale or a compulsory administration is initiated according to the provisions pertaining to enforcement of a monetary claim against an immovable.

d. Enforcement Against other Property Rights

1151. In order to realize other property rights, the court of enforcement issues an order of assignment, order of sale, and order of administration. When the order of administration is issued, the judgment creditor is satisfied by the earnings from the seized property right.

C. Compulsory Enforcement of a Nonmonetary Claim

1. Enforcement of Claims for Delivery of Tangibles

1152. When the debtor is obliged to deliver a specified movable, a real property, a ship, or a specific quantity of fungibles, the enforcement officer enforces the judgment by taking them away from the debtor and delivering them to the creditor (§§257,258(1) CEA).

1153. In principle, the enforcement is impossible when a third party who is not subject to the binding effect of the judgment is in possession of the object to be delivered. In such a case, the court of enforcement may, upon petition by the creditor, issue a decision ordering the seizure of the debtor's right to demand the third party for its delivery and transferring the claim to the creditor (§259 CEA). Based on this order, the creditor may file a lawsuit against the third party seeking delivery of the object.

2. Enforcement by Substitute

1154. Where the debtor refuses to perform his/her obligation prescribed in the judgment but the nature of the obligation does not permit an enforcement, and where it may be fulfilled by a third party because there is no difference depending on who performs the obligation, the trial court which heard the case authorizes a specific person, upon petition by the creditor, to fulfill the obligation at the costs of the debtor (§260(1) CEA). If the court has not designated the person to carry out the obligation, the creditor may do so at the costs of the debtor.

1155. Examples of such obligations include a demolition of a building, removal of the trees planted on a plot of land, and other obligations that can be fulfilled by simple labor. In respect of such obligations, the enforcement authority is the trial court of first instance having heard the case.

3. Indirect Compulsory Enforcement

1156. Where the obligation of an action cannot be carried out by a third party because the action depends exclusively on the will of the debtor, the trial court of first instance having heard the case may, upon petition by the creditor, order the debtor to pay the creditor a certain amount of money according to the period of the delay. The court determines, at its discretion, the time by which the obligation must be fulfilled and the amount of money considered to be reasonable for securing performance of the obligation (§261(1) CEA).

1157. This method of enforcement may be used for the obligation of inaction, such as prohibition of obstructing a passage or that of stalking. In such cases, the court orders the debtor to pay a certain amount of money according to the number of violations or the period during which the violation of the obligation lasts.

4. Enforcement of Obligation to Declare Intent

1158. With respect to obligations to make a declaration of intent or to give a notice, such obligations are deemed to have been performed at the time the judgment has become final and binding (§263(1) CEA). It means that the judgment ordering the debtor to manifest his/her intention is enforced without any enforcement proceedings.

1159. The judgment ordering the debtor to make a declaration of intent or to give a notice is rendered where the debtor is required to do so in order for the creditor to realize his/her claim. For example, in the sale and purchase of a real property, the ownership is transferred to the purchaser when the registration for the ownership transfer is entered in the registration record. If the seller refuses to file for the registration, the purchaser may bring a lawsuit against the seller, seeking registration therefor. When the judgment in favor of the purchaser becomes final and binding, the defendant (seller) is deemed to have manifested his/her intent to file for the registration to the registrar. On the other hand, the assignment of a nominative claim may not be asserted against the debtor or any other third party, unless the assignor gives a notice thereof to the debtor, or the debtor has acknowledged the assignment. If the assignor refuses to give such a notice, the assignee may file a lawsuit against the assignor. When the final and binding judgment ordering the assignor to give such a notice is served on the debtor, the effect of notification takes place.

1160. In case where the declaration of intent depends on the counter-performance being made or is subject to a condition, such effects occur when the enforcement clause is granted to the enforcement title.[227]

§2. Judicial Review

I. Objection Concerning Granting of Enforcement Clause

1161. In a case where the court clerk or the notary public refuses to grant an enforcement clause, the creditor may file an objection with the District Court in the district where the office of the court clerk or that of the notary public is located

227. Supreme Court Decision 77Ma427 decided on May 22, 1979.

(§§34(1),59(1) CEA). To the contrary, when the enforcement clause is granted, the debtor may file an objection to the issuance thereof.

1162. When the court issues a decision ordering the grant of an enforcement clause, it must be granted. Even when the enforcement clause is granted according to the court decision, the debtor may lodge an objection thereto. In such a case, however, the debtor may not appeal the decision because the debtor is not a party in respect of the court decision.[228]

1163. In a case where the debtor's objection to the grant of enforcement clause is well-grounded, the court renders a decision revoking the issuance of the enforcement clause and declaring that the enforcement based on the enforcement clause is prohibited. The court ruling on the objection lodged by the debtor is not subject to an appeal.

II. Lawsuit for Granting Enforcement Clause

1164. The claim to be enforced might be subject to conditions, or the judgment debtor or judgment creditor might not be a party set forth in the judgment because an assignment of the claim, assumption of the obligation, inheritance, etc., have been effected after the close of the oral hearing on the merits. In such cases, the judgment creditor must prove the fulfillment of the conditions or occurrence of such facts by public records or documents to obtain a grant of the enforcement clause (§§30(2),31(1)).

1165. When the public documents necessary to establish such facts are not available, the creditor may file a lawsuit against the debtor, with the trial court of first instance having heard the case, seeking the grant of the enforcement clause (§33 CEA). This lawsuit may be filed even after the objection concerning granting of the enforcement clause filed by the creditor has been dismissed. Also, the creditor may file this lawsuit without requesting the court clerk or the notary public to grant it.

III. Lawsuit to Oppose Granting of Enforcement Clause

1166. When an enforcement clause has been granted in a case where the enforcement depends on the occurrence of certain facts that must be proved by public documents, the debtor may file a lawsuit seeking revocation of the grant of the enforcement clause (§45 CEA). In this lawsuit, the creditor (defendant bears the burden of proving the facts regarding the requirements for the grant of the enforcement clause even though the debtor is the plaintiff.[229]

228. Supreme Court Decision 78Ma249 decided on August 25, 1979.
229. Supreme Court Decision 2012Da111630 decided on January 29, 2015.

1167. The debtor may, at his/her choice, file an objection to the grant of the enforcement clause or file a lawsuit to oppose it. The debtor may file the lawsuit even after the objection lodged by him/her has been denied. However, in a case where the enforcement clause was granted according to a judgment or a judgment dismissing the debtor's claim to oppose it in such a lawsuit becomes final and binding, the debtor may not file an objection due to preclusive effects of the judgments.

IV. Objection to the Disposition of an Enforcement

1168. Such an objection may be filed with the court of enforcement when a decision or an order issued by the court of enforcement, or the measures taken by the enforcement officer is erroneous (§16(1) CEA). Filing an objection to the disposition of an enforcement is not allowed when the procedure for an appeal or objection concerning a specific disposition is prescribed in the provisions of the Civil Execution Act. The objection may be lodged by the debtor, the creditor, or a third party who has a legitimate interest in the disposition of the enforcement.

V. Immediate Appeal

1169. An immediate appeal may be filed against a judicial decision issued by a court of enforcement only in cases where there are special provisions allowing such filings. In general, the Civil Execution Act allows an immediate appeal against decisions which end the enforcement proceedings or have a serious impact on the rights of the parties involved. Examples of such decisions include a decision retracting the enforcement proceedings (§17(1) CEA); a decision for permission or nonpermission of sale in the judicial sale of a real property (§129(1) CEA); and a seizure order (§227(4) CEA), a collection order (§229(6) CEA), and an assignment order (§229(6) CEA) in the enforcement against a monetary claim.

1170. An immediate appeal must be filed by submitting a notice of appeal to the court of enforcement within a week after the judicial decision has been notified (§15(2) CEA). The enforcement proceedings are not stayed just for the reason that an immediate appeal has been filed (§15(6) CEA). The appellant must submit a written statement of reasons for the appeal within ten days after filing the appeal (§15(3) CEA).

VI. Lawsuit Raising an Objection to the Claim Being Enforced

1171. In this lawsuit, the debtor may assert objections to the compulsory enforcement based on an enforcement title by disputing the presence or contents of the claim pertaining to the title. This lawsuit is subject to jurisdiction of the trial court of first instance having heard the case (§44(1) CEA). The judgment rendered in this lawsuit is formative in that it terminates or limits the enforceability of the enforcement title.

1172. With respect to the causes of action, those for an enforcement title having preclusive effects and those for one without these effects are different. Grounds for objections to a final and binding judgment are limited to those that arise after the close of the oral hearing on the merits. When the enforcement title is a document that has the same effect as a final and binding judgment, grounds for objections are those which occurs after it takes effect. The causes of action include a performance of the obligation, a release of the obligation by the creditor, a setoff, a revocation of the contract that created the claim to be enforced, among others. However, where the judgment debtor had a right to revoke or a right to rescind the contract that relates to the enforcement title but he/she did not exercise the right prior to the close of the oral hearing, he/she is precluded from revoking or rescinding the contract on the grounds that he/she was able to assert at the hearing.[230]

1173. Where the enforcement title does not have preclusive effects, grounds for objections thereto are not limited by the time when those have arisen. Thus, even if the claim did not exist from the start or it had extinguished before the enforcement title was established, the debtor may assert the fact as a cause of action. Examples of such an enforcement title include a payment order (§474 CPA), a judicial decision recommending performance of the obligation (§5-7(1) TSCA), an enforcement deed (§56 CEA), among others.

VII. Third-Party Lawsuit Against Enforcement

1174. Enforcement proceedings may be commenced against a property over which a third party has a real right that is not subject thereto and capable of preventing them. It is often the case when the enforcement is carried out against movables. In such a case, the third party may file a lawsuit against the creditor seeking an exclusion of the property from the enforcement proceedings (§48(1) CEA).

1175. This lawsuit falls under the jurisdiction of the court of enforcement. However, when the amount in controversy exceeds KRW 200 million, the case is adjudicated by a judicial panel in the District Court (§48(2) CEA).

1176. In most cases, a third party's right is the ownership. A superficies, lease right which is a real right, as well as the right of retention over a real property might survive the compulsory enforcement of a monetary claim against the property, or might be extinguished thereby depending on their relative priority orders in relation to other rights to be extinguished. As a result, the holders of such a right may not file a third-party lawsuit against enforcements. However, with respect to the enforcement of delivery or surrender of the property, these rights may become a cause of action for a third-party lawsuit.

1177. Even an obligatory claim may become grounds for this lawsuit. For example, a monetary claim was assigned, and the assignor gave the notice of the

230. *Supra* n. 177.

assignment, using an instrument bearing a fixed date, to the debtor. And then, the court of enforcement issues a decision ordering seizure of the claim for a creditor who has a monetary claim against the assignor. In such a case, the assignee may file a third-party lawsuit against the creditor.

§3. Recognition and Enforcement of Foreign Judgment

I. Recognition of Foreign Judgment

A. Definition and Meaning

1178. The prerequisites for recognition of a foreign judgment are prescribed in the provisions of the Civil Procedure Act. However, the provisions regarding the proceedings in which the court examines and recognizes a foreign judgment do not exist. In this context, if the ruling on the case pending in the Korean court should be decided depending on the effects of a foreign judgment, the court examines and finds whether it meets the requirements for recognition.

1179. For example, a Korean husband obtained a judgment of divorce in a foreign country and submitted the judgment document and a report of divorce to the municipality in the area where his domicile in Korea is located. The official at the municipality accepted the report thinking that the foreign judgment is effective. Afterward, the divorced wife filed a lawsuit seeking a declaration of nullity of divorce in Korea. In such a case, the Family Court would examine the foreign judgment of divorce and determine whether it meets the requirements for recognition. If it fails to meet such requirements, the court would render a judgment declaring that the divorce is null and void.

1180. Only a final and binding judgment rendered by a court or other court decision that has the same effects as a judgment may be recognized. Here, the court must have the authority to exercise judicial powers in the relevant foreign nation. In addition, the subject-matter of the case should be civil or commercial, and both parties must have been given equal opportunities to examine the opposing party in the proceedings before the foreign court.[231]

B. Prerequisites for Recognition of Foreign Judgment

1. International Jurisdiction of the Foreign Nation

1181. The foreign court must have international jurisdiction over the case pursuant to the statutes or treaties of Korea (§217(1) CEA). In a case which has foreign elements, when a party or the subject-matter of the dispute is substantively related

231. Supreme Court Decision 2009Da68910 decided on April 29, 2010.

to Korea, a Korean court has international jurisdiction (§2 APIL). With respect to a foreign judgment, the foreign nation must have such a relationship to the case.

2. Provision of Opportunities to Respond to the Lawsuit

1182. The defendant must have been properly served with the notice of proceedings, with sufficient time needed to allow him/her to defend himself/herself, or he/she must have responded to the lawsuit even without having been served such documents (§217(1)① CPA).

3. Public Policy

1183. The effects of a foreign judgment must not be in conflict with the public policy of Korea (§217(1)③ CPA). The Supreme Court upheld the judgment of a lower court that recognized a foreign judgment in a case where the facts are as follows. The grounds for divorce cited by the court in Ontario, Canada, are not adopted in the Civil Act which prohibits no-fault divorces. The foreign court used a method for dividing the marital assets between the divorced spouses, which is different from that of Korea, and the alimony that was awarded by the court is new to the Korean legal system. The Supreme Court, however, held that such differences are not sufficient to conclude the recognition of such a foreign judgment is likely to undermine sound morals or other social order of Korea.[232]

1184. Nevertheless, the Supreme Court opined that, when the money damages awarded in a foreign judgment is excessively large compared with the amount a domestic court would have granted in accordance with Korean law, a Korean court may refuse to recognize all or part of such foreign judgment, especially regarding punitive damages (§217-2 CPA).[233]

4. Mutual Guarantee

1185. A mutual guarantee must exist between Korea and the foreign country, or the requirements for recognition of a foreign judgment in the two countries must have no actual differences (§217(1)④ CPA).

1186. A mutual guarantee may be recognized by comparing statutes, court decisions, and legal practices of the two countries even despite the fact that they have not concluded a treaty concerning recognition of a foreign judgment. The requirements for the mutual guarantee are deemed to have been satisfied if the requirements are not substantively different on critical points. Furthermore, the anticipation

232. Supreme Court Decision 2009Da22952 decided on June 25, 2009.
233. Supreme Court Decision 2015Da1284 decided on October 15, 2015.

that a judgment of the same type rendered by a court in Korea may be recognized in the foreign country, even if actual cases of recognition do not exist yet, is sufficient.[234]

II. Enforcement of Foreign Judgment

1187. When a judgment for performance rendered by a foreign court becomes final and binding, the creditor may file a lawsuit with a District Court to enforce it in Korea. In this lawsuit, the defendant is the debtor. When the foreign judgment satisfies the requirements for recognition, the District Court renders an enforcement judgment which permits the enforcement of the foreign judgment. If not, the lawsuit is dismissed (§27(2) CEA).

1188. An enforcement judgment is rendered without investigating whether the foreign court made any error in ruling the case (§27(1) CEA). According to a Supreme Court decision, the allegation that the foreign court made the decision based on forged, falsified, or discarded documents, or that the witness committed perjury, does not affect the recognition, irrespective of whether such allegations are true or not.[235]

---

234. *Supra* n. 173.
235. Supreme Court Decision 2002Da74213 decided on October 28, 2004.

Part X. Arbitration

Chapter 1. Arbitration Agreement

§1. Arbitrability

I. Domestic Law

1189. According to the Arbitration Act, "any dispute over a property right" and "any dispute over a non-property right that can be resolved through settlement" are eligible for arbitral proceedings (§3① AA). Here, the property rights refer to assets tangible or intangible, including movables, real properties, copyrights, trademarks, patents, monetary claims, bonds, stocks, among others. "Any dispute over a non-property right that can be resolved through settlement" includes cases regarding labor union activities, membership of an association, termination of employment, termination of a contract, among others.

1190. As an individual, association, foundation, municipality, the State and a foreign nation may have assets in Korea, they may also become parties to an arbitration agreement. The sources of monetary claims do not matter, and they may include any contract, laws, unjust enrichment, and tortious acts.

1191. Most of family matters and administrative law cases are subject to exclusive jurisdiction of the Family Court and the Administrative Court, respectively, and they may not be resolved through arbitration.

II. International Treaties

1192. In 1995, Korea became a WTO (World Trade Organization) Member State when the organization was inaugurated. According to Article 21.3(c) of the DSU (Understanding on rules and procedures governing the settlement of disputes), when there is a dispute between Member States concerning violations of obligations as members of the WTO, it ought to be resolved by an adjudication or recommendation of the Dispute Settlement Body (DSB). Such a dispute resolution option includes arbitration. In 2013, Korea, according to the DSU provisions, referred the dispute concerning anti-dumping and countervailing measures taken by the United

States against Korean washing machines to arbitration. As of 2019, the arbitral proceedings to determine retaliatory measures to be taken by Korea are ongoing with respect to this case.

1193. In 2012, the U.S.-Korea Free Trade Agreement went into effect. This agreement included provisions for ISDS (Investor-State Dispute Settlement). According to such provisions, investors who invested in a foreign country and suffered a loss due to the foreign country's violation of obligations under the trade agreement may resort to arbitration in order to get compensation therefor. In 2003, Lone Star Funds, a private equity fund in the United States, purchased shares of Korean Exchange Bank and became the controlling shareholder. In 2012, Lone Star Funds commenced arbitral proceedings against Korea on the grounds that Korean financial authorities hindered the Fund from selling the shares of the Bank at high prices during the period from 2005 to 2011, and that it had to sell them off at much lower prices in 2011. The Fund requested compensation for the damages, and the arbitration case is pending as of September 2020.

III. Review of Arbitrability

1194. An arbitration agreement regarding legal relationships that may not be resolved through arbitration is invalid. An arbitral tribunal examines, on its own motion, whether the pending dispute is subject to the arbitration agreement between the parties, and whether the dispute is arbitrable. If not, the tribunal dismisses the request for arbitration.

1195. In case where the arbitral tribunal renders an arbitral award on the subject-matter that is not arbitrable or is beyond the scope of the arbitration agreement, a party may file a lawsuit with a court, seeking to set aside the award (§36(2) AA). In addition, a party may file a petition with a court for recognition of the arbitral award or permission of enforcement thereof. In this case, the court dismisses the petition if there are grounds for setting aside the award (§§37(1), 38 AA).

§2. Methods of Concluding an Arbitration Agreement

1196. An arbitration agreement is usually contained in a clause or clauses which are part of a commercial contract. In such a case, the arbitration agreement is made in preparation for any potential disputes that may arise later between the parties of the commercial contract. The parties may also agree to arbitrate after a dispute has arisen, in which case, this agreement is referred to as a submission agreement (§8(1) AA).

1197. An arbitration agreement must be in writing (§8(2) AA). However, an arbitration agreement is deemed to exist where each party's intent to arbitrate was declared orally or in any other form, and such a fact is recorded in writing; where it is contained in an exchange of letters, telegrams, telexes, facsimiles, or other means of telecommunication; or where a party alleges, in the request for arbitration or in a reply to the request for arbitration, that the arbitration agreement was concluded, and the other party does not deny the allegation (§8(3) AA).

§3. Effects of an Arbitration Agreement

1198. In a case where a lawsuit was filed to resolve a dispute which is subject to an arbitration agreement, the court dismisses the case without prejudice, provided the defendant raises a defense alleging the existence thereof (§9(1) AA). Such defense must be asserted no later than when the defendant presents its first oral argument during the hearing on the merits (§9(2) AA). If the defendant fails to do so, the case is placed under the jurisdiction of the national court.

1199. Should the defense of an existence of an arbitration agreement be raised before the court, the court examines the validity of the arbitration agreement. If the court finds the arbitral agreement is invalid, is no longer effective, or is unenforceable, the court may opt to render an interlocutory judgment declaring that the defense lacks any ground, or explain to the effect in its final judgment on the merits. In a case where the parties agreed to designate a specific person as an arbitrator in their arbitration clause, the Supreme Court has opined that such agreement is not enforceable if that specific person refuses to perform his/her duty as an arbitrator.[236]

1200. According to the opinion of the Supreme Court, regarding selective dispute resolution clauses which stipulate that a dispute must be resolved through arbitration or mediation, or through arbitration or court adjudication, one party is not bound by the choice of the other party. Thus, in a case where a party selects arbitration proceedings and files a request for arbitration, but the respondent raises a procedural defense based on the absence of an arbitration agreement in its reply, the selective dispute resolution clause is not an effective arbitration agreement. However, in such a case, the clause would be a valid arbitration agreement if the respondent does not do so.[237]

1201. The Supreme Court held that, for an arbitration clause of the charterparty to be incorporated into the bill of lading and to bind the holder thereof, words of "incorporation of an arbitration clause" from the charterparty must be explicitly stated in the bill of lading, and such charterparty must be specifically identified by date and by names of the parties in the bill of lading, unless the holder of the bill of lading knew about the existence of a pertinent charterparty and its arbitration clause.[238]

---

236. Supreme Court Decision 96Da280 decided on April 12, 1996.
237. Supreme Court Decision 2003Da318 decided on August 22, 2003; Supreme Court Decision 2004Da42166 decided on November 11, 2004.
238. Supreme Court Decision 2000Da70064 decided on January 10, 2003.

1202. In a case where an arbitration clause is included in an adhesion contract, such clause is null and void if enforcing the arbitration agreement against a party with comparatively less bargaining power is unfair and contrary to the principles of good faith (§6(1) ARTC).

§4. Separability of an Arbitration Clause

1203. Even when an arbitration clause is contained in a commercial contract, it is considered a separate agreement. Thus, the validity of the arbitration agreement is determined irrespective of that of the contract in which the arbitration clause is incorporated (§17(1) AA). Therefore, when the contract is rescinded due to a defective declaration of intent, or revoked for nonperformance, the arbitration clause is likely to remain effective.

1204. Considering that the parties' purpose of inserting such clauses in a contract is to resolve any dispute that might arise in relation to the contract in the future, such separation is in conformity with the intention of the parties. Even if the arbitration agreement is invalid, the effects of the contract are not affected for the same reason.

Chapter 2. Composition of Arbitral Tribunals

§1. Arbitral Institutions

1205. The Korean Commercial Arbitration Board (KCAB) is an incorporated association founded on March 22, 1966. The Government may provide all or part of necessary expenses for an incorporated association conducting commercial arbitrations and designated by the Minister of Commerce, Industry and Energy or the Minister of Justice (§40 AA).

1206. Currently, KCAB is the only organization designated by the Government as an arbitral institution. According to the Arbitration Act, the parties and the arbitrators may independently determine arbitral procedures without the involvement of an arbitral institution, which is referred to as an ad hoc arbitration. However, in practice, all arbitration cases are administered by KCAB.

1207. KCAB is supervised by the Ministry of Justice. When KCAB creates or revises arbitration rules, they must be approved by the Chief Justice of the Supreme Court (§41 AA).

1208. KCAB has two different sets of arbitral rules: the Domestic Arbitration Rules and the International Arbitration Rules. The former includes clauses that reflect domestic laws and practices, while the latter contains clauses based on internationally accepted rules. Parties to an arbitration agreement may choose either of these by agreement. Most of Korean parties prefer the former to the latter, while foreigners tend to prefer the latter. When there is no agreement as to the applicable rules, the domestic rules are applied to domestic cases, and the international rules apply to cases that have foreign elements.

1209. The number of arbitrators registered with KCAB is 1,418 as of 2020. To be eligible for a registered arbitrator, a candidate is required to meet the qualifications prescribed by the internal rule of KCAB, e.g., at least ten years of experience in legal practice or in business. Of course, a party to an arbitration case may nominate an arbitrator even if the candidate is not among those registered. However, in most of the cases, parties select their arbitrators among registered ones because they know that KCAB accepts only highly qualified experts in its official list of arbitrators. In 2018, 393 arbitration cases were filed with KCAB, and the number was 443 in 2019.

§2. Arbitral Tribunal

I. Number of Arbitrators

1210. An arbitral tribunal presides over arbitral proceedings, hears the case and issues arbitral awards. An arbitral tribunal may consist of a single arbitrator or a panel of arbitrators (§3 AA). The parties may determine the number of arbitrators constituting an arbitral tribunal by agreement (§11(1) AA). Should they fail to reach an agreement on the number of arbitrators, they are to have three arbitrators (§11(2) AA). Where the parties leave the matter of the number unresolved, the secretariat determines the number considering the amount in dispute (r.19(1) Domestic Arbitration Rules of KCAB).

II. Method of Selection

1211. In an arbitration with a sole arbitrator, both parties must select the arbitrator by agreement. Should they fail to reach an agreement, a court or an arbitral institution designated by them appoints the arbitrator (§12(3)① AA). In an arbitration with three arbitrators, each party selects one arbitrator, and the two selected arbitrators nominate the third. If a party neglects to select an arbitrator, or if the two arbitrators fail to agree on the third arbitrator, a court or the arbitral institution designated by the parties appoints the arbitrators (§12(3)① AA). In practice, the court does not engage in the process of appointing arbitrators, leaving the task to KCAB, which is the only arbitral institution in Korea.

1212. When a person is approached in connection with his/her possible selection as an arbitrator or has already been selected as such, he/she must, without delay, disclose all circumstances that are likely to give rise to justifiable doubts as to his/her impartiality or independence (§13(1) AA).

III. Challenging Arbitrators

1213. A party may challenge the appointment of an arbitrator only on the grounds that there exist circumstances where the challenging party has a reasonable doubt about the arbitrator's impartiality or independence. However, the party is prohibited from challenging if he/she selected the arbitrator or participated in the selection process knowing that the circumstances disqualifying the arbitrator have existed (§13(2) AA).

1214. The parties are free to agree on a procedure for challenging an arbitrator or removal thereof (§14(1) AA). Should the parties fail to agree, a party may send a written statement of reasons for the challenge to the arbitral tribunal which decides the procedure (§14(2) AA). If the challenge is unsuccessful, the challenging party may file a petition with the court for decision on the challenge (§14(3) AA).

Chapter 3. The Arbitral Proceedings

§1. Interim Measures and Preliminary Awards

I. Interim Measures

1215. The arbitral tribunal may, at the request of a party, take interim measures or preservative measures as the arbitral tribunal may consider necessary in respect of the subject-matter of the dispute. Interim measures or preservative measures are taken to secure the enforcement of arbitration awards that would be issued in the future or to avoid any substantial detriment or imminent danger that would occur to the claimant with regard to the relationship of rights in dispute.

1216. Such interim measures include: (a) maintaining or restoring the status quo until an arbitral award is rendered on the merits; (b) prohibiting actions that would pose an imminent danger to or impose a negative impact on the arbitral proceedings; and (c) preserving evidence relevant and essential to the resolution of the dispute (§18(2) AA).

1217. An interim measure may be taken if there is a reasonable possibility that the requesting party would obtain an arbitral award on the merits in his/her favor and possibly sustain damage that may not be redressed absent the interim measure. In addition, such damage to the requesting party must be deemed to exceed that to be sustained by the other party due to the interim measure (§18-2(1) AA). The arbitral tribunal may order the requesting party to provide appropriate security (§18-4 AA). Where the requesting party loses the case on the merits and the other party sustains damage due to the interim measure, the latter may get compensation for the loss out of the security.

1218. The arbitral tribunal may, upon motion of a party or *sua sponte* in exceptional circumstances, modify, suspend, or terminate an interim measure it has already taken. In such a case, the parties must be heard prior to issuing an order to this effect (§18-3 AA).

1219. Where the arbitral tribunal finds that the interim measure was groundless, the tribunal may order, in the form of an arbitral award, the requesting party to pay the costs and compensate the other party for the damages caused (§18-6 AA).

II. Enforcement of Interim Measures

1220. A party may file a petition with a court seeking a decision approving the interim measure ordered by the arbitral tribunal. Also, the court may issue a decision permitting enforcement of an interim measure upon petition by the claimant (§18-7(1) AA).

1221. The provisions concerning preservative measures in the Civil Execution Act are applied to the enforcement of interim measures (§18-7(4) AA). Thus, it has been interpreted that interim measures may be enforced without being granted the enforcement clause.

III. Preliminary Awards

1222. There has been discussions about whether an arbitral tribunal, based on its authority to issue interim measures, may order the respondent to pay a certain amount of money to the claimant when the arbitrators are assured that the measure will be included in the arbitral award to be rendered. An injunction providing a temporary status may contain such an order under the Civil Execution Act. However, it is beyond the scope of an interim measure prescribed by Section 18 of the Arbitration Act.[239]

§2. Management of the Proceedings

I. Summary of the Proceedings

1223. When the claimant files a request for arbitration with KCAB, the secretariat serves a copy of the request to the respondent. The arbitration proceedings commence at the time the secretariat receives the request for arbitration (r.14(3) Domestic Arbitration Rules of KCAB).

1224. The request for arbitration must set forth the relief being sought and the claim and the facts supporting it. The respondent must submit an answer that includes admission or denial of all or part of the facts asserted by the claimant and responses to the relief being sought in the request for arbitration (§24(1) AA). Parties may submit the request, the answer, or briefs with the documents and items of evidence they consider to be relevant (§24(2) AA).

1225. Unless otherwise agreed by the parties, an arbitral tribunal may conduct the proceedings without holding oral hearings at its discretion. Absent such an agreement, oral hearings must be held at the request of a party (§25(1) AA). In practice, arbitral tribunals hold oral hearings in almost all cases.

1226. Even if the respondent fails to submit the answer responding to the request for arbitration, the respondent is not deemed to have admitted the facts stated therein. In such a case, the arbitral tribunal finds facts based only on evidence as if the respondent denied the factual allegations of the claimant (§26(2) AA).

239. Young-joon Mok & Seung-jae Choi, *Commercial Arbitration Law* 206 (Parkyoungsa 2018).

1227. In case where an arbitral tribunal is composed of multiple arbitrators, there must be an arbitrator, referred to as the chair, who presides over the proceedings. The chair is elected by agreement of the parties. If the parties fail to agree, then the arbitrators select the chair. If the arbitrators fail to agree, then the secretariat appoints the chair (r.21(4) Domestic Arbitration Rules of KCAB).

II. Examination of Evidence

1228. The types of evidence include a witness, document evidence, inspection, expert examination, and party witness (§§21 (1),27 AA). An arbitral tribunal is authorized to determine admissibility, relevance, materiality, and weight of any evidence presented (§20(2) AA).

1229. Unlike a court, an arbitral tribunal lacks coercive powers to exercise in examining evidence, e.g., summoning a witness and forcing him/her to take an oath. For this reason, the Arbitration Act provides for court assistance in taking evidence in arbitral proceedings. An arbitral tribunal may, *sua sponte* or on motion of a party, commission the court of competent jurisdiction to examine evidence or may request assistance from the court in examining evidence (§28(1) AA).

1230. When commissioning a court to examine evidence, the arbitral tribunal may designate, in writing, the items to be examined (r.37(2) Domestic Arbitration Rules of KCAB). When the court examines evidence for the arbitral tribunal, an arbitrator or the parties may take part upon approval of the presiding judge (§28(3) AA). After taking evidence, the court sends the records of the evidence examination to the arbitral tribunal (§28(4) AA). However, in practice, arbitral tribunals seldom seek assistance from the court.

III. Termination of Arbitral Proceedings

1231. Arbitral proceedings are finalized when, after the close of the hearing, arbitrators make a decision on the case and the tribunal renders an arbitral award (§33(1) AA).

1232. If the claimant withdraws his/her request for arbitration and the respondent does not object to the withdrawal, the arbitral tribunal issues a decision for termination. If the respondent raises objections to the withdrawal and the tribunal finds he/she has a legitimate interest in obtaining a final resolution of the dispute, the tribunal continues the proceedings. The tribunal renders a decision terminating the proceedings when the parties agree thereon or when it finds that the continuation of arbitral proceedings is unnecessary or impossible (§33(2) AA).

§3. Arbitral Award

I. Decision-Making

1233. Unless otherwise agreed by the parties, any decision of an arbitral tribunal composed of multiple arbitrators is made by a majority rule (§30 AA). Should some of the arbitrators fail to take part in the decision-making without justifiable cause, the award may be rendered by the remaining majority of the arbitrators (r.40(3) Domestic Arbitration Rules of KCAB).

1234. If parties settle their dispute during arbitral proceedings, the arbitral tribunal issues a decision for termination of the proceedings. In this case, the arbitral tribunal may, if requested by the parties, record the terms of the settlement in the form of an arbitral award (§31(1) AA). An arbitral award made and rendered in this manner has the same effect as any other award issued on the merits of the case (§31(2) AA).

1235. An arbitral tribunal makes an award by finding facts and applying law to the facts. The provisions of law applicable to the arbitration case are designated by agreement of the parties. Absent such an agreement, the tribunal applies the law of the nation to which, the tribunal finds, the subject-matter of the dispute is most closely related (§29(2) AA).

II. Form of the Arbitral Award

1236. An arbitral award must be in writing and be signed by the arbitrators (§32(1) AA). This means that all the arbitrators of the arbitral tribunal must participate in writing the award. Generally, one of the arbitrators makes an initial draft, and other arbitrators review and leave comments on the draft. Reflecting opinions of all arbitrators, the form of the award is completed. The writer of the draft is determined by agreement of the arbitrators. In most of the cases, the chair writes the award.

1237. An arbitral award must set forth the names of the parties, the place of arbitration, the relief sought, the operative provisions of the award, and the reasons upon which the award is based (r.41(1) Domestic Arbitration Rules of KCAB). Where there is an agreement between the parties, or the arbitral award is based on a settlement agreement, the reasons for the award may be omitted (§32(2) AA). In an arbitral award based on agreed terms of a settlement, the relief sought, grounds of the request, and the fact that settlement was reached must be stated.

Chapter 4. Filing Suit to Vacate an Arbitral Award

§1. Arbitral Awards to Be Vacated

1238. The nonprevailing party may file a lawsuit with a court to set aside an arbitral award on the grounds prescribed in the Arbitration Act. The judgment setting aside the arbitral award is a formative one in that the award is made void retroactively when the judgment becomes final and binding. Only a final award may be set aside, excluding an interim measure or an interlocutory award.

1239. It has been debated whether the claimant may file a lawsuit to set aside an award dismissing the request for arbitration on the procedural grounds. The Supreme Court held that the grounds for setting aside an award, which are enumerated in Section 36 of the Arbitration Act, are premised on the fact that the arbitral tribunal rendered the award on the merits, and therefore only such an award may be set aside.[240]

1240. A party may not file a lawsuit to set aside the arbitral award provided a court in Korea rendered a decision recognizing the award or a decision permitting enforcement thereof, and the decision became final and binding (§36(4) AA).

§2. Grounds

I. Grounds to Be Asserted by the Plaintiff

1241. The judgment setting aside an arbitral award is to be rendered by the court when the plaintiff successfully asserts and proves one of the following causes (§36(2)① AA).

(a) a party to the arbitration agreement was incapable of contracting, or the said agreement is invalid;
(b) the plaintiff was not given proper notice of the appointment of an arbitrator or of the arbitral proceedings or was otherwise unable to present his/her case;
(c) the award has dealt with matters that are not subject to the arbitration agreement; or
(d) the composition of the arbitral tribunal or arbitral proceedings were not in accordance with the agreement of the parties.

II. Grounds to Be Examined by the Court *Sua Sponte*

1242. The court examines *sua sponte* whether the subject-matter of the arbitration case is not eligible for arbitration under Korean law, or whether the award is in

240. Supreme Court Decision 2003Da70249,70256 decided on October 14, 2004.

conflict with public policies of Korea. If the case lacks arbitrability, or the award contradicts public policies of Korea, the court renders a judgment setting aside the arbitral award (§36(2)② AA).

§3. Effects of a Judgment Setting Aside an Arbitral Award

1243. When a judgment setting aside an arbitral award becomes final and binding, it has formative effects and preclusive effects. Due to the formative effects of the judgment, the effects of the arbitral award end retroactively. It is deemed that the arbitral award has never existed.

1244. A judgment setting aside the award has the preclusive effects on the grounds upon which it is based. For example, should the arbitral award be set aside on the ground that the arbitration agreement is invalid, the preclusive effects apply to the invalidity of the agreement. Henceforth, the parties may not dispute such fact. In such a case, the claimant cannot but bring the case to court to have the respondent perform its obligation.

1245. If the arbitral award was set aside on the ground that there had been a procedural defect, the arbitral tribunal may conduct the proceedings anew, this time without any procedural error. Where any part of an arbitral award is beyond the scope of the arbitral agreement, and it is separable, the part would be set aside. In such a case, the claimant may file a lawsuit seeking performance of the obligation in respect of that part. Where the arbitral award was vacated because the dispute is not arbitrable under the Korean law, the claimant may bring the case to court.

Chapter 5. Recognition and Enforcement of Arbitral Awards

§1. Domestic Awards

1246. Prerequisites for recognition or enforcement of an award and grounds for setting aside one are two different sides of the same coin. However, the proceedings are different in that an arbitral award is recognized or enforced by a court decision, whereas it is set aside by a judgment. The court may issue a decision without holding a hearing, but a hearing for oral argument is a must in proceedings for judgments.

1247. Where a party filed a petition for recognition or enforcement of the award, the other party who opposes it must assert and make a prima facie showing that there are grounds for setting aside the award, and that it was not recognized or enforcement thereof was not granted by a final and binding court decision. If such requirements are met, the court denies the petition for recognition or granting enforcement of the award (§38① AA).

1248. If there are the grounds for setting aside, which are to be examined *sua sponte*, the court examines them in the same manner and denies the petition for recognition or grant of enforcement (§38② AA).

§2. Foreign Arbitral Awards

I. A Member State of the New York Convention

1249. Where a foreign award is subject to the Convention on the Recognition and Enforcement of Foreign Arbitral Awards ("New York Convention"), the requirements and procedures for recognition or enforcement thereof are regulated by the New York Convention (§39① AA). In 1973, ROK joined the New York Convention which had been effectuated in 1959. Article V of the New York Convention enumerates the grounds on which Member States may refuse to recognize or enforce a foreign award. These grounds are very similar to those stipulated in the Arbitration Act.

II. A non-Member State of the New York Convention

1250. With respect to recognition and enforcement of a foreign award that is not bound by the New York Convention, the relevant provisions of the Civil Procedure Act (§217) and the Civil Execution Act (§§26(1),27) regarding foreign judgments are applied. Please refer to Part IX. Chapter 2. §3 of this book for more details on recognition and enforcement of foreign judgments.

Part XI. Mediation

Chapter 1. Introduction

§1. Definition and Meaning

1251. Mediation is a procedure in which dispute resolution experts, including judges, standing mediation commissioners of a court and members of various mediation committees participate to lead the disputing parties to amicably reach an agreement for resolving their dispute. Mediation is mainly conducted in courts. However, many government agencies and municipalities have respective mediation committees, and there are institutions that operate mediation committees dealing with disputes arising in each specialized area.

1252. The Civil Mediation Act regulates mediation procedures for civil disputes, which are conducted by judges and mediation commissioners in courts. This Act is usually applied to the procedure in other mediation committees associated with government agencies, municipalities, and others according to the statutes that established them.

1253. In court-supervised mediations, a mediation settlement agreement concluded by the parties has the same effects to those of a judicial settlement (§29 JCCDA). A judicial settlement is a legally binding agreement reached before the court which has the same effects as a final and binding judgment rendered by a court (§220 CPA).

1254. Agreements reached through mediation in some institutions are legally binding while agreements reached through mediation in other institutions are non-binding. Mediation institutions in the former category include the Consumer Dispute Mediation Committee (§60 FWAC), the National Environmental Dispute Resolution Commission (§5 EDMA), the Industrial Technology Dispute Mediation Committee (§23 APDOIT), the Broadcasting Dispute Conciliation Committee (§35-3 BA), and the Medical Dispute Mediation and Arbitration Committee (§19 ARIMD).

1255. It can be said that there are no mediators by profession in Korea. Various mediation committees established by numerous statutes are composed of mediation commissioners appointed by each agency. They are mostly experts in specialized areas with good social reputation and legal experts including attorneys. In this part, explanations of mediation focus on the procedures conducted in a court.

§2. Disputes That May Be Subject to Mediation

1256. Considering that a mediation settlement agreement and a judicial settlement have the same effect as a final and binding judgment, and also that mediation and settlement are dispute resolution procedures through an amicable agreement of the parties to the dispute, legal relationships and/or rights that are not suitable for settlement may not be subject to mediation, either.

1257. The legal rights eligible for mediation are the ones that can be disposed of by the holders thereof at will. They must not be related to the public interest. Family relationships are created by marriage or birth, and a particular right based thereon are not subject to settlement. Thus, disputes over such rights are not suitable for mediation.

1258. However, mediation may be a viable dispute resolution mechanism for disputes over divorce, damages for pain and suffering due to divorce, division of marital assets upon divorce, division of the estate among heirs, designation of a custodian, and claims for child support.

1259. According to a decision of the Supreme Court, the final and binding judgments revoking a resolution of a shareholders' meeting, affirming nullity thereof, or affirming the nonexistence thereof are formative, and they have an *erga omnes* effect that binds a third party. Therefore, a mediation settlement agreement or a judicial settlement concluded in such cases is invalid.[241]

§3. Mediation Organization Within a Court

I. Mediation Judge

1260. The president of each level court, except the Supreme Court, must designate at least two judges dedicated to mediation cases in the court. A mediation judge serves for two years generally. He/she presides over mediation proceedings, organizes and supervises mediation panels for specific cases, educates mediation commissioners, among other duties.

1261. A mediation judge may mediate cases by himself/herself, or have a standing mediation commissioner or a mediation panel do so (§7(2) JCCDA). When a mediation panel conducts mediation proceedings, the mediation judge or the standing mediation commissioner becomes the chair of the panel (§9 JCCDA).

241. Supreme Court Decision 2004Da28047 decided on September 24, 2004.

II. Standing Mediation Commissioner

1262. The Minister of the National Court Administration appoints standing mediation commissioners for each of High Courts, District Courts, and Branch Courts nationwide (r.2-2(1) RMC). To be qualified as a standing mediation commissioner, one must have at least ten years of career experience as a judge, prosecutor, attorney, or member of faculty of law at a university (r.2-2(2) RMC).

1263. A standing mediation commissioner receives a salary and works full time. The commissioner may not have another job concurrently unless the Minister of the National Court Administration permits (r.9-2 GACM). A standing commissioner has the same authority as a mediation judge in dealing with mediation cases allotted to him/her (§7(4) JCCDA).

III. The Trial Court Hearing the Case

1264. The trial court which is a judicial panel or a single judge may, if it deems necessary, refer the case pending therein to mediation by a judicial decision (§6 JCCDA). In principle, the mediation judge takes the referred case. However, the trial court may mediate such cases on its own when the court deems it appropriate (§7(3) JCCDA). In a case where a judicial panel handles a mediation case, one or two judges of the panel may be delegated to preside over the mediation proceedings (r.8 GACM).

IV. Mediation Committee

1265. The president of a court appoints mediation commissioners for the court (r.2 RMC). The number of mediation commissioners for each court is determined depending on the size of the court and the number of mediation cases. The term of office of a mediation commissioner is two years (§10(2) JCCDA). The mediation committee is composed of such commissioners. The president of a court may designate mediation commissioners dedicated to a specific judicial panel in the court, considering their profession, experience, expertise, and others (r.6(1) GACM).

1266. A mediation panel, which is composed of a chair and commissioners who are members of the mediation committee, is formed ad hoc for a specific mediation case. The chair of the mediation panel is a judge or a standing mediation commissioner. The parties may select the mediation commissioners by agreement. If they fail to agree, the chair selects the commissioners (r.7(1) GACM).

1267. Even when the trial court has referred a case to mediation and then decided to mediate the case on its own, the court may form a mediation panel. In this case, the presiding judge or a delegated judge becomes the chair of the mediation panel, and other panel members are selected by the chair among the mediation commissioners dedicated to the judicial panel (r.6(1) GACM).

Chapter 2. Mediation Proceedings

§1. Commencement

1268. There are two ways to initiate mediation proceedings. A party to the dispute may file a petition for mediation with a court of first instance (§§3(1),5(1) JCCDA). On the other hand, the trial court may refer the pending case therein to mediation on its own motion (§6 JCCDA). In the latter case, the litigation proceedings are suspended until the mediation proceedings are closed (r.4(2) RCM).

§2. Management of the Proceedings

1269. Once mediation proceedings commence, the chair of the mediation panel designates and notifies the date for a hearing to the parties (§15 JCCDA). The parties to the case must make an appearance at the hearing in person. However, in special circumstances, a party may have a representative appear at the hearing on his/her behalf or accompany an assistant (r.6(1) RCM). In such a case, a party must obtain permission of the mediation judge in order to have a representative or assistant participate in the proceedings if the representative is not an attorney (r.6(2) RCM). In case where the trial court referred a case to mediation, the attorney of record in the litigation proceedings may represent the party in the mediation proceedings only upon authorization by the party to do so (§6(3) RCM).

1270. Multiple parties with a common interest may appoint one or more parties from among themselves to stand as the petitioner or the respondent on behalf of them (§18 JCCDA). A third party who has a legitimate interest in the result of the mediation may participate in the proceedings upon permission of the mediation judge (§16 JCCDA).

1271. A mediation judge hears the parties and a third party with a legitimate interest in the mediation. If deemed necessary, the judge may examine evidence by appropriate means (§22 JCCDA). The mediation proceedings are not open to the public (§20 JCCDA). The statements made by parties or third parties in mediation proceedings may not be presented or used as evidence in other proceedings (§23 JCCDA). The exchange of candid opinions with the opposing party and disclosure of facts are made during the course of negotiations on the premise that what they do, say, or communicate remain confidential. Therefore, using such statements in litigation proceedings goes against the principle of good faith and allowing use of such would thwart the settlement and mediation system.

§3. TERMINATION OF MEDIATION PROCEEDINGS

I. Failure to Reach an Agreement

1272. Where the hearing date for mediation cannot be notified to a party, the mediation judge may dismiss the petition for mediation in the form of a decision (§25(1) JCCDA). If the petitioner fails to appear at the hearing, another hearing date is designated and notified. Should the petitioner fail to appear on the new hearing date or one of the subsequent hearing dates, the petition for mediation is deemed to have been withdrawn (§31 JCCDA). Should the respondent fail to appear at the hearing, the mediation judge may, on its own motion, issue a decision in lieu of mediating the matter (§32 JCCDA).

1273. When the case is deemed not suitable for mediation due to its nature, the mediation judge may issue a decision terminating the proceedings (§26(1) JCCDA). Should the parties fail to reach an agreement in the proceedings, the mediation judge may issue a decision in lieu of mediating the matter or a decision terminating the proceedings (§27 JCCDA).

II. Conclusion of a Mediation Settlement Agreement

1274. When the parties conclude an agreement in the mediation proceedings, the terms of the agreement are entered in the record of the hearing (§28 JCCDA). The mediation settlement agreement entered in the record has the same effect as a judicial settlement or a settlement before the court (§29 JCCDA). This means that the legally binding agreement is enforceable and has effects of precluding claim(s).

1275. In addition, the agreement has the nature of a settlement which creates a new legal relationship with respect to the subject-matter of the dispute. Therefore, the legal rights and obligations based on the previous legal relationship are extinguished at the time the mediation settlement agreement takes effect. The parties are precluded from disputing the effects of the settlement agreement. The record of the hearing in which the mediation settlement agreement is entered is an enforcement title when a party enforces his/her claim set forth in the agreement.

III. Issuing a Decision in Lieu of Mediation

1276. Where the parties fail to conclude an agreement or the agreement concluded between the parties is inappropriate and unreasonable, the mediation judge may, on its own motion, provide the terms of agreement in the form of a decision, taking into account the legitimate interests of the parties and all the relevant circumstances (§30 JCCDA).

1277. A party may file an objection to the decision within two weeks after a copy of the decision is served (§34(1) JCCDA). Where no objection has been raised, or where the objection filed is withdrawn, the decision in lieu of mediation becomes final and binding. In this case, the parties are deemed to have agreed to the terms set forth in the decision (§34(4) JCCDA). The final and binding decision has the same effect as a judgment or a mediation settlement agreement.

IV. Resuming to Litigation Proceedings

1278. Where the mediation judge issues a decision not to mediate the case or a decision terminating the mediation proceedings, or a party files an objection to the court decision providing the terms of agreement, the petitioner is deemed to have filed a lawsuit at the time the petition was filed (§36(1) JCCDA). If any of the above circumstances arises to the case referred to mediation by the trial court, the case is returned to the court, and thereby the litigation proceedings are resumed.

Bibliography

(Books)

Chung, Dong-yoon et al. *Civil Procedure Law* (Bobmunsa 6thed. 2017).
Jang, Young-soo. *State Organization Theory* (Hongmunsa 2005).
Kim, Hong-yup. *Civil Procedure* (Parkyoungsa 5thed. 2014).
Kim, Neung-hwan et al. *Civil Procedure Commentaries (I)* (Judicial Administration Association 2003).
Kim, Sang-won et al. *Commentary on Civil Procedure Act (I)* (Association of Judicial Administration 2003).
Lee, Jae-sang & Cho, Gyun-seok. *Criminal Procedure* (Parkyoungsa 11th ed. 2017).
Lee, Si-yoon. *New Civil Procedure Law* (Parkyoungsa 9th ed. 2015)
Mok, Young-joon & Choi, Seung-jae. *Commercial Arbitration Law* (Parkyoungsa 2018).
Seoul Administrative Court Practice Research Association. *Theory and Practice of Administrative Litigation* (Judicial Development Foundation 2014).
History of Courts (National Court Administration 1995).
Court Practice Summary Civil Procedure (I) (National Court Administration 2017).
Court Practice Summary Civil Procedure (II) (National Court Administration 2017).

(Periodicals)

Ha, Myung-ho. *Relationship between an administrative lawsuit for civil remedies and a civil action* 380 Human Right and Justice 52 (2008).
Lee, Young-seob. *Reading Summary of Publishing Civil Procedure Act,* 4-3 Beob Jeong 4 (1949. 3.).

Table of Cases

(Supreme Court)

Supreme Court Decision 63Da111 decided on May 15, 1963.
Supreme Court Decision 66Da842 decided on January 31, 1968.
Supreme Court Decision 69Da2449 decided on March 25, 1969.
Supreme Court Decision 68Da1798 decided on May 27, 1969.
Supreme Court Decision 69Da1888 decided on January 27, 1970.
Supreme Court Decision 70Ma103 decided on March 20, 1973.
Supreme Court Decision 74Ma71 decided on July 23, 1974.
Supreme Court Decision 74Ma281 decided on May 23, 1975.
Supreme Court Decision 76Da1365 decided on September 14, 1976.
Supreme Court Decision 76Da1623 decided on October 29, 1976.
Supreme Court Decision 76Da1488 decided on December 14, 1976.
Supreme Court Decision 77Ma284 decided on November 9, 1977.
Supreme Court Decision 77Ma427 decided on May 22, 1979.
Supreme Court Decision 78Ma249 decided on August 25, 1979.
Supreme Court Decision 80Ma403 decided on September 26, 1980.
Supreme Court Decision 80Ma445 decided on November 25, 1980.
Supreme Court Decision 80Da2751 decided on July 7, 1981.
Supreme Court Decision 81Da124 decided on June 23, 1981.
Supreme Court Decision 81Nu230 decided on October 13, 1981.
Supreme Court Decision 80Da916 decided on May 11, 1982.
Supreme Court Decision 82DaKa317 decided on August 24, 1982.
Supreme Court Decision (*en banc*) 82DaKa1533 decided on March 22, 1983.
Supreme Court Decision 83Ma214 decided on June 21, 1983.
Supreme Court Decision (*en banc*) 83DaKa1489 decided on December 13, 1983.
Supreme Court Decision (*en banc*) 83DaKa1981 decided on February 28, 1984.
Supreme Court Decision 84Da552 decided on April 9, 1985.
Supreme Court Decision 87DaKa1728 decided on October 25, 1988.
Supreme Court Decision 88DaKa17181 decided on September 29, 1989.
Supreme Court Decision 87DaKa2478 decided on June 27, 1989.
Supreme Court Decision 90DaKa20548 decided on November 27, 1990.
Supreme Court Decision 88DaKa19002,19019 decided on January 15, 1991
Supreme Court Decision 90Nu5153 decided on September 10, 1991.
Supreme Court Decision 91Da4096 decided on December 10, 1991.
Supreme Court Decision 90DaKa1158 decided on December 13, 1991.

Table of Cases

Supreme Court Decision 92Da2585 decided on July 14, 1992.
Supreme Court Decision 91Da41897 decided on July 28, 1992.
Supreme Court Decision 92Nu5096 decided on September 25, 1992.
Supreme Court Decision 92Da31453 decided on January 15, 1993.
Supreme Court Decision 92Da33008 decided on June 25, 1993.
Supreme Court Decision 93Da11050 decided on June 29, 1993.
Supreme Court Decision 93Da22074 decided on August 24, 1993.
Supreme Court Decision 92Da24899 decided on September 14, 1993.
Supreme Court Decision 92Da55794 decided on September 28, 1993.
Supreme Court Decision 93Da41938 decided on November 23, 1993.
Supreme Court Decision (*en banc*) 93Ma524 decided on December 6, 1993.
Supreme Court Decision 93Da39225 decided on February 25, 1994.
Supreme Court Decision 94Ma536 decided on May 26, 1994.
Supreme Court Decision 93Da52808 decided on August 12, 1994.
Supreme Court Decision 94Meu246, 94Meu253 decided on October 28, 1994.
Supreme Court Decision 93Da31993 decided on November 4, 1994.
Supreme Court Decision 94Da12517, 94Da12524 decided on November 25, 1994.
Supreme Court Decision 92Da22473, 92Da22480 decided on December 27, 1994.
Supreme Court Decision (*en banc*) 94Ma1961 decided on January 20, 1995.
Supreme Court Decision 94Ma1059, 1060 decided on May 15, 1995.
Supreme Court Decision 95Da12125 decided on May 26, 1995.
Supreme Court Decision (*en banc*) 94Da34265 decided on July 11, 1995.
Supreme Court Decision 94Da50274 decided on February 9, 1996.
Supreme Court Decision 94Da61649 decided on February 9, 1996.
Supreme Court Decision 96Da280 decided on April 12, 1996.
Supreme Court Decision 96Nu2699 decided on May 28, 1996.
Supreme Court Decision 94Da53006 decided on June 14, 1996.
Supreme Court Decision 96Da37176 decided on November 22, 1996.
Supreme Court Decision 95Da40038 decided on December 23, 1996.
Supreme Court Decision 96Da21188 decided on March 14, 1997.
Supreme Court Decision 96Da41649 decided on May 28, 1997.
Supreme Court Decision 96Da56115 decided on June 13, 1997.
Supreme Court Decision 96Da16896 decided on September 9, 1997.
Supreme Court Decision 96Da12276 decided on October 24, 1997.
Supreme Court Decision 95Da29895 decided on December 12, 1997.
Supreme Court Decision 97Da45532 decided on February 27, 1998.
Supreme Court Decision 98Da2051 decided on June 26, 1998.
Supreme Court Decision 96Da99 decided on July 24, 1998.
Supreme Court Decision 99Da1789 decided on May 25, 1999.
Supreme Court Decision 97Da54024 decided on September 17, 1999.
Supreme Court Decision 97Da57733 decided on November 26, 1999.
Supreme Court Decision 99Da67703 decided on March 10, 2000.
Supreme Court Decision 2000JaeDa87 decided on August 18, 2000.
Supreme Court Decision 2000Da46399 decided on December 22, 2000.
Supreme Court Decision 2000Da58668 decided on March 9, 2001.
Supreme Court Decision 2001Da5654 decided on April 24, 2001.
Supreme Court Decision 2000Da4050 decided on April 27, 2001.

Supreme Court Decision 2001Da59033 decided on April 26, 2002.
Supreme Court Decision 2002Ma1156 decided on May 10, 2002.
Supreme Court Decision 2001Da60491 decided on July 26, 2002.
Supreme Court Decision 2002Da34666 decided on September 6, 2002.
Supreme Court Decision 2002Da34581 decided on September 10, 2002.
Supreme Court Decision 2000Ma282 decided on September 25, 2002.
Supreme Court Decision 2002ChoGi113 decided on September 27, 2002.
Supreme Court Decision 2002Da44014 decided on December 6, 2002.
Supreme Court Decision 2000Da70064 decided on January 10, 2003.
Supreme Court Decision 2002Da65929 decided on February 11, 2003.
Supreme Court Decision 2000Da24856 decided on March 28, 2003.
Supreme Court Decision 2002Da59481 decided on April 11, 2003.
Supreme Court Decision 2003Da318 decided on August 22, 2003.
Supreme Court Decision 2001Da53349 decided on March 25, 2004.
Supreme Court Decision 2004Da28047 decided on September 24, 2004.
Supreme Court Decision 2003Da70249,70256 decided on October 14, 2004.
Supreme Court Decision 2002Da74213 decided on October 28, 2004.
Supreme Court Decision 2004Da42166 decided on November 11, 2004.
Supreme Court Decision 2004Mu54 decided on November 24, 2004.
Supreme Court Decision 2005Da41443 decided on November 10, 2005.
Supreme Court Decision 2005Ma902 decided on March 2, 2006.
Supreme Court Decision 2004Ma1148,1149 decided on June 2, 2006.
Supreme Court Decision 2004Da44506 decided on September 28, 2006.
Supreme Court Decision 2004Da69581 decided on October 27, 2006.
Supreme Court Decision 2007Ma346 decided on November 15, 2007.
Supreme Court Decision 2007Da49960 decided on February 29, 2008.
Supreme Court Decision 2006Da68209 decided on March 13, 2008.
Supreme Court Decision 2007Da25261 decided on July 24, 2008.
Supreme Court Decision 2006Da86597 decided on September 25, 2008.
Supreme Court Decision 2008Da79340 decided on January 30, 2009.
Supreme Court Decision 2006Da34190 decided on May 14, 2009.
Supreme Court Decision 2009Da12399 decided on June 11, 2009.
Supreme Court Decision 2009Da22952 decided on June 25, 2009.
Supreme Court Decision 2006Da73966 decided on July 9, 2009.
Supreme Court Decision 2009Da37138,37145 decided on September 10, 2009.
Supreme Court Decision 2009Ma1482 decided on November 13, 2009.
Supreme Court Decision 2009Da56603,56610 decided on December 10, 2009.
Supreme Court Decision 2010Ma215 decided on March 22, 2010.
Supreme Court Decision 2009Da68910 decided on April 29, 2010.
Supreme Court Decision 2010Da18355 decided on July 15, 2010.
Supreme Court Decision 2009Da68941 decided on February 10, 2011.
Supreme Court Decision 2010Da99040 decided on March 10, 2011.
Supreme Court Decision 2010Ma1001 decided on June 30, 2011.
Supreme Court Decision 2009Da90856 decided on July 28, 2011.
Supreme Court Decision 2011Ma62 decided on September 29, 2011.
Supreme Court Decision 2009Da16766 decided on December 13, 2011.
Supreme Court Decision 2011Da73540 decided on December 22, 2011.

Supreme Court Decision (*en banc*) 2010Da95390 decided on January 19, 2012.
Supreme Court Decision 2010Da81315 decided on January 27, 2012.
Supreme Court Decision 2011Da45521 decided on February 16, 2012.
Supreme Court Decision 2011Da1828 decided on April 13, 2012.
Supreme Court Decision 2010Da28604 decided on May 17, 2012.
Supreme Court Decision 2012Do6027 decided on August 30, 2012.
Supreme Court Decision 2012Da55198 decided on October 11, 2012.
Supreme Court Decision 2012Da44471 decided on November 29, 2012.
Supreme Court Decision 2011Da21556 decided on February 28, 2013.
Supreme Court Decision 2011Da95564 decided on March 21, 2013.
Supreme Court Decision 2012Da102629 decided on March 28, 2013.
Supreme Court Decision 2011Da18864 decided on July 11, 2013.
Supreme Court Decision 2011Da60759 decided on July 11, 2013.
Supreme Court Decision 2006Da17539 Decided July 12, 2013.
Supreme Court Decision 2011Du20321 decided on July 12, 2013.
Supreme Court Decision 2013Da19571 decided on July 12, 2013.
Supreme Court Decision 2013Da45457 decided on September 13, 2013.
Supreme Court Decision 2011Da98426 decided on October 31, 2013.
Supreme Court Decision 2012Da7571 decided on April 10, 2014.
Supreme Court Decision 2010Da84932 decided on April 10, 2014.
Supreme Court Decision 2013Da95964 decided on June 12, 2014.
Supreme Court Decision 2014Da11376 decided on June 12, 2014.
Supreme Court Decision 2012Da111630 decided on January 29, 2015.
Supreme Court Decision 2014Da34041 decided on January 29, 2015.
Supreme Court Decision 2013Da88829 decided on March 20, 2015.
Supreme Court Decision 2014Da34126 decided on September 10, 2015.
Supreme Court Decision 2015Da1284 decided on October 15, 2015.
Supreme Court Decision 2015Ma4147 decided on December 21, 2015.
Supreme Court Decision 2015Da207747 decided on January 28, 2016.
Supreme Court Decision 2014Da210449 decided on April 2, 2016.
Supreme Court Decision 2015Da217848 decided on June 10, 2016.
Supreme Court Decision 2015Da224469 decided on October 26, 2017.
Supreme Court Decision 2015Da73753 decided on December 22, 2017.
Supreme Court Decision 2017Ma5829 decided on February 9, 2018.
Supreme Court Decision 2017Da21411 decided on May 30, 2018.
Supreme Court Decision 2018Da229564 decided on August 1, 2018.

(Constitutional Court)

Constitutional Court Decision 90HunBa1 decided on January 20, 1995.
Constitutional Court decision 2004HunNa1 decided on May 14, 2004.
Constitutional Court decision 2005HunGa21 decided on November 27, 2008.
Constitutional Court decision 2013HunDa1 decided on December 19, 2014.
Constitutional Court decision 2016HunNa1 decided on March 10, 2017.

(U.S. Supreme Court)

The Schooner Exchange v. McFaddon, 11 U.S. 116 (1812).
Shaffer v. Heitner, 433 U.S. 186, 204 (1977).

Index

The numbers here refers to paragraph numbers.

Index

www.ingramcontent.com/pod-product-compliance
Ingram Content Group UK Ltd.
Pitfield, Milton Keynes, MK11 3LW, UK
UKHW020134290926
15471UKWH00003B/471

9 789403 526737